Stalwart Peasants, Undesirables, Refugees:
Central and Eastern European Immigration to Canada
Edited by Balázs Venkovits

Stalwart Peasants, Undesirables, Refugees: Central and Eastern European Immigration to Canada

Edited by Balázs Venkovits

sciendo

ISBN 978-83-67405-47-8
e-ISBN (PDF) 978-83-67405-45-4
e-ISBN (EPUB) 978-83-67405-46-1

Library of Congress Cataloging-in-Publication Data
A CIP catalog record for this book has been applied for at the Library of Congress.

Published by De Gruyter Poland Ltd, Warsaw/Berlin
Part of Walter de Gruyter GmbH, Berlin/Boston
The book is published with open access at www.degruyter.com.

www.sciendo.com

Cover illustration: "Canadian Passific / Railway / (Atlantic Steamship Lines) / to Canada [...]",
Collectie Stad Antwerpen, Letterenhuis. Available at: https://dams.antwerpen.be/asset/
ggGwCNGLBSTec8QYBsZNj7j3#id

Contents

Balázs Venkovits
Introduction

Emigration has been an integral part of the historical experience of people from Central and Eastern Europe with millions leaving their homes in different eras from what is today the Czech Republic, Hungary, Poland, Russia, Slovakia, and Ukraine in search of better lives. At the same time, the significance of immigration in shaping North American history remains profound, with Canada welcoming millions of newcomers who have been pivotal in shaping the fabric of a culturally diverse society. The confluence of push and pull factors at various times initiated waves of migration from the former region to the latter, establishing a strong, albeit occasionally intricate and not entirely unproblematic, relationship between these two parts of the world. The nine essays included in this interdisciplinary volume of *HJEAS Books* provide fascinating insights into this dynamic interplay and the history of migration from Central and Eastern Europe to Canada, spanning a period of approximately one hundred years and introducing fresh perspectives and methodological approaches that enrich the scholarly discourse in this field.

The chapters were written by an international group of scholars from Canada, Belgium, France, Slovenia, the Czech Republic, and Hungary studying novel aspects of migration associated with these nations, while extending their analyses to include perspectives also encompassing the United States, Ukraine, and Russia. The chapters not only illuminate differences in the migration trajectories of people from Central and Eastern Europe, but also reveal a shared narrative of immigrants bound for Canada from this region. This is often characterized by shifting labels applied to these people over time, ranging from "stalwart peasants in sheepskin coats," to "non-preferred" and "undesirable," to "likely to become public charge" or "illegal." The predominantly negative labels (perhaps with the exception of the description of people arriving during the Cold War, for example, after 1956 and 1968) serve as intricate reminders of the often bad perception of Central and Eastern Europeans; as the essays in this volume confirm, however, this representation and relationship is much more complex than what such simplistic labels could express.

In the context of scrutinizing emigration from this area to North America, scholarly attention has predominantly converged upon the United States because of the substantial influx of people who immigrated there since the second half of the nineteenth century, in comparison with which Canada could appear more marginal. Studying immigration to Canada therefore requires an inter-American approach that is also mindful of events and migration policy in the United States. Although this is true for the nine essays included in this volume as well, they clearly show that we also need to be aware of the distinctive trajectory experienced by immigrants in the Canadian context. The authors add often overlooked perspectives that provide valuable insights for migration studies in general, as well as the history of the

Americas and Central and Eastern Europe, while reflecting on the cultural and social interconnections between these geographical realms.

The chapters build on a great variety of approaches from the fields of history, cultural studies, and literary analysis, relying on scrupulous archival work. They offer a scrutiny of migration policy and its international impact, which facilitates a comprehensive exploration of the social challenges on both sides of the Atlantic from the era of early settlement through the interwar period to the Cold War era. The question of immigration to Canada is studied from a diverse spectrum of vantage points and, among others, the authors address the following topics:

- the complex trajectory of migration from the place of origin to the new land and the introduction of key players along the way;
- the similarities and differences in the migration experience of people from various countries of Central and Eastern Europe;
- the impact of race and ethnicity on immigration and the immigrant experience in the new country;
- connections between religion and immigration;
- inter-American aspects of immigration to Canada;
- the influence of international migration policies on migration pathways;
- the contribution of immigration to the evolving image(s) of Canada in Central and Eastern Europe;
- the complicated nature of the relationship with the country of origin after emigration;
- representations of immigration and emigration in literature, arts, and music.

The various migration waves between Central and Eastern Europe and Canada affected millions of people, and while often stressing hardship, the essays reveal the valuable contributions of Central and Eastern Europeans to the emergence of a successful multicultural Canada. Today, although their number has decreased since the previous census, there are more than 300,000 people in Canada who indicated their ethnic origin as Hungarian, 1,200,000 as Ukrainian, 98,000 as Czech, 68,000 as Slovak (with another 33,000 indicating Czechoslovak), and 548,000 as Russian, to mention only those groups that are studied in more detail in this volume ("2021 Census Canada"). We hope this collection contributes to a better understanding of their rich history in the diaspora and elucidates a profound narrative that reverberated across the lives of countless individuals and resonates with the broader narrative of Canada and North America.

Reflections on migration history, policy, and the legacy of immigrants

The migration of people from Central and Eastern Europe to Canada could, of course, vary to a great extent depending on individual circumstances, social status, national context, ethnic and religious background, but despite the diversity of this group we are able to identify certain similarities both in terms of the key waves of migration from countries as well as the reception and life of immigrants in Canada. These include shared push factors of historical turmoil, poverty, religious persecution, and social malaise as well as a positive perception of North America as the land of opportunities, often fueled by immigration propaganda. People from this region were, in most cases, regarded as non-preferred immigrants in Canada but they began to arrive in larger number between the 1870s and World War I already, initiating a long history of migration between the two regions of the world.

The period between Canadian Confederation in 1867 and World War I brought territorial as well as economic expansion for Canada, and it gradually became an attractive destination for immigrants. Similarly to its southern neighbor, the country became a transcontinental nation with the addition of Manitoba, British Columbia, Prince Edward Island, as well as Saskatchewan and Alberta to the Confederation, with Newfoundland joining only later in 1949 as the tenth province. The development of the Canadian West was considered to be the key to the country's progress and leaders of the nation believed that immigration was to play a major role in this regard.

The building of a transcontinental railway fueled these aspirations, with trains carrying settlers to the west and products from there to the east. The Canadian Pacific Railway was completed in 1886, while simultaneously with this, a network of immigration halls was also established to facilitate the migratory flow and make sure immigrants reached their place of settlement (Vineberg 8). These developments resulted in a population boom to a great extent due to immigration. The United States proved to be the most attractive destination for immigrants from the region of Central and Eastern Europe, with the largest number arriving during the period of New Immigration from the 1880s to World War I. Within this period, approximately four million people left Austria-Hungary alone for the United States and although exact figures are almost impossible to specify due to the varied categories under which people were registered upon their arrival, about 2.5 million Polish immigrants and 500,000 Ukrainians also arrived among many others (for the statistics on the immigration of various groups mentioned here, see Powell). Although the United States remained the number one destination of immigrants throughout this period, between 1896 and 1914, three million people settled in Canada and between 1901 and 1911 the population increased by 43 percent (Knowles 107-24).

From the first immigration act in 1869, the Canadian government tried to make the Western provinces more attractive for immigration. At first, based on the Dominion Lands Act of 1872, any male head of family of at least 21 years of age could obtain 160 acres of public homestead for a 10 USD registration fee and six months' residence for the first three years of the claim (Powell 46). While general programs aimed at colonization failed, they were more successful in attracting specific groups of immigrants especially when the necessary infrastructure was also made available (as seen in the chapters by Eric Wilkinson and Peter Bush). Here, the Minister of the Interior Clifford Sifton was the key figure. He not only emphasized the need for the settlement of the Prairie Provinces but at different times also encouraged immigration from Central and Eastern Europe (using the famous expression of "stalwart peasants in a sheep-skin coat" to refer to these people in 1922 when he had already retired from politics) with immigration propaganda playing a key role in popularizing the region through the image of the "Last Best West" (Vineberg 11, Dreisziger 62).

Despite these efforts, Canada could not compete successfully with the United States and compared to the southern neighbor fewer people arrived, as even despite the activities of immigrant agents no large-scale settlement took place (Knowles 82-83). Although the country appeared attractive due to the benefits offered by the Canadian government, the difficulties associated with settlement were also often discouraging, especially in comparison with the United States. In fact, at the beginning of the period, more people left Canada (for the US) than immigrated there (Powell 45).

To encourage the settlement of the western provinces Canada at some points and with regard to certain groups left behind its immigration and colonization policy that preferred immigrants from Great Britain, the United States, and Northern Europe (Knowles 69). However, while Sifton argued that sturdy immigrants should be brought from "Central Europe, particularly from Hungary and Galicia" (Knowles 141), his successor, Frank Oliver, supported mostly British and American immigration, and members of the East-Central European group were often considered undesirable. Many argued for stricter regulation against mass immigration, which was also reflected by the regulations. The Immigration Act of 1906 greatly expanded the scope of undesirable immigrants, strengthened control of the US-Canadian border, and increased the government's relevant powers (Knowles 107-10); the Immigration Act of 1910 allowed for immigration to be regulated on the basis of ethnicity or occupation; while other measures sought to reduce the number of immigrants from Central and Eastern Europe specifically (Knowles 110-112). These measures, however, did not stop arrivals from the region, which continued until World War I.

Studying this pre-War Era in his chapter, "The Success of Jewish Agricultural Colonies in Western Canada," Eric Wilkinson from McGill University introduces the history of Jewish agricultural settlements. The earliest colonies were founded following the 1881 Russian pogroms, at which time Canada's Jewish community tried to resettle refugees in Western Canada. The result was the establishment of over a dozen farming colonies at the turn of the nineteenth and twentieth centuries. Wilkinson not only provides an overview of the history of the farming colonies established between 1884 and 1891, but he also reconstructs the lives of the colonists and examines how various organizations facilitated their settlement. His study investigates documents available for twelve different communities that span the Prairies. He takes detailed note of the various impediments to their success, including inexperience, poor soil, natural disaster, anti-Semitism, poor administration, and financial hardship but reconsiders the usual presumption that their colonies were bound to ultimately end in failure and re-evaluates the legacy of such settlements, claiming that the decisive factor which brought an end to the colonies was upward social mobility. They were victims of their own success, unable to maintain their numbers as younger generations moved away and parents joined them when they retired.

Also examining Eastern-European settlement in Canada before World War I, Peter Bush (Independent Scholar and Teaching Elder, St. Andrew's Presbyterian Church, Fergus, Ontario) surveys the period when the first immigrants from the region now called Ukraine arrived in Canada. Ukrainians (mostly from Galicia and Bukovina) also fit into the plans of Prime Minister Wilfrid Laurier and especially those of Minister of the Interior Clifford Sifton for populating the West as already detailed. At the time approximately 170,000 persons migrated to Canada from present-day Ukraine, mostly settling in Manitoba, Saskatchewan, and Alberta. Bush examines the immigration experience of these people through the study of the Independent Greek Church in Canada, representing a middle ground between The Presbyterian Church in Canada, which desired to bring the growing Ukrainian diaspora into the Presbyterian fold, and the Ukrainian immigrant intelligentsia, which envisioned a culturally and linguistically independent, Protestant church for themselves. Using the work of Richard White on middle ground and the work of Lamin Sanneh on non-dominant cultures' agency in missionary contexts, the chapter offers a new interpretation of the history of the Independent Greek Church in Canada: one that valorizes the agency of the Ukrainian participants and stresses the role of religion in the immigration process, while also revealing that as a middle ground, the denomination was too unstable to survive long and the growing uniformity of Canadian Presbyterianism ended this unexpected pairing on the Canadian Prairies.

Bram Beelaert (a scholar from the Red Star Line Museum in Antwerp, Belgium) contributes a chapter that provides a link between the pre-war and the interbellum eras; in "On the Way to the Last Best West: Antwerp as a Transit Port for Central and Eastern European Immigrants to Canada, 1870-1930," the author presents the rise of Antwerp as an emigration port from the 1840s to the 1930s, with an emphasis on Canada. Complete with fascinating illustrations providing insights into the migrant journey, the chapter focuses on the European part of the immigrant experience and shows how the shipping business also had a crucial role in the migration process. From the moment their passengers bought their shipping tickets in their hometown up until they arrived in the new country, shipping companies and their agents shaped the migrant experience. Meanwhile, Beelaert also underlines how the settlement of the Canadian West necessitated and came hand in hand with an international, transatlantic network of actors working with and in line with the regulations of the Canadian government. The shipping companies played a crucial role in the selection process between wanted and unwanted newcomers, as destination countries such as Canada adopted a policy of "remote control" and attempted to organize the selection process as far from their borders as possible. In the second part of the chapter, Beelaert provides insights into the experiences of emigrants from Central and Eastern Europe on their way to and in the port of Antwerp, highlighting the determining (but often overlooked) role of the transport industry during their journey to the sea and even on the decision to leave.

As noted already, Canadian immigration in many ways needs to be studied in an inter-American context that considers the impact of US immigration policy on Central and Eastern European immigration. This is especially true in the wake of World War I and the strict US restrictions introduced in the 1920s that several chapters in this volume refer to as a turning point and which are discussed in more detail in the chapter written by Balázs Venkovits. The anti-immigrant and nativist sentiment that appeared in the United States as a result of the influx of millions from the non-preferred region of Central and Eastern Europe culminated in demands for a general restriction of immigration (for a detailed overview, see Daniels). From the 1880s onwards, more and more restraints were introduced, ending the former free immigration policy of the country and barring various groups from entering the US. The Great War gave a boost to these mainly because of the fear of enemy aliens in the country and doubts about their loyalty, and in 1917 a literacy test was introduced. This did not stop another major wave after the war, as a result of which a growing number of people demanded the introduction of quotas. The Emergency Quota Act was passed in 1921, followed by the 1924 Johnson-Reed Act, which effectively ended New Immigration from Central and Eastern Europe by establishing a quota for each country in a way that clearly showed that restrictions targeted immigration from these regions.

The Canadian governments introduced various restrictions earlier as well and the situation was further complicated during the Great War due to the peculiar position of enemy aliens (resulting in their disenfranchisement and with many of the "foreigners" even being placed in internment camps). Immigration from enemy countries was banned in 1914, and the Immigration Act of 1919 introduced even more restraints (widening the list of inadmissible immigrants) and specifically excluded immigration from countries that fought against Canada in the war. As Knowles argues, "the opposition to immigration from central and eastern Europe was promoted by leading educators, journalists, and politicians, who took the view that immigrants from that part of Europe resisted assimilation into mainstream Canadian society and that encouraging their immigration would only lead to the 'balkanization' of Canada" (136). And yet, as the United States shut its gates tight after the war, Canada opened its borders and offered new opportunities for people from previously non-preferred countries, bringing about the reversal of former measures barring immigration. As a result, Canada clearly became one of the favored targets of immigrants in the 1920s, as shown in several chapters in this volume.

The impact of US quotas on Canada was varied: as the quotas did not apply to people born in Canada, many citizens moved to the south, but more importantly for this volume, the country becoming a possible new target was actually facilitated by the reversal of former measures. In 1923 the regulation restricting the entry of immigrants from Germany and her wartime allies was repealed and in 1925 the Canadian Pacific Railway and Canadian National Railways were authorized to recruit European agriculturalists, even from previously non-preferred countries. In line with these measures, a major wave of Central and Eastern European immigration to Canada started at the very time the United States quotas were introduced. The chapters written by Beelaert and Balázs Venkovits provide a more detailed overview of this era and these regulations: Beelaert reveals how it impacted the migration pathway and the business of shipping companies, while Venkovits (Institute of English and American Studies, University of Debrecen, Hungary) examines a little-studied aspect of Hungarian immigration to Canada as he presents how the US regulations and quotas not only resulted in Canada becoming more attractive for Hungarian immigrants but also how they contributed to illegal immigration across the US-Canada border. After an overview of the changing regulatory environment in an inter-American and transatlantic context, he assesses the extent to which illegal border crossing could be present in Hungarian immigration and using examples from archival sources, newspaper articles, and other publications he scrutinizes the representation of the topic in Hungary. Besides providing insights into so far neglected issues in the era, the chapter also provides a reminder of how recent discourse in the Americas on illegal immigration, restrictions, deportation, and border control has historical roots at the Canada-US border one hundred years ago.

Lukáš Perutka (Palacký University Olomouc and Charles University in Prague, the Czech Republic) in his intriguing chapter on "Czechoslovak Resistance in Canada During World War II" also shows how this growth impacted Czechoslovak-Canadians. By the time of the war, the Czechoslovak community in Canada was the second largest outside of Europe, preceded only by the one in the United States of America and it grew especially in the interwar period thanks, in part, to the restrictive policies of the US government. Perutka also examines a topic that thus far has received less scholarly attention and introduces the activities of Czechoslovaks in Canada during World War II that goes beyond the presentation of the military mission there. Based on a thorough analysis of extensive archival materials, Perutka focuses on so far neglected actors and assesses their roles in and contributions to the renewal of the independent Czechoslovak state in Central Europe. Importantly, besides studying key organizations and their leaders, Perutka also emphasizes that the minorities (traditionally ignored in the historical works about the second Czechoslovak resistance) should not be excluded from the resistance narrative.

With the end of World War II and the emergence of the Cold War with most of Central and Eastern Europe trapped east of the Iron Curtain, immigration from the region decreased overall. However, turbulent events in countries like Hungary (1956) and Czechoslovakia (1968) contributed to new (albeit short) waves of migration to Canada and shaped the perception of the nation in Central and Eastern Europe. The last four chapters in the volume examine exactly this era, with three essays related to the 1956 Hungarian revolution, which resulted in a brief but significant influx of Hungarian refugees, and one paper providing a study from the post-1968 era.

By December 1958, Canada had admitted almost 38,000 Hungarian refugees who were forced to flee their country after Soviet forces crushed the October 1956 uprising. Scholars have written extensively about the events in Hungary, the reception of Hungarians both in Canada and the United States, but the chapters in this volume add to this discourse by analyzing innovative aspects from so far little-studied perspectives. Sheena Trimble (Université catholique de l'Ouest, Angers, France) addresses such a topic in "Shaping Destinies: Women and the Hungarian Refugee Movement to Canada (1956–1958)" with her analysis of the evolving roles and actions of women, both Canadians and refugees, in Canadian society at the time, stressing their symbolic power and agency in the movement. Her meticulous archival research reveals that Canadian women expressed opinions and took on a variety of roles related to the Hungarian refugee movement. This examination not only offers an original perspective on Canada's response to the refugee crisis, but it also provides insights into the evolving roles of women in Canadian society. The weight of intersectionality often muted the voices of women of Hungarian origin, yet refugee women were accorded a symbolic power that played its own role in the movement, and they found ways to exercise their agency to achieve their desired admission and settlement outcomes.

Many arriving in and after 1956 left a clear mark on Canada and contributed to Canadian culture; two chapters illustrate this through examples from the fields of literature and music. Mária Palla affiliated with the Institute of English and American Studies, Pázmány Péter Catholic University, Budapest, studies the life writing of two Hungarian-Canadian authors, each of whom focuses on their thinly disguised autobiographical self, in "Food Memories Across Borders: Narratives of Emigration from Hungary to Canada." Béla Szabados (1942-) and Erika Gottlieb (1938-2007) fled Hungary and escaped to Canada in 1957 and 1958, respectively. The events recounted in a personal voice by Szabados in his *In Light of Chaos* (1990) not only include those he witnessed during World War II but also the events of the Hungarian Revolution of 1956 together with those of his and his family's arrival in Montréal as refugees. Gottlieb's *Becoming My Mother's Daughter: Survival and Renewal* (2008) is an account of the Jewish-Hungarian protagonist Eva Steinbach's border crossings, into which the intersubjective narrative of four generations of her family is incorporated. The journeys recalled involve multiple ways in which the two books' respective protagonists are impacted by various forces of history and intercultural encounters ultimately leading to the characters' re-evaluation and reconstruction of their personal and ethnic identities. Striking in both life narratives is the presence of embodied memories related to food, signifying climactic emotional moments and turning points. Szabados's life writing offers itself for an analysis of how the psychological responses given to the somatic experience of eating express the protagonist's position in his socio-political environment, while in Gottlieb's narrative the complexity of the relational identity is explored through food memories.

Gábor Hegedűs, whose family escaped from the Russian invasion of Hungary in 1956, settled in Toronto leaving his mark on the Canadian (and international) music scene under the stage name B. B. Gábor with his most popular songs being satiric commentaries on culture and politics, comparing life in the USSR and in Canada. In "'Outsider': The Influence of Migration Experience on the Life and Work of Hungarian-Canadian Songwriter BB Gábor," Victor Kennedy and his colleagues Kristian Kolar and Neža Bojnec Naterer (University of Maribor, Slovenia) introduce the life and work of B.B. Gábor. His songs and the themes addressed in them drew most attention from audiences and critics, and earned them international airplay, most notably on Radio Free Europe. The chapter analyses his difficulties coping with life as a refugee and as an immigrant to Canada resulting in personal tragedy, while the analysis of lyrics and interviews reveals how his work was unmistakably influenced by his migration experience and his position of being caught between East and West, enabling him to provide satirical commentaries on culture, politics, and life on either side of the world. His ability to express the difficulties of life in his songs left a lasting legacy in both Canada and his native Hungary.

The final chapter of the volume returns to the Czech perspective from the time period following the Prague Spring in 1968, when 12,000 Czechs were admitted to Canada and which thus, similarly to 1956 in Hungary, represents an important dividing line in the history of Canadian immigration from the region. Ludmila Čiháková (archivist at the State Regional Archives Litomerice, the Czech Republic) introduces the life and books of Josef Novotný, a language teacher working in northern Alberta at a local high school during the 1969/1970 school year who published his experience in books that went through three editions. Čiháková reveals how migration contributed to mutual transatlantic perceptions and the evolution of the image of Canada in the Czech Republic. Her chapter, "From Communist Czechoslovakia to Canada and Back: The Story of a Teacher from Czechoslovakia in Alberta," reconstructs and examines Novotný's life story thoroughly for the first time based on extensive research and adds valuable insights into the history of Czech immigration to North America during communist times, presenting the narrative as a typical cultural product of "normalization".

The objective of the HJEAS Books series is to reflect high-standard scholarship in the areas covered by the *Hungarian Journal of English and American Studies*. This is true of this volume that indeed grew out of a special section of the journal published in the fall of 2022. The essays by Wilkinson and Bush first appeared there, while the chapters by Trimble, Kennedy et al., and Palla represent revised or expanded versions of papers in the issue. The other chapters supplement these nicely and provide a multifaceted view of the history of immigration to Canada from Central and Eastern

Europe. Over the past two years many people have worked on making the publication of this volume possible. I would like to take this opportunity to express my gratitude to the authors for their contributions and their work throughout the lengthy publication process. I wish to thank those scholars who vetted the submissions, provided feedback to the authors, and helped improve the essays. I would like to thank Marianna Gula and Mariann Buday for their work with the journal issue in 2022 and Kálmán Matolcsy for copy editing the manuscript. This volume, and the book series overall, could not have become a reality without the professional and financial support of the University of Debrecen and the Faculty of Humanities (especially dean Róbert Keményfi and deputy dean Péter Csatár), as well as several colleagues of the Institute of English and American Studies. Most importantly, let me thank Donald E. Morse for not only establishing the book series but also offering scholarly and personal guidance throughout the publication of this volume and working together with Dorottya Mózes, making the publication of the Book Series with DeGruyter/Sciendo possible.

Works Cited

"2021 Census Canada, Ethnic or Cultural Origin by Gender and Age: Canada, Provinces and Territories." *Statistics Canada*. https://www150.statcan.gc.ca/t1/tbl1/en/tv.action?pid=981003 5501&geocode=A000011124. Web. 22 Aug. 2023.

Daniels, Roger. *Coming to America: A History of Immigration and Ethnicity in American Life*. New York: Perennial, 2002.

Knowles, Valeria. *Strangers at Our Gates: Canadian Immigration and Immigration Policy, 1540–2006*. Toronto: Dundurn Press, 2007.

Powell, John. *Encyclopedia of North American Immigration*. New York: Facts on File, 2005.

Venkovits, Balázs. "Introduction." *Hungarian Journal of English and American Studies* 28.2 (2022): 373-77.

---. "'The New Mecca of Immigrants': Hungarian Emigration to Canada and the Role of Immigration Propaganda." *Minorities in Canada: Intercultural Investigations*. Ed. Miklós Vassányi, et al. Budapest/Paris: L'Harmattan, 2020: 99-121.

Vineberg, Robert. *Responding to Immigrants' Settlement Needs: The Canadian Experience*. Dordrecht: Springer, 2012.

Eric Wilkinson

The Success of Jewish Agricultural Colonies in Western Canada

The history of Jewish agricultural colonies in Western Canada is often recounted as one of failure. As Harry Gutkin wistfully remarks, "all these colonies begun in hope and determination, dwindled into extinction . . . the dream of a Jewish agricultural society had vanished" (66). Never was there a mass agrarian movement, and by the mid-twentieth century each of the Jewish farm colonies had disappeared. The question of whether the history of these colonies is one of failure can be answered by juxtaposing the farmers' goals with the conditions that led to a decline in Jewish agriculture in Canada. This requires examining each colony's history and identifying the reasons for its decline. If the goals of the colonists are compatible with the ultimate demise of their communities, then the colonies should not be called failures. As the colonists primarily sought religious freedom and the opportunity to build a better life—rather than the utopian agricultural project envisioned by some of their supporters—it is possible they achieved this end without the colonies surviving into perpetuity. This reframes the history of Jewish farm settlement in Western Canada as a generational success.

Planning the agricultural colonies

The history of Jewish farm settlement in Western Canada begins with the Russian pogroms that themselves began in 1881. In the early 1880s Imperial Russia was pervaded by anti-Semitism that coincided with an economic recession and weak, irresolute tsarist governance (Aronson 235). Following the assassination of the moderate Czar Alexander II in 1881, Jews in Russia became the targets of violent rioting fueled by the erroneous, anti-Semitic conspiracy theory that claimed that the Jewish community was responsible for the Czar's assassination. Moreover, on May 10, 1882 the Russian government imposed the May Laws, limiting the rights and mobility of Jews in Russia. These events prompted the mass emigration of Jews from the Russian Empire in the late nineteenth and early twentieth centuries (Aronson 62), with many of the emigrants traveling to North America.

In response to the pogroms, the Lord Mayor of London, John Whittaker Ellis, organized a meeting at Mansion House in February 1882. In attendance was Sir Alexander Galt, Canada's High Commissioner in London. This meeting established the Russo-Jewish Committee, with a mandate to resettle Jewish refugees. Galt proposed large-scale Jewish colonization in Western Canada and lobbied the Canadian government to create a dedicated district in the Prairies for Jewish colonists, while conferring with Canada's Jewish community (Sack 193–94). At Galt's urging, the committee would in 1884 finance the founding of the first Jewish farm colony in Western Canada: Moosomin.

In 1881 Hermann Landau, a Jewish philanthropist who had made a fortune on the London Stock Exchange, independently conceived of a colonization scheme for Jews facing the pogroms. Landau would directly finance the Wapella settlement and provide his friend the Baron de Hirsch with funding for the Young Men's Hebrew Benevolent Society (YMHBS) in Montréal (Chiel 55). Landau imagined creating a large-scale Jewish society in the Canadian West through agricultural settlement and promoted the idea to Canadian lawmakers. In 1897, Prime Minister Wilfrid Laurier is alleged to have said to Landau: "If you will take up the question seriously and select any part of Manitoba, the Dominion will grant the Jews a measure of self-government as will enable them to make their own by-law, substituting Saturday for Sunday" (Chiel 55). The idea of a large, autonomous district in Canada would prove enticing but elusive to those coordinating the Jewish farm colonies.

Montréal's YMHBS began receiving financing from Baron Maurice de Hirsch in 1890. To honor their patron, the YMHBS was renamed the "Baron de Hirsch Institute" in 1900 (Belkin 39). The organization met with Prime Minister John C. Abbott and his Minister of Agriculture in 1892 to discuss the mass settlement of Jews in Western Canada. After the meeting, the Institute submitted a fourteen-point memorandum asking if there was land for 2,000 families or 10,000 Jewish persons. The government responded positively and recommended the colonists select land from that which was already allocated for settlement (Sack 225–26). However, nothing came of the proposal for a mass settlement due to a "lack of synchronization between the major forces involved" (Chiel 55). While the Canadian government was open to permitting immigration of individual Jewish settlers, they opposed the creation of the autonomous district desired by those funding Jewish colonization.

The Baron de Hirsch would also create the Jewish Colonization Association (JCA) in Paris in 1891, with the mandate to found agricultural colonies throughout the world for Jewish refugees. JCA Director Dr. Sigmund Sonnenfeld was receptive to the YMHBS project aimed at mass Jewish settlement in Western Canada (Leonoff, *Jewish Farmers* 24). Although the JCA became the main organization providing support to the Jewish farm colonies in Western Canada, the relatively autonomous Jewish district imagined by the JCA and YMHBS never materialized. When historians lament the demise of the dream of a Jewish agricultural society in Canada, it is often the dreams of these groups to which they refer, as the aspirations of colonists were different.

No people are homogenous in their aspirations, so describing the dreams of the Jewish farm colonists collectively is impossible. Nevertheless, there are basic commonalities in their narratives. Rarely did the Jewish colonists, most of whom were fleeing pogroms in Eastern Europe, envision a movement spanning the Canadian prairies. The dreams of the agriculturalists were more modest. The perspective of the farmers is typified by the stated goal of an anonymous colonist at a meeting in Edenbridge, who had "hoped to build a home in this country where, when he was older and not so strong, he could live without fear of being driven out" (Usiskin 46). Jews fleeing Eastern Europe sought freedom, and the opportunity to build a future for themselves and their children. The virtue of agricultural living from a social perspective—championed by Am Olam and similar movements that associated farming with Jewish religiosity—largely did not motivate the colonists (Belkin 53).

The zest for freedom that grounded this common sentiment had its roots in the oppressive societal conditions the colonists were escaping. William Leonoff describes this shared attitude: "My father said he wouldn't want his children to live the type of life that he lived. The government was corrupt. A Jew had no chance whatsoever. And he said he doesn't care what he's going to do—if he has to carry stones" (6). In addition to illustrating a desire for liberty, this quote exemplifies how the colonists understood their work to be an extension of their freedom. As an unnamed Edenbridge farmer explained: "Here there is always plenty of work, and the fruits of my labour at least belong to me" (Usiskin 38). The Jews connected the hardships of farming to the freedoms and equality they had in their new home. Another anonymous farmer insisted that "[t]here is no place on earth where people are more equal than right here" precisely because the hardships of farm life were considered equalizing (Usiskin, 30).

A Jewish settler could aspire to positions in society that were unheard of in Eastern Europe, and even difficult to attain for Jews elsewhere in Canada. For instance, some colonists at Rumsey-Trochu became Justices of the Peace or School Board trustees, while those at Edenbridge became reeves (equivalent to mayor) and Justices of the Peace (Rubin 334). Not only were Jewish colonists free to practice their religion, but they also reported that their gentile neighbors treated them with respect. The challenges of farm life required cooperation that transcended religion, ethnicity, or language.

Additionally, the colonists sought to maintain a Jewish life, though Orthodox Judaism was difficult to maintain in the farming colonies. The formation of a *minyan*, which is meant to consist of ten adult Jews—usually men for Orthodox practitioners— was necessary for prayer and reading the Torah (Katz and Lehr 52). There was also the need to maintain the synagogue and *mikveh* (ritual baths). A functioning community also required a *shochet* (ritual slaughterer), a *mohel* (one qualified to perform circumcisions), and preferably a rabbi. Finally, there was a need for education, requiring schools. Many Orthodox settlers made short term concessions while working towards the creation of the institutions necessary to fully practice their faith. Every colony approached these challenges differently. As the colonists intended to live freely *as Jews*, these were all crucial.

Understanding the aspirations of the colonists is key to assessing whether the colonies can be considered failures. There are seven factors which affected the decline of the settlements:

Factor:	Description:
• Agricultural experience	The degree of agricultural training that colonists arrived with
• Quality of the land/soil	The suitability of the allocated land for farming
• Frequency of natural disaster	The frequency of fires, frosts, droughts, and other disasters
• Relationship to neighbors	Support from neighbors, and the incidence of anti-Semitism
• Religious institutions	The capacity of a settlement to offer a Jewish religious life by maintaining a synagogue, *mikveh*, rabbi, *shochet*, *mohel*, etc.
• Colony administration	The quality of administration and available financial support
• Population replacement	The ability to attract new colonists or train the young

In both the autobiographical writings of the colonists and records of the organizations promoting Jewish settlement, these seven factors emerge as the chief challenges facing the Jewish colonies. By understanding which of these factors were decisive in the ultimate decline of the settlements, it is possible to determine whether the aspirations of the colonists were frustrated and unrealized.

The farm colonies

Discussing the historical record of the Jewish farming colonies in Western Canada is made complicated by two factors. First, the settlements were collections of loosely aligned family farms with no clearly demarcated outer boundaries. Secondly, the names used for the same colonies differ depending on the source and were often changed. Settlements like Edenbridge, where the colonists founded their own community, are exceptional for being referred to by a single, recognized name. Frequently the names for settlements were borrowed from the village or town nearest to the farms. For instance, the Qu'Appelle colony took its name from the existing municipality of Qu'Appelle. However, some sources call the Qu'Appelle colony Cupar or Lipton, two *different* nearby towns.

In what follows, the colonies that were adjacent to each other, such as Sibbald/Alsask/Empress or Rumsey-Trochu, are counted together because they shared educational and religious institutions. Though some documents and maps differentiate between these colonies, the fact that they were located alongside each other and shared their institutions makes differentiating between them unnecessary. When the names that refer to the same locations are consolidated, we are left with thirteen colonies.

Name of Colony:	Date of Establishment:
• Moosomin / New Jerusalem	1882
• Wapella	1886
• Hirsch	1891
• Pine Lake	1892/1893
• Qu'Appelle / Lipton / Cupar	1901
• Bander Hamlet / Narcisse	1902
• Rumsey-Trochu	1906
• Edenbridge	1906
• Hoffer-Sonnenfeld	1906
• Sibbald / Montefiore / Empress / Alsask / Eyre / Compeer	1910
• Camper / New Hirsch	1911
• Winnipeg Settlements	Various

Of the thirteen colonies, the colony of Rosetown is omitted from the present analysis. It is only known to exist on one map, and no other information is available about the settlement beyond it being located near the municipality of the same name in Saskatchewan (Katz and Lehr 51). There were also at least seven minor colonies surrounding the city of Winnipeg, which are assessed here collectively as the economic structure and institutions of these individual "colonies" were shared.

Moosomin ("New Jerusalem")

Following the meeting at Mansion House in 1881, Sir Alexander Galt wrote Prime Minister John A. Macdonald recommending the admission of Russian Jews to Canada. Galt suggested using land in Western Canada that had been set aside for Mennonites or private colonization companies and reallocating it to the Jewish settlers. The first twenty-seven Russian Jews arrived in Winnipeg on May 26, 1882, with two-hundred and forty-seven more arriving six days later. The government was slow to provide homestead lands, and many drifted into other occupations before the land was ready in 1884. Twenty-six families settled twenty-five miles southwest of the town of Moosomin in what would become Saskatchewan. The colony was given the moniker "New Jerusalem" either by the Jewish colonists themselves, or their neighbors (Paris 223; Leonoff 2–3). The Russo-Jewish Committee gave the colony $15,000 in loans, with each farmer receiving between $259 and $485.

The history of the colony was one of successive disasters (Gutkin 57). In 1884, there were early frosts and the settlers' shelters were inadequate when faced with the cold, wind, and snow of winter. Another early frost in August 1885 caused more crop failure, and general drought swept the region in 1886. Between 1885 and 1886 the colony made some progress, constructing a small synagogue and Hebrew school, but these advances were lost when the settlement's rabbi and teacher was stuck in a blizzard and had his feet amputated due to frostbite. The settlement held on until 1889 when its hay crop was consumed by a wildfire. The colonists suspected arson and were dissatisfied with the police investigation. By 1890 the colony was depopulated, with many leaving for Winnipeg. Of the two-hundred Jews who had settled at Moosomin, only one remained by 1901.

Adversities that would be overcome in later settlements were encountered at Moosomin in greater magnitude. Among these were inadequate funding, lack of training, and perpetual disaster. The Russo-Jewish Committee was not prepared to provide financial support to the settlers beyond the initial $15,000. Future colonies that found themselves without funding would have access to umbrella organizations that offered consistent financing. A lack of agricultural training was common among Jewish farm colonists in Western Canada, but all subsequent colonies included at least some settlers who had some experience before emigrating or had some assistance from gentile farmers. Finally, while virtually all of the Jewish farm colonies would face natural disasters, there remained occasional periods of success and relative prosperity. The Moosomin colony never had a reprieve that would have enabled it to shore up resources against future periods of adversity. Each of these factors, which would later prove individually surmountable in other colonies, were faced all at once and to a more devastating degree at Moosomin. Colonization efforts in the area by other ethnic groups failed for similar reasons in the same period despite greater expertise and support (Rosenburg 218).

Wapella

When looking to establish a Jewish farm colony, Hermann Landau handpicked the Heppner family of two men and three women, as well as six men who knew English and were familiar with farming (Leonoff, *Early Jewish Agricultural Colonization* 3). This group settled six miles northeast of the town of Wapella in 1886. In 1887, Wapella's Liberal Conservative Association complained to the government that "[n]ot only are Jews an undesirable class of settlers but they are keeping a number of desirable settlers out" (Leonoff, *Jewish Farmers* 10). An inspector was dispatched to assess the colony and later reported from Moosomin that "the English settlers speak highly of these Jews, and don't desire better neighbours. . . . A class of settlers such as these men cannot but be beneficent to the country" (Leonoff, *Early Jewish Agricultural Colonization* 6). Within a year of settlement, the six men had departed in search of brides, leaving only the Heppner family. Luckily, in 1888, Abraham Klenman came from Bessarabia to Montréal with his family, including his son-in-law, Solomon

Barish. Klenman had overseen an agricultural estate while Barish came from the Russian-Jewish colony of Dombroveni (Leonoff, *Wapella* 4). Klenman learned about the Heppner family and traveled to join them, bringing more experience to the colony. Between 1889 and 1892 twenty-eight other Jewish families joined them in Wapella.

The Wapella colony began without financial aid. Not until 1901 when crops were destroyed by frost did twenty-seven farmers obtain loans from the Jewish Agricultural Society of New York, which were repaid within seventeen years (Leonoff, *Jewish Farmers* 16). In 1889, Edel Brotman and his sons took up homesteads at Wapella. Having been a rabbi in Galicia, Brotman would provide religious services to the colony. With no synagogue or *mikveh*, Wapella had limited religious institutions compared to other colonies. The colony peaked at fifty families and potential for expansion was limited because of a lack of homesteads available in the district and rising land values (Leonoff, *Wapella* 32). When Jewish soldiers from the Russo-Japanese War of 1905 passed through they only found temporary work before moving on to find cheaper land. The colony lasted until the 1960s when after Klenman's son had died and Barish's sons retired (Leonoff, *Jewish Farmers* 17), at least one fourth-generation family still farmed in the district in 1984.

The success of Wapella contrasts with Moosomin, which was only thirty miles away. The land was forested with fertile black soil (Leonoff, *Wapella* 4), which made it both suitable to farming and provided lumber. Though the protestations of the Liberal Conservative Association constituted an instance of organized anti-Semitism, it was ineffectual. Once established, the settlers befriended the neighboring farmers, including some signatories of the anti-Jewish resolution (Leonoff, *Jewish Farmers* 17). The independence of Wapella also facilitated its success, with Leonoff claiming that the involvement of government and aid organizations in the founding and maintenance of other colonies caused them to get "bogged down in official red tape" compared to Wapella (Leonoff, *Jewish Farmers* 16). Despite never having its own institutions other than basic religious services, retaining these basic religious activities was key to maintaining its viability as a Jewish community.

Hirsch

In 1891 the YMHBS, with financing from the Baron de Hirsch, dispatched two non-Jews, Charles McDiarmid, the manager of the prospective colony, and Ignatius Rotth, to scout land for a settlement (Belkin 71). Although they liked the land at Moosomin, where the earlier farm colony had been, the land had reverted to prairie and the district was twenty-five miles from the railroad. In 1888, the Jewish farmer Jacob Pierce had settled at Oxbow in what would become the southeast corner of Saskatchewan. His son Ascher Pierce recommended the area to the YMHBS. Land was selected twenty-one miles west of Oxbow, and the new colony was named Hirsch in honor of the Baron de Hirsch, and sometimes called Oxbow-Hirsch in recognition of the settlers at Oxbow.

In April the first twenty-seven men arrived by rail from Montréal. With more coming from Montréal, Winnipeg, and Regina, there were forty-nine families in Hirsch by the end of the month (Leonoff, *Jewish Farmers* 28). By July there were seventy-three homesteads in the colony. The first three years proved difficult; the YMHBS Colonization Committee in Montréal had underestimated the capital needed to establish farmers. The JCA in Paris, who were providing the funding, were also ignorant of the costs of maintaining the colony. There were three years of crop failure from drought, hail, and grasshopper plagues. Many colonists left or relocated closer to Oxbow, although others refused to be dislodged. In 1892 the school and the first synagogue in Saskatchewan were built. In the fall of 1895, the fortunes of the colony finally turned around with the harvest of their first bumper crop. This continued with another good harvest in 1896 and the arrival of five more families from Red Deer (Belkin 73). In November 1899, Rabbi Marcus Berner arrived with another fifteen families. He would serve for thirty-two years as rabbi, *shochet*, school board chairman, and municipal councilor for the colony. The JCA would take direct administrative control in 1900 before transferring that authority to the Jewish Agricultural Society of New York in 1903. By the time of Louis Rosenberg's survey in 1939, there were two schools and synagogues in the community (220). Descendants of the original colonists were still farming in Hirsch in 1984.

Hirsch faced early challenges from natural destruction of crops. Additionally, the YMHBS in Montréal and the JCA were too far removed to understand what was necessary for its success, leading to mismanagement. Nevertheless, the inexperience of the colonists was overcome through help from the pre-existing Jewish farmers at Oxbow. The establishment of a synagogue and arrival of Rabbi Berner also marked a turning point for the colony. Hirsch illustrates how inexperience, natural calamity, and poor management could be overcome if a colony could survive until a strong harvest. The establishment of religious institutions is also notable, as the settlers would have been less likely to have persevered if they did not at least have access to the basic rudiments of Judaism.

Pine Lake

Pine Lake was located in central Alberta, far from Moosomin, Wapella, and Hirsch, which were all located in southeast Saskatchewan near the Manitoba border. The colony was established in either 1892 or 1893. While the precise date of its founding is unknown, it is known that nobody lived in the vicinity of Pine Lake in the spring of 1892 (Dawe 8). Fifteen Jewish families with seventy individuals settled in a rough ring around Blank's Lake. Rabbi Blank, the community's leader, had a modest cabin built on the southwestern lake edge. The settlers had no farm training and only seed potatoes, no seed grain. Henry Alford tried to assist by supplying the settlers with wild game, but others purportedly gave the Jews pork they had said was deer meat as a cruel joke (Dawe 10). The local Dominion Lands agent Jerry Jessup disparaged the Jewish colonists and withheld assistance. In May 1894 the Russo-Jewish Committee, having learned about the colony, sent them $400. The Committee would send more funds in the spring, but after a poor potato crop and a frozen oat crop from the previous season, only six residents remained, with the remainder leaving that year. Rabbi Blank would settle in Winnipeg while the others are speculated to have also returned to Winnipeg. Some moved to the United States and took up poultry farming in California (Armstrong, Par. 10).

The colony's isolation relates to the Dominion Lands Act, which controlled colonization. The Act required immigrants to claim a quarter-section of land they would improve, reside on for at least six months every year, and receive full title to only after three years. This system effectively settled the prairies, but the residency requirement precluded the formation of the sort of settlement the Pine Lake colonists preferred. Those at Pine Lake had sought to create a communally governed colony under the leadership of a rabbi (Armstrong, Par. 9), modeled after the *shtetls* of Eastern Europe. This explains why they traveled so far, as they correctly assumed that the remoteness of the colony would discourage interference from the government. A later attempt to emulate a *shtetl* at Bender Hamlet has also been scrutinized for being impractical for farming in Canada (Chiel 55). Thus, the structure of the colony contributed to its demise, along with inexperience, disaster, and antipathy.

Qu'Appelle/Lipton/Cupar

Qu'Appelle was the "first and only attempt in Canada to delegate to Government officials the founding and administration of a Jewish agricultural settlement" (Rosenburg 220). The JCA approached the Canadian government about establishing the colony and it was determined that the immigration agent in London would select a number of Romanian Jewish families and the JCA would pay for their travel. A thousand francs were provided to the government by the JCA for each family in order to purchase livestock, farm equipment, and building materials. A district twenty-five miles north of the railway station at Qu'Appelle was selected with conditions "suitable to mixed farming" (Belkin 76). A first group of forty-nine Jewish families arrived in 1901, and with the assistance of the nearby Métis community they constructed houses and prepared for winter.

The supervisors chosen for the colony were anti-Semitic and could not communicate with the colonists who spoke Yiddish, Romanian, and German (*Belkin*, 76). They misspent money, buying food instead of farm equipment. Several families departed, but the colony was replenished by more arrivals in 1902, raising the total population to three-hundred and sixty-five. The colony attracted some Jewish immigrants from Russia who brought their farming experience and capital. The JCA constructed three schools and recruited a *shochet*. No synagogue was in the colony itself, although one was built in the town of Lipton and religious services were held in schools (Rosenberg 221). The government was relieved of responsibility for the colony in April 1903, and the JCA had its New York affiliate reorganize the colony on a more productive basis. In 1906, the Canadian Pacific Railroad extended fourteen miles north of the colony causing new stations to appear at Lipton and Cupar. The portions of the colony nearest either station came to be referred to by the village names. The colony persisted into the mid-twentieth century, though its decline seems to be undocumented.

The takeaway from Qu'Appelle relates to administrative mismanagement. While in Hirsch there was a disconnect between the colony and the distant YMHBS and JCA, neither were anti-Semitic or wholly incompetent like the initial government managers at Qu'Apelle. The assumption of administrative control by the JCA in 1903 alleviated this issue, and Qu'Appelle was fortunate not to face any major natural disasters during its early history. Like Hirsch, the institutional strength of the colony helped it flourish after the construction of schools, a synagogue, and a rail line nearby.

Bender Hamlet/Narcisse

Founded in 1902, Bender Hamlet attempted to emulate the *shehtl* communities of Eastern Europe: single-street villages with houses on one side, fields on the other (Katz & Lehr 52). Jacob Bender, who hailed from a *shtetl* community in Ukraine, arrived in Winnipeg in 1902 and traveled to the Interlake region in search of land. Bender was impressed by the brush of the area since wood was coveted in Ukraine, but the chosen land was poor for farming. He went to England and Eastern Europe to recruit eighteen families who arrived between 1902 and 1904. They sought government approval to divide a quarter-section of land into nineteen strips of eight and a half acres each. The settlers built their houses in a row on these sections, and each took up a homestead on the perimeter.

In December 1912 the Canadian Northern Railway built a station two miles north of the colony which the colonists named after Narcisse Loven, President of the JCA. The railway would help the farmers ship their goods to Winnipeg. The colony peaked in 1915 with thirty-nine families enjoying relative prosperity. However, a severe economic blow would be dealt by the fall in cattle prices after World War I (Chiel 64). Lehr believes these economic difficulties caused the population to drop below the threshold required to maintain a Jewish religious life, leading to an exodus (25). After three years of torrential rains washed out crops between 1924 and 1926, the last of the colonists left in 1927. This combination of poor soil and falling cattle prices affected not only the Jewish colony, however, as nearby Ukrainian and Scandinavian colonies were also abandoned.

Unlike the two other Jewish colonies that dispersed before the 1930s—Moosomin and Pine Lake—Bender Hamlet suffered not only from natural conditions but also market ones. Katz and Lehr argue that the communal *shtetl* arrangement was uneconomical as farmers had to commute to their homesteads every day (139). Some colonists even ended up relocating to their homesteads. In response to the poor quality of the soil the colonists adapted by focusing on livestock. However, this left the colony more vulnerable to the interwar fluctuations in cattle prices. This caused the population losses that would put the community below the threshold needed to maintain a Jewish religious life, and with religious rites unavailable within the colony the remaining settlers departed.

Rumsey-Trochu

A colony was created in central Alberta near Trochu in 1906. The JCA had sent seventeen Jews from Montréal to farm the fertile land along the Red Deer River (Gutkin 64). A year after the initial group arrived, another group appeared just east of Trochu at Rumsey. Although identified by some authors as separate colonies, they shared the same religious institutions and functioned as one colony. The colony lacked a *shochet* or a rabbi, but a homesteader, Judah Shumiatcher, served as Hebrew teacher (Rubin 333). Rumsey-Trochu would become one of the more successful colonies—in 1906 there were only eleven homesteaders, but within three years this number doubled.

J. A. Guttman and Max Waterman were appointed as Justices of the Peace and trustees of the Tolman School District, becoming the first Jews in Alberta to hold such positions (Rubin 334). In 1916, the JCA funded the construction of a synagogue and a school; the colony proved unable to attract a rabbi, but the synagogue still served religious and social functions. After World War I the colony absorbed several Polish Jews, though a lack of farming experience, combined with drought between 1921 and 1923, led many to leave. A serious blow to the colony was how farmers had overextended their credit as a result of a land boom that followed World War I. In 1922, a JCA inspector described the case of one farmer who purchased a half-section of land for $20,000 and still owed $10,000 despite the land now only being worth $6,000–7,000 (Rubin 334–35). The colony lost over half its families in the twenties, with most moving to Calgary because of debt, and their children leaving the colony for education or spouses (Armstrong Par. 13). The Depression would wipe out the remaining colonists, and by World War II only two Jewish families remained.

Rumsey-Trochu suffered from its small size, which made its existence precarious when too many individual farmers left. The failure to attract a rabbi limited its ability to attract new Jewish colonists, as despite the synagogue and some other facilities, the colony could not provide the kind of religious life many emigrants expected. This weakness made the colony susceptible to the credit crisis its farmers faced in the interwar era, which depleted it in a manner similar to Bender Hamlet.

Edenbridge

The first Jews to settle Edenbridge had escaped Lithuanian pogroms by moving to South Africa in the late 1890s (Paris 242). The Vickar family, near the end of 1904, had read an article in an American Yiddish newspaper written by a textile worker who left the city to farm in North Dakota. As there were few homesteads left in North Dakota, he advised Jews to look to Canada (Leonoff, *Jewish Farmers* 48). In February 1906 Louis and Fanny Vickar, their families, and nine other Jews, set out for Canada. Two went ahead to Saskatchewan by rail-line to a stop called Star City and selected land fifteen miles north along the Carrot River. When the inexperienced homesteaders arrived in 1906, they met two Englishmen, George Ellis and Isaac Brass, who taught them to farm. In 1907 when a post office was built, the Jews were asked to name the colony. The settlers proposed names such as "Israel Villa" or "Jew Town" that were rejected by the government, who disallowed names based on ethnicities (Usiskin 62). The name "Edenbridge" was selected as a pun on Yidden (Jew's) bridge, referencing a bridge that had been built by the community across the Carrot River.

A cemetery was registered in 1906 and two years later the settlers constructed a synagogue (Leonoff, *Jewish Farmers* 54). The Beth Israel Synagogue served the community for sixty years until 1968 when a *minyan* could no longer be maintained. The colony advertised in a Winnipeg newspaper to locate a rabbi and Max Shallit responded, taking up a homestead and becoming *shochet* and teacher for the community as well. The colonists also wrote to overseas newspapers in the hope of attracting more immigrants. A group of Jews working in sweatshops in Whitechapel, England, took interest, and the first arrived in 1911. The Edenbridge Jewish Co-operative Credit Union was formed in 1910 and was loaned $1,000 by the JCA. In November 1912 the rural municipality of Willowcreek, which included Edenbridge, was established. David Vickar served as reeve (mayor) for twenty-two years, as would his son Charles. Edenbridge School No. 2930 was opened during the fall term of 1913, and eventually two public schools served the settlement. The population peaked at about fifty families in the early 1920s. By the late 1970s the only remaining farmers were two old, unmarried brothers who tended the cemetery and synagogue.

Edenbridge benefited from significant institutional strength. The synagogue, credit union, post office, schools, and services of Rabbi Shallit provided amenities that discouraged people from leaving. The colony was also able to maintain its population by recruiting new farmers in foreign newspapers. Like other successful colonies, its decline was not the result of a natural or economic calamity, but a lack of generational continuity. Although some families farmed for four generations, the children of most farmers eventually left to pursue education (Paris 261). With decreased Jewish immigration and the end of homesteading, there were no farmers to replace those who left or retired.

Hoffer-Sonnenfeld

In 1906 another Jewish farm settlement appeared in the southwest corner of Saskatchewan. The account of the settlement's founding in most histories recounts how several young men, trained in agriculture by the JCA at its Agricultural School and led by Moses Hoffer, settled in the area (Belkin 61). Anna Feldman challenges this narrative in her essay "Sonnenfeld." She explains that there were Jews already established in the area when the group from the agricultural school arrived; the community was named New Herman after a colonist named Mr. Herman, whose legs had frozen in a blizzard while he protected his young son (38–39). When Moses Hoffer arrived in 1907, he advised the name to change to Sonnenfeld, but "New Herman" was used as late as 1912.

By 1909 the colony had fifty-eight people on twenty-five farms, owning 6,400 acres. In 1910 a post office was built a few miles northeast of the colony. This was followed in 1912 by a building to house a synagogue, a Hebrew school, and accommodations for a teacher (Feldman 43). A credit union was established in 1917 with $2,000 in start-up capital raised with JCA help. Excellent crops in 1912 and 1913 and high wartime wheat prices were followed by dropping prices between 1920 and 1923, and five crop failures in a row from 1917 to 1921 (41). Encouraged by harvests later in the twenties, the JCA brought in thirty-one families from Eastern Europe. The Depression hit the colony hard. The crops of 1931 and 1934 were failures; those of 1930, 1932, and 1933 were insufficient to meet harvesting costs; and no new settlers arrived as immigration was halted during the following war. Nonetheless, the attrition rate of the Jewish farmers compared favorably to their neighbors. Only four of twenty-six farmers that remained in 1939 had lived in the colony less than nine years, and in 1936, 58.33 percent of farmers' sons stayed on the family farm (49). The colony benefited from strong institutions that helped it retain its population during periods of hardship. Its end only came as children departed for education and their retiring parents joined them elsewhere.

Sibbald/Montefiore/Empress/Alsask/Eyre/Compeer

A series of adjoining colonies appeared along the Alberta-Saskatchewan border beginning in 1910. These colonies are prone to confusion as authors sometimes distinguish between adjoining communities or use different names for the same communities. Sibbald is often used to collectively refer to these colonies, although some authors who differentiate between the communities use it to refer specifically to some farmers on the Albertan side of the border (Rubin 329). Sibbald is also sometimes called Montefiore and, confusingly, "Alsask North." John Lehr's map of Jewish farm colonies places a community named Empress to the south of Sibbald but identifies it as smaller (Lehr 21). On the Saskatchewan side of the border is Alsask, and Lehr's map locates Eyre southeast of Alsask. Leonoff refers to this community as "Eyre (Alsask)" (Leonoff, *Jewish Farmers* 70). Finally, Palmer lists "Compeer" alongside the other communities in the area, although it appears on no maps, so the precise location of this part of the colony is unknown (Palmer 128).

This colony was founded by farmers from North Dakota who moved due to poor farming conditions. The land at the new colony also had poor natural vegetation, soil, and rainfall (Rubin 335). The colonists constructed a community hall that served educational and religious functions. A house was also built for a rabbi and the settlement attracted three over the course of its existence. The specifics of the colony's decline are unclear, though Rosenberg blames the quality of the land (223). The farmers appealed to the JCA for assistance, but during the Depression many colonists fled their farms. Rosenburg reported in 1939 that six Jews still clung to their farms, but the others had returned to the United States to take up poultry farming in the Petaluma district of California.

Camper/New Hirsch

In 1911 several Russian Jews took up homesteads near Camper, Manitoba, in the Interlake region. The colony was named New Hirsch but is also referred to on occasion by the name of the nearby town of Camper. The soil quality of the land was poor (Belkin 82), so the farmers devoted themselves to cattle-raising and dairy-farming. Like Bender Hamlet, New Hirsch suffered from the fall in cattle prices following World War II (Chiel 56). But the colony itself had dissolved, with most farmers relocating to Trancona and Kildonan, Jewish farm communities near Winnipeg.

Winnipeg settlements

According to Arthur Chiel, the "Jewish farmers in Manitoba that were most successful for the longest period of time were those who settled near Winnipeg" (56). These colonies included Gimli, Rosenfeld, Bird's Hill, Transcona, Kildonan, Rosser, Lorette, and Ste. Anne (Katz and Lehr 51; Leonoff, *Pioneers* 10). These farmers focused on dairy farming, poultry raising, and truck-farming to supply Winnipeg. Due to their proximity to the city, they had access to the Winnipeg Jewish community, which alleviated the pressure of isolation. Even so, Bird's Hill and Kildonan were large enough to have their own synagogues constructed. At its height Kildonan— also called "West Kildonan"—had fifty farm families and supplied a large portion of Winnipeg's milk supply (Leonoff, *Pioneers* 11). The eventual decline of the Jewish farms around Winnipeg is attributable to a lack of continuity. The Depression hurt farmers generally, and with a city nearby the enticement to leave was magnified. Immigrants aspiring to be farmers were more likely to seek out larger, isolated colonies, so the continuation of the Winnipeg colonies depended on the children of the existing farmers, but few children chose to continue in the farming tradition.

The decline of the colonies

My examination of these colonies reveals what conditioned their success or failure. While most settlers were inexperienced in agriculture, this impediment did not itself cause a colony to fail. On occasion, some settlers would bring farming knowledge with them, such as Abraham Klenman and Solomon Barish at Wapella, or the trained arrivals at Hoffer-Sonnenfeld. Some colonists were also assisted by their neighbors, including the Métis at Qu'Appelle, or English farmers at Edenbridge. Finally, many learned from trial and error. In no instance did inexperience cause a colony's demise.

The quality of land and soil presented a related challenge to the colonists. Although lands were occasionally chosen by the JCA or other organizations, frequently farmers selected land for themselves, the quality of which varied from colony to colony. This, however, was not a decisive factor for survival: Moosomin and Wapella were founded close to each other, both on rich soil, yet the former failed and the latter prospered. Bender Hamlet and New Hirsch, founded on poor soil, persevered by diversifying through livestock farming, though this hurt them when the cattle market collapsed. Land quality was reportedly the main factor in the decline of Sibbald, though this is not well documented. The quality of the land was therefore rarely decisive, although it definitely contributed to the demise of Bender Hamlet and directly to Sibbald.

Natural catastrophes, including frosts, droughts, torrential rains, and grasshopper plagues, damaged several colonies but were not usually deciding factors in their demise. The only colony where natural forces prevailed entirely over farmers was Moosomin, which faced worse conditions than any other colony. Hirsch and Rumsey-Trochu survived periods of crop failure spanning years through outside financial support, institutional strength, and eventual successes. A more pertinent factor for some colonies was financial disaster. In Rumsey-Trochu this involved the over-extension of credit during the land boom of World War I, whereas the fall in cattle prices hurt Bender Hamlet and New Hirsch. While the Depression would see the general deterioration of the colonies, even during that period Jews were less likely to abandon their farms than other farmers in Canada.

The fourth factor affecting the colonies was anti-Semitism and general relations with non-Jews. Recorded instances of anti-Semitism included the rumored arson that ruined the Moosomin colony and the complaints of the Liberal Conservative Association at Wapella. The anti-Semitism encountered often sprang from ignorance rather than malice, however, and was mitigated through contact. This is typified by one anecdote about a Jewish settler working as a farmhand before establishing his own farm (Paris 245). The farmhand declined to attend church with his employers, explaining that he was Jewish. The family did not believe he was Jewish because they believed that Jews had horns. They produced a biblical image of Abraham, and the farmhand found that they had confused the placement of Abraham's hands for horns. Instead of attending church, the gentile couple ended up staying home to learn about their Jewish neighbors from the farmhand. This episode captures the kind anti-Semitism Jews encountered in Western Canada where most had never encountered a Jewish person before and revised their view once they encountered the colonists. Incidents of anti-Semitic cruelty like that experienced at Pine Lake were rare, and settlers more often recorded being helped.

The administration of the colonies also contributed to success or failure. The lack of "red tape" allowed Wapella to flourish, as it avoided seeking outside support for five years after creation. The administration of Hirsch by the YMHBS and JCA was inhibited by distance and their lack of understanding the realities in the colony. Likewise, the Canadian government's administration of Qu'Appelle was hampered by the managers' anti-Semitism. The successful colonies were largely independent but received arms-length support in difficult times. Additionally, colonies organized to emulate the *shtetls* of Eastern Europe proved uneconomical in Western Canada (Rosenberg 224). At both Pine Lake and Bender Hamlet this form of colony failed, although Simon Belkin speculates that "[h]ad it been on a larger scale and in a better agricultural area, it would have perhaps produced much better results" (79). Regardless, sound administration had an impact on a colony's success.

The maintenance of religious institutions was also crucial. The survival of Hirsch despite a prolonged crop failure is owed to the construction of a synagogue and the recruitment of a rabbi. At Edenbridge and Sonnenfeld multiple synagogues and schools were constructed. Communities that provided religious and social institutions were more successful, as they encouraged settlement and prevented colonists from leaving to find amenities their colony lacked. The relationship between the presence of religious institutions and colonists was indeed reciprocal: without sufficient institutions colonists would leave, and without a "critical mass" of colonists the Jewish religious institutions and rites could not operate (Katz and Lehr 63), which further disintegrates a community.

The Depression depleted the colonies not because Jews left their farms in greater numbers than their neighbors, but because when the population fell below the threshold necessary for basic religious services, the remainder would often leave all at once. This happened more often during the Depression because, in addition to the associated hardships, restrictions on immigration meant that nobody was coming to replenish a colony's numbers. After World War II and the eventual establishment of Israel Jewish immigrants no longer looked to Western Canada as a destination. The only remaining source of continuity was the children of previous farmers. As the colonies only offered an elementary education, children often left and remained in cities rather than return to the farm. Most colonies thus faded away as farmers retired and moved to the city to join their children.

Having uncovered the conditions of decline for the farm colonies, it may be asked whether this amounts to failure in light of the goals of the farmers. The Jewish farm colonists sought liberty and equality, and despite setbacks they found them in the farm colonies. More crucially, the colonists sought to build a better life for their families through agriculture. When one observes that the cause of decline for most colonies was that the children of the farmers left the colonies to pursue a better education and find employment, the effort of the colonists to ensure a better life for their families cannot but be said to have been a success. Success for the colonies did not consist in their existing in perpetuity. In any case, the family homestead only existed for a time before being replaced by large commercial farms. The decline of this way of life was inevitable, yet the colonists achieved what they intended to before its demise. Insofar as the dream of Jewish farm colonists was carving a better life out of the soil of Western Canada, their history is that of heroic generational success.

Works Cited

Archives Consulted

Alex Dworkin Canadian Jewish Archives, Montréal.
Library and Archives Canada, Ottawa.

Primary Sources

Hoffer, Clara, and F. H. Kahan. *Land of Hope*. Saskatoon, SK: Modern Press, 1960.
Rosenberg, Louis. *Canada's Jews*. Montréal, QC: McGill-Queens UP, 1993.
Usiskin, Michael. *Uncle Mike's Edenbridge*. Trans. Marcia Usiskin Basman. Winnipeg, MB: Peguis Publishers, 1983.

Secondary Sources

Armstrong, J. A. "From Pogrom to Prairie: Early Jewish Farm Settlements in Central Alberta." *Alberta Museums*. https://wayback.archive-it.org/2217/20101208180652/http://www.albertasource.ca/aspenland/eng/society/article_pogrom_to_prairie.html. Web. 1 Sept. 2022.
Aronson, Michael. *Troubled Waters: The Origins of the 1881 Anti-Jewish Pogroms in Russia*. Pittsburgh: Pittsburgh UP, 1991.
Belkin, Simon. *Through Narrow Gates*. Montréal, QC: Eagle Publishing, 1966.
Chiel, Arthur A. *The Jews in Manitoba*. Toronto, ON: University of Toronto Press, 1961.
Dawe, Michael. "Blank's Lake Jewish Colony." *Heritage* 11.3 (Summer 2009): 8–10.
Feldman, Anna. "Sonnenfeld: Elements of Survival and Success of a Jewish Farming Community on the Prairies, 1905–1939." *CJHSJ* 6.1 (1982): 33–53.
Gutkin, Harry. *A Journey into Our Heritage*. Toronto, ON: Lester & Orphen Dennys, 1980.
Katz, Yossi, and John C. Lehr. "Jewish and Mormon Agricultural Settlements in Western Canada: A Comparative Analysis." *The Canadian Geographer* 35.2 (June 2008): 128–42.

---. "Jewish Pioneer Agricultural Settlements in Western Canada." *Journal of Cultural Geography* 14.1 (1993): 49–67.

Lehr, John C. "'A Jewish Farmer Can't Be': Land Settlement Policies and Ethnic Settlement in Western Canada 1870–1919." *Jewish Life and Times* 9 (2009): 18–28.

Leonoff, Cyril Edel. "Early Jewish Agricultural Colonization in Saskatchewan." *Saskatchewan History* 36 (1983): 58–69.

---. *Pioneers, Ploughs and Prayers: The Jewish Farmers of Western Canada*. Vancouver, BC: The Jewish Historical Society of British Columbia, 1982.

---. *The Jewish Farmers of Western Canada*. Vancouver, BC: Jewish Historical Society of British Columbia, 1984.

---. *Wapella Farm Settlement*. Winnipeg, MB: Manitoba Historical and Scientific Society, 1975.

Paris, Erna. *Jews: An Account of Their Experience in Canada*. Toronto: Macmillan of Canada, 1980.

Rubin, Max. "Alberta's Jews: The Long Journey." *Peoples of Alberta*. Ed. Howard and Tamara Palmer. Saskatoon, SK: Western Producer Prairie Books, 1985. 328–47.

Sack, B. G. *History of the Jews in Canada*. Trans. Ralph Novek. Montréal, QC: Harvest House, 1965.

Peter Bush

The Independent Greek Church in Canada, 1903–1912: A Middle Ground on the Canadian Prairies between Ukrainian Immigrants and Presbyterianism

The Independent Greek Church (IGC) in Canada was a middle ground shaped on the Canadian Prairies by Ukrainian immigrant intelligentsia and leaders in The Presbyterian Church in Canada. Both the Ukrainian intelligentsia and the Canadian Presbyterians had something to gain from this relationship, but each side needed the other in order to achieve their goals. The middle ground required not only negotiations with the other party, but also each side needed to convince their own constituencies that this was the way forward to the hoped-for conclusion. While scholars have depicted the Independent Greek Church as a tool of assimilation imposed on Ukrainian immigrants by Canadian Presbyterians, the story is more nuanced with members of the Ukrainian intelligentsia exercising agency in the shaping of this middle ground. In fact, without the initiative of the Ukrainian intelligentsia in Canada, the Independent Greek Church would not have been created. The agency exercised by Ukrainians complicates previous accounts of the Independent Greek Church presenting a connection between two parties, each of whom had power in the relationship. That the Independent Greek Church was a contingent middle ground is demonstrated through tracing the agency exercised by Ukrainian leadership, the negotiated development of both a constitution and a catechism, and the complexities of funding and authority. The middle ground, which is always contingent, collapsed in this case for a variety of reasons, a primary one being the inability of nascent bureaucratic systems in The Presbyterian Church in Canada to allow such middle ground to exist.

Ukrainian immigration to Canada

The first immigrants from the region now called Ukraine arrived in Canada in 1891. The 1896 election of Prime Minister Wilfrid Laurier's Liberal government saw Clifford Sifton become the cabinet minister responsible for Canada's immigration policy. Sifton believed the peasant stock of Eastern Europe would do well on the Canadian prairie; between 1891 and 1914 approximately 170,000 persons migrated to Canada from present-day Ukraine, most settling in Manitoba, Saskatchewan, and Alberta. The new arrivals came most frequently from the provinces of Galicia and Bukovyna. Ethnic Ukrainians living in Russia seldom made their way to Canada and Ukrainians from Transcarpathia were more likely to emigrate to the mining regions and urban centers in the United States. In Galicia, Ukrainians were known as Ruthenians (rusyny), and the term "Ruthenian" came to be an identifier for all those of Ukrainian ancestry. Between 1891 and 1914 the identifiers of Galician and Ruthenian were frequently used in the Canadian press (Martynowych 4). The term "Ukrainian" is used in this chapter, unless the sources being discussed use other terms.

The vast majority of Ukrainians were Uniates (Greek Catholic), that is, Eastern-rite Christians who, while recognizing the supreme authority of the Roman Pontiff, used the Orthodox (Greek/Byzantine) rite and liturgy. This denomination was known as the Ruthenian Greek Catholic church or the Ukrainian Greek Catholic church. Only after 1918 did the Ukrainian Greek Orthodox church arise, a split in response to fears that the Ukrainian Greek Catholic church was becoming too Latinized (Martynowych xxviii). In Ukraine, tensions had arisen between the nationalist aspirations of the Ukrainian intelligentsia, who were progressive in their thinking, and Ukrainian Catholic priests, the intellectual leaders of the villages, who were generally more traditional in their views. Many of the intelligentsia following the thinking of Mykhailo Drahomanov (1841–1895) had sought to combat clerical influence by reviving traditions of lay initiatives in church matters and telling Ukrainian peasants about the more democratic and egalitarian practices of Protestant denominations (15). The intelligentsia were primarily young men who were schoolteachers, small entrepreneurs, and professionals in their communities. They sought to maintain a distinct Ukrainian culture and identity even in diaspora (xxviii, xxix). Few priests were among the first immigrants arriving on the Canadian Prairies. Into the gap caused by the non-presence of priests stepped the small group of Ukrainian intelligentsia who had come with the first wave of immigrants. The new arrivals came as family groups, often with three or four children. The appearance of hundreds of children in rural areas of the Canadian Prairies put pressure on the education system. It was in teacher training programs in Winnipeg that the future leaders of the IGC came into contact with Canadian Presbyterians.

The Presbyterian Church in Canada's primary roots are among the Scottish Presbyterians who arrived in Canada in various waves of immigration from Great Britain starting in the eighteenth century. With a theology rooted in the writings of John Calvin and one of Calvin's disciples, John Knox, Canadian Presbyterians developed spiritual practices based on the Westminster Confession of Faith and the Larger and Shorter Westminster Catechisms. Their church sanctuaries were devoid of images or icons and into the late nineteenth century did not use musical instruments in worship beyond a pitch pipe or tuning fork. The center of worship was the sermon. The Lord's Supper (the Eucharist) was celebrated as rarely as once a year in some congregations. Congregations were led by elders selected from the members of the congregation, who, together with the minister, oversaw the life of the congregation including exercising church discipline. By 1896 The Presbyterian Church in Canada (PCC) was the largest Protestant denomination in the country.

Describing a middle ground

The IGC was a form of middle ground, as defined by historian Richard White. White's exploration of the relationship between the French and the Algonquin (one of the Indigenous groups present when the French arrived and started to settle the land) between 1650 and 1815 demonstrates three aspects of a middle ground. The French did not become indigenous or give up French values, nor did the Algonquin become French or give up Algonquin values. The two groups "nonetheless had to deal with people who shared neither their values nor their assumptions about the appropriate way of accomplishing tasks. They had to arrive at some common conception of suitable ways of acting" (White xxi). Each side needed to find a way to relate to the other, since the other side was present and was not going away, a mutually agreed way forward had to be found. Such a way forward was not built on having achieved "widespread mutual understanding and appreciation" of the other, rather it was simply a way to live together (xxi). This common conception was built on seeming congruences between the two cultures. White's second important point is that these "often seemed—and, indeed were—results of misunderstandings or accidents" (52). Congruences "no matter how tenuous, can be put to work" to produce a cohesion of shared interest. These perceived congruences often arise from the assumption that the meanings attached to words and actions by one side are the meanings attached to those same words and actions by the other. Not surprisingly, a middle ground is a non-permanent place, "a realm of constant invention, . . . just as constantly presented as convention" (52). The third point to be gleaned from White's work is that an agreed upon set of conventions when met by the exigencies of a new situation become new ground over which a further set of struggles take place until a new middle ground can be defined. A middle ground is contingent and the conventions governing it are constantly shifting.

Despite the tensions and tenuousness White describes, a middle ground provides a place where two diverse cultures can find a way to work together, even if their purposes are not congruent, and the relationship is strained. Such a situation existed between those Ukrainians willing to enter into the middle ground of the IGC and the leaders of the PCC similarly prepared to enter it. A middle ground exists where each party believes it is possible to achieve at least some of their purposes even if they are unable to achieve all their goals, where both parties exercise agency even as their freedom of action is constrained by the agency of the other. The competing agencies and incongruent goals which mark the history of the IGC demonstrate that White's typology of middle ground applies to understanding contexts beyond Algonquin-French relations.

Missiologist Lamin Sanneh, in *Religion and the Variety of Culture*, discusses the ways Christian missionaries brought and imposed their form of Christian faith on people living in Sub-Saharan Africa. His insights aid in further understanding the nature of middle ground. Sanneh rejects the suggestion that Western Christianity was synonymous with "the whole Western enterprise." He is not denying that Western Christianity caused "real destruction and harm . . . including missionary denigration of non-Western cultures." However, the gaps that existed between the "Western enterprise," on the one hand, and Western Christianity, on the other, introduced "some ambiguity into cultural encounter, such that there would be ambivalence, paradox, and other unintended consequences resulting from the encounter." One such ambivalence arose as Western missionaries recruited "translators, interpreters, . . . , colporteurs, teachers, writers, preachers, catechists, secretaries." All these persons had some level of agency. These local agents played pivotal roles in their societies leading to unintended, at least as far as Western church leaders were concerned, consequences. Sanneh is particularly interested in how the use of the mother tongue preserves and even valorizes the non-dominant culture. He writes, "It is impossible that missionaries should devote so much time and effort to mother tongues without being aware at some point or other of the wider consequences of what they were doing." The preservation of vernacular languages, in worship, schooling, and even the press, created space for the aspirations of the non-dominant culture to grow. Sanneh's work complicates the questions of assimilation, agency, and control regarding the IGC. As this church maintained Ukrainian as the language of communication and worship, space was made available for the aspirations of the non-dominant Ukrainian community to grow (Sanneh 62–65).

Previous writing about the Independent Greek Church

The claim that the IGC was a form of middle ground challenges the widely held view that the denomination was a creation of the PCC as a means of assimilating Ukrainians into a Protestant Canada. The argument that Ukrainian voices had agency in the creation of middle ground in the IGC seeks to add nuance to the commonly recounted narrative. In the absence of a Ukrainian Greek Catholic clergy among the Eastern European immigrants arriving in Canada, the Roman Catholic Church in Canada regarded the growing Ukrainian community as their mission field. The Canadian Roman Catholic community of the first decade of the twentieth century was outraged by the actions of the Presbyterians, describing the IGC as a "deception of a simple people, this trickery, this fraud" (Karwchuk 212). Presbyterians responded to those charges by noting that *The Acts and Proceedings of the General Assembly* of The Presbyterian Church in Canada carried annual reports from the IGC. In addition, the Synod of Manitoba, a regional Presbyterian body, regularly heard about the work among Ukrainians including hearings from representatives of the IGC. Reports of the Synod's meetings were published in the *Winnipeg Tribune* and Presbyterians argued it was not a secret that they were involved in the IGC.

The narrative that the Presbyterians kept their assimilationist agenda hidden has appeared in the scholarly writing about the IGC. Educator and college principal

Roman Yereniuk describes the three key leaders of the IGC—John Bodrug, John Negrych, and Cyril Genyk—as "secretly" making arrangements with Presbyterian church leaders. He argues that "the major obstacle for the IGC was the manipulation of the Presbyterians" (Yereniuk 117–18). Historian Vivian Olender argues that the IGC used "symbolic manipulation" in its "proselytizing of Ukrainians," contending that the full constitution was not introduced to potential supporters of the IGC and therefore those not party to the negotiations with the Presbyterians were not aware of the assimilationist agenda (Olender 195). Orest Martynowych also argues that the constitution of the new denomination was done "secretly" between Protestant-leaning Ukrainians and leaders in the Presbyterian Church. He contends that the Presbyterian Church "could be accused of deception by not stating clearly at the outset that the new church was intended as a bridge to Protestantism" (Martynowych 191, 218). Such arguments limit the agency of the Ukrainian immigrants who were seeking to create a middle ground with the Presbyterian Church. Further, the scholars named above fail to appreciate the flexibility Canadian Presbyterians showed through funding the IGC with its Eastern Christian liturgy if only on a temporary basis. Historian Paul Yuzyk, known as "the father of multiculturalism" in Canada, comes closest to the complexity of the situation when he describes the IGC as "a sensational movement which shocked many a devout Protestant." Yuzyk emphasizes the agency of the Ukrainian leadership of the IGC claiming that "these priests broke away from [Bishop Seraphim's] church and secretly became a subsidiary body of the Presbyterian Synod in Canada" (1953, 73). This analysis opens the possibility of understanding the IGC as a middle ground. In a personal reflection on his academic career, Yuzyk wrote in 1989, "to my knowledge, no authentic scholarly studies have appeared on the Protestant church among Ukrainians" (3). This chapter does not claim to fill that gap, but it does use the Presbyterian Church as a lens through which to view the IGC as middle ground.

Presbyterian interest in Ukrainian immigrants

As the flow of Ukrainian immigration to the Prairies became a flood following 1896, the PCC, along with other Christian denominations in Canada, was concerned about reaching this new group of arrivals. They did so in ways that sought to Christianize and Canadianize. In October 1898 Ivan (John) Bodrug and Ivan (John) Negrych, two members of the Ukrainian intelligentsia in Canada, came to the Presbyterian leadership indicating their desire to make the Presbyterian Church their spiritual home. They had reached this decision because they preferred the understandable, intelligent sermons and the dignity that marked Presbyterian worship over the emotional piety of Methodism and the ritualism of Anglicanism (Bodrug 9–12). The next day, Bodrug and Negrych began courses at Manitoba College, the Presbyterian post-secondary institution, receiving free tuition and living expenses. As James

Robertson, the superintendent of missions for the Presbyterian Church in western Canada told the *Winnipeg Free Press*, "The two young men who commenced their studies in Manitoba College this morning are shrewd and intelligent and eager to learn; if they are fair specimens of their race, the Galicians are desirable additions to our population." By the spring of 1899 Bodrug and Negrych had left Manitoba College and were working as translators among Galician, Ruthenian, and Doukhobor settlers on the Prairies. Later that same year, James Robertson convinced these two and Ivan Danylchuk, also part of the Ukrainian intelligentsia, to become teachers at Ukrainian language schools in the Dauphin, Manitoba, area which were funded by the Presbyterian Church. These three were the first Ukrainian school teachers in Canada. Bodrug would subsequently say that it was Robertson who "found him and induced him to turn his attention to teaching" ("Minutes," Sub-Committee). The focus on education was quickly joined by health care with the Presbyterians building small hospitals and medical dispensaries in Ukrainian-speaking communities. In 1900 Dr. J. T. Reid opened a hospital in Sifton, Manitoba; in 1902 Alexander Hunter opened one in Teulon, Manitoba; and the following year hospitals were opened in Ethelbert, Manitoba, and Wakaw, Saskatchewan. Combining education and medical care was the default mission practice of Christian churches at the time. This practice fit well with James Robertson's understanding of the church's task. He wrote to the Rev. David McQueen, an influential Presbyterian minister in Edmonton, in 1899:

> Watch the Galician settlements and tell me what can be done to meet the wants of the people. Until we can get some of their own people trained, can anything be done thro' interpreters? We must not leave large lumps of undigested foreigners in the stomach politic else there is trouble ahead, nor can we afford to have the religious views of the Greek Church, any more than the Roman, influencing the religious tone of the country, else religion will decline. And since many of the Galician women are sure to become mothers of no small part of the next generation, the homes must be Christian. (Robertson)

Robertson did not regard Ukrainian Greek Catholics as Christians; they needed to become Protestants or else Canada was at risk both spiritually and politically. To that end education was essential, as he had demonstrated in recruiting three teachers for Presbyterian-funded schools using the Provincial education curriculum. This standard approach to the evangelization and assimilation of non-Protestants into an Anglo-Protestant worldview was re-imagined in 1903 by the agency of the Ukrainian intelligentsia.

Ukrainian overtures towards Presbyterians

Orthodox Church liturgy and Canadian Presbyterian Church theology are an unlikely pairing, but that unusual pairing took place on the Canadian Prairies in the form of the IGC in the first decade of the twentieth century. A Presbyterian woman from Ontario after worshiping in an IGC congregation wrote:

> An onlooker finds difficulty in seeing a Presbyterian element in their service, for with their crosses, candles, incense, etc., one would think them of the Roman Catholic faith. They have no seats in their church, and remain standing throughout their long service, which lasts from 8 a.m. to 1 or 2 p.m. They prostrate themselves and the minister intones much of the service, as the Independent Greek Church has not discarded the Ritual of John Chrysostom of the Orthodox Greek Church. They get their ritual from John Chrysostom, but their theology from Manitoba College. (Story of Anna Turnbull Hospital)

Rural Ukrainian culture was anchored in the religious life of the local parish. The church was a source of cultural identity, nationalist philosophy, and spiritual support. Thus, the way towards a truly independent Ukrainian identity had to include a religious component. A significant number of the intelligentsia had religious dispositions that were Protestant and were desirous of a truly independent Ukrainian church, free from hierarchies in both Rome and St. Petersburg. Among these Protestant-leaning promoters of Ukrainian identity were Bodrug, Negrych, and Danylchuk. By 1903 they and others in the Ukrainian intelligentsia had "earned the lasting enmity of Catholic and (Russian Orthodox) missionaries and acquired a reputation as 'atheists' among many immigrants" (Martynowych 174). With such a reputation it was hard to develop a hearing among the rural Ukrainian population of the Prairies.

What made their task easier was that few priests had come with the influx of immigrants to Canada and the newly arrived community was without spiritual moorings (Ustvolsky). Stephan Ustvolsky, a Russian Orthodox priest who claimed to have the authority to ordain priests and establish a North American Orthodox church, although that claim was contested, arrived in Winnipeg in April 1903. Ustvolsky, known as Bishop Seraphim, drew thousands of Orthodox to the Eastern/Greek Rite liturgy and his preaching (Bodrug 34). He was prepared to ordain as cantors, deacons, and priests those who were selected by their communities to those responsibilities and who were able to pay his fee of twenty-five dollars (Martynowych 174).

Cyril Genik, part of the intelligentsia but unconnected to the church, feared that Bishop Seraphim's "ignorant priests will bring about religious chaos among our people" (Bodrug 36). He urged Bodrug and others to take up the task of providing leadership to the All-Russian Patriarchal Orthodox Church that Bishop Seraphim had created. Bodrug was uncertain but willing, replying to Genik that "[i]f there were any possibility of creating a reformed Christian church out of Orthodoxy, then for the sake of the idea I would leave everything, and go forth to serve God and my people" (37). Bodrug was committed to the Reformed theological understanding, which arose from the teachings of Jan (John) Hus and Jean Cauvin (John Calvin). Bodrug and Negrych met with Genik to plan their approach; they agreed the two would seek ordination under Bishop Seraphim and "would accord him due respect. But, having once established leadership over his priests, would undertake to preach not

Orthodoxy, but Evangelical [Protestant] Christianity. As for the forms and traditions in the Church ritual, we would honor those which did not conflict with the spirit of Christ and the teaching of the Apostles" (37). Respect for Bishop Seraphim would attach to his person, but little of what he stood for would be honored, as Bodrug and Negrych hoped to establish their leadership over the priests, essentially undermining Bishop Seraphim's authority. No sources indicate that anyone inside The Presbyterian Church in Canada was aware of these plans.

Plan in place, Bodrug and Negrych met with Bishop Seraphim, having been introduced by Genik, in late April 1903. The only record of the conversation is Bodrug's memoirs written years after the event, a source which other scholars have treated as an accurate account of the events. Bodrug remembered Seraphim asking if they "had the willingness and the call to become Orthodox priests," to which Bodrug and Negrych replied they "were Protestants by conviction." Bodrug records Bishop Seraphim saying, "We will make fine Orthodox priests out of you." The conversation demonstrates the awkward position of each side. Bishop Seraphim needed the abilities these two and the other intellectuals would bring to the denomination he was building. The intelligentsia, in order to effectively lead the Ukrainian community into the future they envisioned, needed the status Bishop Seraphim offered them through ordination (Bodrug 38–39).

In an action-packed week in May 1903 Bodrug and Negrych were made deacons and then priests by Bishop Seraphim and also entered into negotiations with the Presbyterian leadership located in Winnipeg. On Bodrug's account, it was only after Bishop Seraphim had set the date for Bodrug and Negrych's ordination that they approached Principal William Patrick of Manitoba College seeking "moral and material support from the Presbyterian Church in realizing our project" (Bodrug 39). Patrick, newly arrived from Scotland, had offered encouragement to a variety of experiments across theological lines. Upon reading the "sketch" of the denomination's proposed constitution, Bodrug recorded Patrick as saying, "You, young people know your countrymen and are planning to open a new page in the religious history of our young Dominion" (40). Patrick, who was not the initiator but an encourager of the idea, was responding to an existing document prepared by Bodrug and Negrych. He did, however, recognize how unusual the proposal was, hence his referring to it as "a new page." The language used by both Patrick and Bodrug suggests significant agency on the part of the members of the Ukrainian intelligentsia in imagining what Bodrug called "our project." In his 1912 interview with the Sub-Committee on the Reception of Ministers of the Independent Greek Church, Bodrug spoke of being "induced" into teaching school, going on to say, "[I]n due time the Independent Greek Church was organized and he became one of its ministers" ("Minutes," Sub-Committee). The shift in language is notable: becoming a teacher was something he had to be convinced to do; but, on the other hand, organizing and joining the IGC was something into which he willingly entered.

This meeting with William Patrick and the subsequent meeting with leaders of the Presbyterian Church in Winnipeg have been identified as *the* secret meeting in which the plan to create a duplicitous church structure was developed. What Bodrug called "our plan" proposed initially drawing Orthodox worshippers into the IGC due to the familiar liturgy, but which over time would become increasingly Protestant (Presbyterian). Bodrug envisioned this plan resulting in an independent Protestant Ukrainian Church; he did not envision a Canadianized church.

Just as Patrick was not expecting the plan Bodrug and Negrych proposed, neither were the Presbyterian leaders Patrick gathered to hear it. Bodrug arrived at the meeting with a constitution prepared. The desire was to name the denomination "The Ruthenian Independent Greek Orthodox Church of Canada," a name which clearly stated the goal of the Ukrainian intelligentsia: a Ukrainian-language church independent of Rome and of St. Petersburg. The name identified to ethnic Ukrainians the church's cultural heart, but as Bodrug and Negrych had told Bishop Seraphim, it would be theologically Protestant. "Ruthenian" in the name was a non-starter for the Presbyterians, and Bodrug had to give that up. Giving up the name did not change the goals of the Ukrainian leadership, but the Presbyterians thought the removal of the name removed the risk that they were funding an ethnically nationalistic denomination inside Canada. One of the misconceptions frequent in the building of middle ground had become a "convention" (Bodrug 41).

Bodrug proposed that worship gatherings in the IGC would "shorten the Divine Service of St. John and other rituals, so that they would not last longer than an hour and a half." The Presbyterians pushed back stating that the worship should follow "on the lines of the Reformed Christian Churches." Bodrug rejected this idea stating that Ukrainians had no psalms and hymns in Ukrainian, and over time such patterns could be introduced, but "in the meantime, we would have to use liturgical forms of service with prayers and sermons." Here again a contingent middle ground was created in which each side could claim a convention had been set. The Ukrainians were given an unspecified amount of time to introduce psalms and hymns, and the Presbyterians were able to state that a commitment had been made to transition to Reformed worship practice (Bodrug 42–43).

It was in the area of church polity, however, that the two sides most misunderstood each other. Bodrug proposed a system of a minister and at least three elders elected by the congregation being the decision-making body at the congregational level. This fit with the Session structure Presbyterians were used to. At the level of the Consistory, however, which was "the supreme governing body over the entire Independent Greek Church," misunderstandings arose. The Consistory's control was limited when the majority of the funding for the IGC came from the PCC; as the funder, the PCC expected to have a role in directing the IGC. Further, as the IGC submitted annual reports which were reviewed and approved by the General Assembly of the PCC, the Consistory's claim to be "the supreme governing" over the IGC was contingent. Both sides chose to leave these questions of church polity and independence unanswered.

The constitution based on Bodrug and Negrych's work was a middle ground between Protestant-leaning, educated Ruthenian leaders and the leaders of the PCC. While the leaders on both sides were content with the approach, both sides had constituents who also needed to affirm the plan if it was going to be successful. For Bodrug and Negrych, those constituents were not only Protestant-leaning Ukrainian-speakers, but it was also rural parishioners who were thoroughly rooted in Eastern rite and liturgy and who were desperate for religious gatherings and spiritual care that was also rooted in that practice. For the Presbyterian Church leaders present at the meeting in Winnipeg, the constituents they needed to be concerned about included the nascent denominational bureaucracy and the advocates for the development of uniform Canadian Presbyterian worship practice.

At the urging of leaders within the All-Russian Patriarchal Orthodox Church, Bishop Seraphim went to St. Petersburg in early 1904 to get clarification of his role and authority and to obtain financial support. By the time of his return, Bodrug and Negrych had mounted a take-over and virtually all the priests Bishop Seraphim had ordained were part of the IGC.

The ministers of the Independent Greek Church

The IGC, by 1907, had grown to 15,000–20,000 adherents with twenty-four ministers and missionaries, all financed by the Presbyterian Church's Board of Home Missions. In addition to the paying of stipends for the ministers/priests, the Presbyterians also funded the construction of church buildings in the architectural style of churches in Galicia and Bukovyna. Furthermore, Manitoba College started a theological course in Ukrainian to educate ministers for the IGC. Up until this point Ukrainians enrolled in the school were being trained as teachers. Michael Sherbinin, a Russian who spoke Ukrainian and German, was hired by the college in February 1904 to begin a class teaching the clergy and prospective clergy of the IGC. He had been educated in Russia and grew up Russian Orthodox, but after converting to Protestantism, he left Russia. He arrived in Canada in 1901, and by early 1903 was employed by the Presbyterian Church working among Doukhobors and Ukrainians.[1] Having made the journey from Orthodoxy to Presbyterianism, his theological story shaped him into a helpful teacher for the clergy of the IGC, who were taking similar theological journeys. Sherbinin believed the best way to learn another language was to know one's own language well; therefore, he insisted that much of his teaching be in Ukrainian and that his students encourage the use of Ukrainian in the congregations of the IGC.

---

1 The Doukhobors are a Christian ethnoreligious group of Russian origin dating back to the early eighteenth century. Some emigrated to Canada where they hoped to practice communal land holding and pacifism, which were central spiritual practices.

The theological course began as an evening class so students could hold down employment and still study. But it quickly evolved into a regular academic timetable, although many students attended only one of two terms of classes before being sent out to serve congregations. The starting date of the Ukrainian language theological classes is significant: February 1904 was after Bodrug and Negrych had led the split which created the IGC. The Presbyterians were trying to catch up with the fast-moving developments initiated by the leaders of the IGC (Knysh 14, 22).

In the fall of 1912, as the IGC was being wound down, a committee of the Presbyterian Church interviewed twenty-two ministers from the IGC to determine their fitness to be ministers of the PCC. The notes taken provide a thumbnail sketch of those interviewed. Of the twenty-one ministers who gave their ages to the interviewing committee, five were in their twenties, thirteen were in their thirties, only three were over the age of forty. The data is skewed by the fact these are interviews with ministers who wished to join the Presbyterian Church, which is approximately half of the clergy of the IGC. What is missing are the reasons why half the ministers of the IGC chose to not move to the Presbyterian Church. A significant number of those moving into the Presbyterian Church were born in Galicia, which was consistent with the immigration patterns that saw a majority of Ukrainian immigrants coming from that region.

Bodrug's voice so dominated the history of the IGC at times that it is assumed he spoke for all the leadership, but the story is more complicated. The pastoral leadership of the IGC was diverse in its social and educational background as well as in its goals. Some ministers joined the IGC because of their Protestant leanings, others resonated with Bodrug's rhetoric promising a church free from the interference of Rome and St. Petersburg, and still others were drawn to the stability offered by a guaranteed stipend. Bodrug, a nationalist and a Protestant, wanted a distinctly Ukrainian expression of church that would be Protestant and free from interference from any non-Ukrainian authority. As a nationalist he saw among Protestant polities a way to create an independent denomination. Even in 1912, when Bodrug saw the writing on the wall for the Independent Greek Church, he still sought to create space for what he called the Ruthenian Presbyterian Church, which would have its own newspaper, "Ranok" (Bodrug to Farquharson).

Bodrug's vision stands in contrast to the vision of the Rev. Maxim Balizniak, minister of the Independent Greek Church in Edmonton. Balizniak described to the Rev. Dr. James Farquharson, Convenor of the Synod Missions Committee, his ministry approach:

> I explained to the people what the Independent Greek Church is, who supports her and what future this Church must have. Then I introduced the people to the dogma and the doctrine of the Presbyterian Church and after awhile they understood that the Independent Greek Church is just a bridge to the Presbyterian and of course it is no use to continue any longer to be Independent, but we must be real Presbyterians. (Balizniak)

For Balizniak the IGC was a bridge; the sooner the people crossed the bridge to the other side—joining the Presbyterians, which meant rapid adoption of Presbyterian liturgical and doctrinal approaches—the better. With this would come assimilation into the dominant Canadian culture and the loss of a distinctly Orthodox religious and cultural expression.

In addition to these approaches, other streams of thought can be discerned among the ministers of the IGC. Quite a few of them had "leanings to Protestantism" while still in Ukraine but had had no forum in which to explore those "leanings," which are likely to have been encouraged by the work of Drahomonov and his students, who introduced Ukrainians to Protestant thinking. Upon arrival in western Canada and with the presence of the IGC, they had the opportunity to seek out a theological home with which they were more comfortable. The Rev. Glowa, aged thirty and born in Galicia, had been in a Basilian monastery in Europe for three years but left the monastery feeling it was not where he belonged. After coming to Canada by way of the United States, a Roman Catholic priest urged him to study at St. Boniface College in Winnipeg. While there, he taught classes in singing and met A. Baczynski, who was a cantor before leaving Galicia and had Protestant leanings. As a result of Baczynski's influence, Glowa left the Church of Rome. He "felt that he must preach the Gospel as he understood it," which was "in accordance with the Bible." The Rev. A. Baczynski—who was sixty-five years old, making him the oldest minister in the IGC—was ordained by Bishop Seraphim seven years after his arrival in Canada. Although ordained by Seraphim, he articulated a thoroughly Protestant understanding of Christianity; teaching that people "became Christians by believing in Christ," he "assured all that Christ would receive whosoever came to him." The Rev. J. Danylchuk, also from Galicia, had done well in school to the point that a wealthy woman offered to become his patron funding his education if he would enter the priesthood. But Danylchuk "declined because of his difficulties regarding the doctrines of the Roman Catholic Church." Four years after his arrival in Canada, the Presbyterian Church contacted him to be a teacher in one of their schools that opened the door to his becoming a minister in the IGC in 1903. The Rev. N. Sekora, also from Galicia, joined the IGC "because he had been favorably impressed with Protestantism before leaving his Native land." For these individuals the Prairies and more specifically the IGC became a place to follow through on theological leanings they had had in their homeland but never had a context in which to explore fully ("Minutes," Sub-Committee).

Another group within the IGC had been comfortable with the Greek Orthodox practices while in Galicia or Bukovyna, but arrival in Canada had dislocated their theological frame. The Rev. A. Wylchinski had trained in the Greek Catholic Church to be a cantor and teacher of catechism. Upon his arrival in Canada his desire to address the spiritual needs of "his fellow countrymen" led him into the IGC. That experience had changed him; "when he began to preach he followed the liturgy of the Orthodox Church pretty thoroughly but gradually abandoned the use of the objectionable parts." The new context of Canada provided a venue in which to examine the practices and theology of the Orthodox Church. The Rev. E. Eustafiewicz had also been moved by the spiritual needs of "his own people" upon his arrival in Canada. In Canada he obtained a Bible and read it. That experience made him dissatisfied with both "the Greek Church" and the Roman Catholic Church. The Rev. A. Maximchuk "rather than be compelled to become a soldier . . . escaped to Canada." Sometime after his arrival he became concerned with people's spiritual well-being and would read the Bible to people in need and explain it to them as best he could. His motivation in being a preacher was "his desire to give the people light concerning Jesus Christ." The Rev. J. Zazulak had been a Church Teacher in his parish in Galicia and had spent a year in a Roman Catholic monastery before coming to Canada. His moving into a church role in Canada was consistent with his previous life, and the IGC was a logical place for him to continue his vocation of being a spiritual mentor and support. Seeing the spiritual needs of those around them and recognizing that the spiritual models that had worked in Ukraine might not be applicable on the Canadian Prairies, these individuals adjusted their theological practice to fit a new reality ("Minutes," Sub-Committee).

Being a minister in the IGC was a challenging vocation as the life of the Rev. Joseph Czerniawski demonstrates. Czerniawski had some education in Galicia and worked as a customs agent before he, his parents, and siblings emigrated to Canada. In 1903 when Bodrug was in Vegreville, Alberta, recruiting priests for a church free from the influence of Rome and St. Petersburg, the senior Czerniawski was supportive and encouraged his son to be ordained. Ordained by Bishop Seraphim, Joseph Czerniawski followed Bodrug into the IGC. There he became a respected minister, working for the spiritual well-being of his congregation and seeking to be an advocate for Ukrainian immigrants and the Ukrainian language. His public advocacy was in line with Bodrug's vision for the IGC. Tragically, in the contested religious context of the early twentieth century, a member of the community took exception to Czerniawski and he was murdered in March 1912. Orest Martynowych, in his analysis of this tragic series of events, suggests that Czerniawski's death "brought to a climax a crisis that had been brewing for years" inside the IGC (Martynowych).

The Catechism of the Independent Greek Church

The Presbyterian Church in Canada is a confessional church, which means that Presbyterians are formed in the faith through learning, studying, and living out the creeds, confessions, and catechism of the church. When the Rev. Charles Gordon, long-time member of the Synod of Manitoba's Mission Committee and a supporter of the IGC, was asked in 1912 to outline the history of the Independent Greek Church for his Presbyterian colleagues, he began by stating that the Apostles Creed, the Nicene Creed, and the Athanasian Creed were its doctrinal bases. He knew this was the fastest and best way to give legitimacy to the church in the eyes of those who were skeptical about the IGC. A further way to add legitimacy in the Presbyterian worldview was the creation of a catechism (*Christian Catechism* 1–16).

Instead of choosing to translate the Westminster Shorter Catechism and its 107 questions, a catechism most Presbyterian young people were taught and had memorized, the team of IGC pastors and members of the Presbyterian Home Missions Committee agreed, on Bodrug and Negrych's recommendation, to make the recently published (1899) catechism drafted by members of the various Evangelical Free Churches of England the basis for the Catechism of the IGC (*The Independent* 439–41). This newer catechism, put together by a team including Presbyterians, Baptists, and members of five different branches of Methodism, had as its lead author J. Oswald Dykes (1835–1912), a Presbyterian and Principal of Westminster College, Cambridge. Among the goals of the new catechism to demonstrate the unity between churches, albeit in this case between Protestant denominations, was key. Choosing an ecumenically written catechism as the basis of the IGC catechism was an attempt to signal the IGC was seeking to build a tent larger than just Presbyterianism; in fact, it desired to be a Protestant Ukrainian church. This particular catechism was heralded for its simplicity. "It is in the language of today," wrote the editor of *The Independent*, a New York based Christian periodical, going on to say, "[T]here are no theological formulas in semi-medieval phrases to puzzle" readers (433).

The Ukrainian translation of the Catechism stays close to the original version. Olender is correct when she notes it is a Protestant catechism which at times offers a little space for Greek Catholic expressions of Christianity (204). In those places where the IGC catechism breaks with the original text evidence can be seen of a middle ground being built. By accident Question 19 in the original asks, "What is the mystery of the blessed Trinity?" This phrasing sounds far more Orthodox than Presbyterian. Neither the word "blessed" nor "Trinity" appear in the Shorter Westminster Catechism. Without even trying to accommodate the Orthodox tradition, a little space was found. In response to Question 21 "What is it to repent?" the English answer is: the one "who truly repents of their sin not only confesses it with shame and sorrow, but above all turns from it to God with sincere desire to be forgiven." The Ukrainian translation speaks of the one making the confession of sin being absolved and having a "steadfast purpose to sin no more." In using the language of absolution, the Ukrainian translation opens the door to Orthodox practices. Intentionally or unintentionally, space was made for two understandings of repentance to co-exist. Two questions later "providential discipline" became in Ukrainian "the ways of God's providence." This is a softening of the Reformed theological edge by holding up the Orthodox commitment to God's providence. In the cases of these two questions the translation team provided opportunity for Orthodox understandings to find a footing.

Two questions from the original document were not included in the IGC version: "What is the duty of the Church to the State?" and "What is the duty of the State to the Church?" (*The Independent* 440). For Scottish, Irish, and Canadian Presbyterians, the removal of any discussion of Church–State relations was to set aside three hundred years of bitterly argued theological debate and not a little bloodshed. By not including those questions, the priests and others in the IGC who dreamed of a Ukrainian church free of interference from outsiders were given the opportunity of silence in which to dream. For both Canadian Presbyterians and Ukrainians, the silence allowed for unspoken expectations to flourish in what each side believed was a convention of the middle ground between them.

Most surprising, however, were the questions about sacraments. Following a fairly standard description of the sacraments as "[s]acred rites instituted by our Lord Jesus to make more plain by visible signs the inward benefits of the Gospel," Question 40 of the catechism asked: "How many Sacraments are there?" The original document gave as answer: "Two only—Baptism and the Lord's Supper." The answer provided in the IGC catechism was: "The Orthodox Greek Church say seven, namely: 1 Baptism, 2 Unction with Chrism, 3 Penitence, 4 Communion, 5 Anointing of the sick, 6 Orders, and 7 Matrimony." All seven sacraments of the Orthodox Greek Church were recognized as having value; the listing did not even locate Communion and Baptism as first and second, with the rest following. However, as Olender notes, the next question did put a Protestant flavor on the answer: "What are the principal Sacraments?" The answer given was "Baptism and the Lord's Supper, called also Eucharist." The language is important here. Nowhere was there criticism of the other five sacraments, for they simply are not among the principal sacraments. The Catechism made fuzzy what had been clear lines drawn as a result of the debates of the Reformation. That softening points to the flexibility with which certain parts the PCC approached the challenge of showing hospitality to Ukrainian immigrants.

Further space was created in describing the meaning of the Lord's Supper. Olender argues that the catechism provided an explanation "of Communion as a memorial, thus denying the Real Presence in the Eucharist" (Olender 204), which suggests that no middle ground was given by the Presbyterians on the meaning of the Eucharist. The original catechism had answered the question "What is signified by the bread and the wine?" with: "By the Bread is signified the Body of our Lord Jesus Christ in which he lived and died; and by the Wine is signified His Blood shed once for all upon the Cross for the remission of sins." The bread and the wine were symbols, with the catechism using typical Protestant memorial language. The IGC catechism, however, provided a different answer to the question: "This question is most effectively answered by the Apostle Paul, who in the tenth chapter of his First Epistle to the Corinthians does write: 'The Cup of Blessing which we bless, is it not the Communion of the Blood of Christ? The Bread which we break, is it not the Communion of the Body of Christ? For we being many are one bread and one body; for we are all partakers of that one Bread.'" The Protestant Presbyterians and Ukrainians of the IGC in struggling to find mutually agreeable space on this matter turned to the Biblical witness and quoted without explanation one of the Apostle Paul's more mystical passages. The I Corinthians 10:16–17 passage is open to widely divergent interpretations, for it is not a narrowly memorialist text. Given the passage quoted in the IGC catechism, the answer to the next question, which originally would have sounded memorialist, takes on the possibility of a more mystical interpretation, as it says, "[Those who eat and drink] feed spiritually upon Christ as the nourishment of the soul, by which they are strengthened and refreshed for the duties and trails of life." Having participated in the "Communion of the Blood of Christ" and the "Communion of the Body of Christ," this may not be real presence, but the spiritual feeding is not mere memorial either. The IGC catechism had created a middle ground in which neither memorial nor real presence were endorsed.

The Catechism was used to introduce some elements of Presbyterian worship to the IGC. The Catechism was designed to be used with children, and the printing of some metrical psalms and hymns along with the Catechism was introducing the next generation to elements of Reformed worship (*Christian Catechism* 18–39). Two of the metrical psalms, which are designed to be sung, Psalms 100 and 103, had the same meter in both Ukrainian and English, allowing them to be sung bilingually, a practice the psalter encouraged. The hymns were all originally in English with Ukrainian translations and included a number of well-known nineteenth-century hymns such as "Onward Christian Soldiers," "When I Survey the Wondrous Cross," and "Blessed Assurance." The expected hymn tunes would have been the tunes which English-speaking congregations commonly sang. The development of twelve hymn texts that could be sung bilingually required skill and commitment on the part of the translators. Determining how widely the metrical psalms and hymns were used, if at all, has not been possible. Bilingual singing preserved Ukrainian as a language of worship, and the hymns and catechism not only taught English to Ukrainians, but also exposed children to Ukrainian in the context of worship. The Catechism was the first book in Ukrainian published in Canada.

The end of the Independent Greek Church

A variety of motivations had brought together Ukrainian immigrants and the PCC in the IGC, but it did not last. The contingent and contested nature of middle ground meant the IGC could not withstand a series of changes that began in 1908. The departure of John Bodrug for the United States left a leadership vacuum which no one was able to fill and with the creator of the middle ground gone, it started to fray. In addition, there was growing pressure on all Presbyterian congregations in Canada to adopt common worship practices, including the use of English. The limitations on vernacular practices and languages of worship sought to create a uniform worship style so Presbyterians moving from one community to another in Canada could attend any Presbyterian congregation and be comfortable with a recognizable worship style (Bush 2004). Thirdly, the attention of the Roman Catholic community had been drawn to the spiritual needs of the Greek Catholic community in diaspora in Canada, and in 1912 a Greek Catholic bishop, Nykyta Budka, was appointed to Canada. His arrival opened the way for Greek Catholic priests to be trained and ordained in Canada, and he also recruited priests from Galicia. This move meant that large numbers of IGC parishioners were able to access Ukrainian language worship in the ritual and theology they knew from their homeland. All of the above were factors in the decline of the IGC.

A further significant factor, often overlooked by scholars, was the rise of bureaucratic systems within the PCC. In the years leading up to World War I, the Canadian Presbyterian Church became increasingly committed to business models in all aspects of its ministry, including its mission on the Prairies (Bush 2012). This control was exercised through the centralized management of finances. The new systems could not allow for the freedom the leadership of the IGC enjoyed to open new congregations, hire additional personnel, and even launch building campaigns. Previously the Presbyterian Church was expected to finance all these actions without being able to exercise control over the decisions to spend the money. Under the new centralized management, not only did the IGC have less financial freedom, but there was also less freedom to have patterns of church that were outside the "normal," that is Presbyterian, ways of being a church. The Rev. Dr. Andrew S. Grant, the recently appointed full-time paid Convenor of the Home Missions Committee and the person charged with building on the increasingly bureaucratized systems in the church, chaired a meeting of the Home Missions Committee of the Presbyterian Church in Winnipeg on May 29, 1912. The meeting's purpose was to develop a path by which clergy within the IGC would become fully recognized ministers within The Presbyterian Church in Canada, thereby regularizing the relationship the clergy of the IGC had with the Presbyterian Church. In so doing, the leadership of the Presbyterian Church would achieve the goal that "any further extension of the work among the Ruthenian people should be under Presbyterian supervision, and that in general closer supervision of work among the Ruthenians is desirable" (Minutes, Home Missions Committee). The IGC clergy would be brought under Presbytery control, and any new initiatives would come through Presbytery processes, including the determination of what funding would be made available. The autonomy of decision-making the IGC had enjoyed was to be eliminated. The Rev. J. A. Carmichael, a Superintendent of Missions for The Presbyterian Church in Canada and a supporter of the IGC, had died in 1911, leaving the IGC without one of its champions (Grant 1, 3). The Rev. Dr. Charles Gordon (Ralph Connor), a member of the committee that met in May 1912, spoke against the transfer of IGC clergy into the Presbyterian church. Gordon supported the work the IGC had done and did not believe its work was finished; he believed that it was still needed and should be "still strengthened and supported by the warm sympathy and financial aid of the Presbyterian Church" (Grant 1, 3). Yet, realizing his argument would not carry the day, Gordon was unable to do anything but express his opposition to the move and make his displeasure clear. Notably, no representative from the IGC was present at this meeting. The IGC had come into existence through a conversation between Protestant-leaning Ukrainian leaders and Presbyterian Church leaders, but the end came through a bureaucratic process at which only Presbyterian leadership was present.

In October 1912 twenty-two clergy of the IGC appeared one-by-one before a sub-committee of the Home Missions Committee to tell their story and answer questions examining their theology to determine if it was sufficiently Protestant. Those approved by the sub-committee were allowed to become ministers in the Presbyterian Church without further requirements. At the 1913 General Assembly of the Presbyterian Church, fifteen clergy from the IGC were welcomed as ministers of the Presbyterian Church—John Bodrug was not among them. His vision of an independent Ukrainian church living in middle ground had failed.

A. J. Hunter, a Presbyterian minister, who served in the largely Ukrainian community of Teulon, Manitoba, reflected on the IGC after its demise,

> They [the Presbyterians] did not wish to induce the mass of Ukrainians to turn Presbyterian: this they knew would be impossible in any short space of time. They did want the Ukrainians to study the Bible and to give serious consideration to the arguments in favor of the evangelical [Protestant] interpretation of Christianity, yet they saw that for years to come the religious feelings of the majority would demand their ancestral form of worship. (Hunter 35)

The patience Hunter describes as being present among the Presbyterian leaders involved in the establishment of the IGC allowed for the creation of a middle ground, contingent as it was. However, the bureaucratizing impetus within the Presbyterian Church was not patient and was not willing to have such an ill-defined and, at times, unmanageable entity connected to the denomination. The IGC was not able to survive the pressure to become uniform like the rest of the Presbyterian Church, for in that uniformity there was no room for middle ground. In that uniformity there was no room for a Ukrainian expression of Protestant Christianity to arise which used the liturgy of John Chrysostom and the theology of John Calvin.

Works Cited

Balizniak, Maxim. "To James Farquharson." 29 May 1912. Board of Home Mission and Social Service, Presbyterian Church, United Church in Canada Archives: Box 3, File 34.

Bodrug, John. *Independent Orthodox Church: Memoirs Pertaining to the History of a Ukrainian Canadian Church in the Years 1903 to 1913*. Trans. Edward Bodrug and Lydia Biddle. Toronto: Ukrainian Canadian Research Foundation, 1980.

---. "To James Farquharson." 2 March 1912. Board of Home Mission and Social Service, Presbyterian Church, United Church in Canada Archives: Box 2, File 13.

Bush, Peter. "Sir Sandford Fleming and Presbyterian Worship." *Canadian Society of Church History Papers* (2004): 33–51.

---. "Developing a Denominational Structure: The Introduction of a Unified Budget." *Canadian Society of Presbyterian History Papers* (2012): 17–33.

Christian Catechism for the Use of School Children and Young People. Winnipeg: Independent Greek Church in Canada, 1904.

Goa, David J., ed. *The Ukrainian Religious Experience: Tradition and the Canadian Cultural Context*. Edmonton: Canadian Institute of Ukrainian Studies, University of Alberta, 1989.

Grant, John Webster. "The Presbyterian Approach to the Ukrainian." *Historic Sites and Archives Journal*. Alberta and Northwest Conference Historical Society 5.1 (May 1992): 1, 3.

Hunter, A. J. *A Friendly Adventure: The Story of the United Church Mission Among New Canadians at Teulon, Manitoba*. Toronto: Board of Home Mission. United Church of Canada, 1929.

"The New Catechism." *The Independent* (New York) 51.2619 (9 Feb. 1899): 433; 439–41.

Karwchuk, Andri. "Between a Rock and a Hard Place: Francophone Missionaries among the Ukrainian Catholics." *Canada's Ukrainians: Negotiating an Identity*. Ed. Lubomyr Luciuk and Stella Hryniuk. Toronto: University of Toronto Press, 1991. 206–17.

Knysh, George. *Michael Sherbinin in Winnipeg: A Preliminary Study*. Winnipeg: Ukrainian Academy of Arts and Sciences in Canada, 1994.

Martynowych, Orest. "Czerniawski, Joseph." *Dictionary of Canadian Biography* 14 (1911–1920). Web. 29 June 2021.

---. *Ukrainians in Canada: The Formative Years, 1891–1924*. Edmonton: Canadian Institute of Ukrainian Studies, University of Alberta, 1991.

McGowan, Mark George. "A Watchful Eye: The Catholic Church Extension Society and Ukrainian Catholic Immigrants, 1908–1930." *Canadian Protestant and Catholic Mission, 1820s–1960s: Historical Essays in Honour of John Webster Grant*. Ed. John S. Moir and C. T. McIntire. New York: Peter Lang, 1988. 221–43.

"Meeting of Synod of Manitoba." *Winnipeg Tribune* 8 June 1911.

"Minutes." Home Mission Committee of the General Assembly, PCC. Winnipeg, 29 May 1912. Board of Home Mission and Social Service, Presbyterian Church. United Church in Canada Archives: Box 2, File 13.

"Minutes." Sub-Committee on the Reception of Ministers of the Independent Greek Church into the Presbyterian Church, 24 Oct. and 28 Oct. 1912. Board of Home Mission and Social Service, Presbyterian Church. United Church in Canada Archives: Box 2, File 13.

Olender, Vivian. "Symbolic Manipulation in the Proselytizing of Ukrainians: An Attempt to Create a Protestant Uniate Church." Goa 191–207.

Robertson, James. "To McQueen." Spring 1899. *Papers of Charles William Gordon*. Archives and Special Collections, University of Manitoba Library: MSS 56, Box 37, File 2.

Sanneh, Lamin, *Religion and the Variety of Culture: A Study in Origin and Practice*. Valley Forge, PA: Trinity Press International, 1996.

"The Story of the Anna Turnbull Hospital at Wakaw [Saskatchewan]." Pamphlet. Women's Home Missionary Society. Presbyterian Church in Canada Archives.

"Ustvolsky, Stefan, Bishop Seraphim." *Dictionary of Canadian Biography*. Vol. 13 (1901–1910). Web. 29 June 2021.

White, Richard. *The Middle Ground: Indians, Empires, and Republics in the Great Lakes Region, 1650–1815*. Cambridge: Cambridge University Press, 2011.

"Ukrainian Students to Enter Manitoba College." *Winnipeg Free Press* 11 Oct. 1898.

Yereniuk, Roman. "Church Jurisdictions and Jurisdictional Changes Among Ukrainians in Canada, 1891–1925." Goa, ed. 109–27.

Yuzyk, Paul. *The Ukrainians in Manitoba: A Social History*. Toronto: University of Toronto Press, 1953.

---. "A Personal Reflection." Goa 1–3.

Bram Beelaert

On the Way to the Last Best West: Antwerp as a Transit Port for Central and Eastern European Immigrants to Canada, 1870–1930

. . . O Dinska Bronska,
you leave for Canada:
the rusty steamer waits for you along the quay.
You read on an almanach
of the "Red Star Line"
that Canada has bigger apples,
oh, and higher and yellower grain than Plocka.
It must be much better in Canada!
Oh, Dinska Bronska,
with your very big fingers:
it is so difficult for you to write that letter. . . .

Traces of the past

There used to be a time in Antwerp when schoolchildren read the poem "Dinska Bronska" by Flemish poet Karel van den Oever about a Polish girl writing her last letter to her family before leaving Europe to start a new life in Canada. The lines reflected the feelings of many, as at the height of transatlantic migration between 1873 and 1934 nearly two million Europeans went to Antwerp to board a ship set to North America (Vervoort and Beelaert 18). As the Belgian-American Red Star Line catered to the continental market and Belgian overseas emigration was small in comparison to other countries, the overwhelming majority of the passengers came from Central and Eastern Europe, making Antwerp a key port of transit for these people. The emigrant departure halls of the shipping company still stand today housing the Red Star Line Museum that shares the story of transatlantic European emigration through the port of Antwerp.[1]

For the most part of this period, the majority of the passengers embarked for the United States, and Canada was perceived as a less attractive destination. However, when in 1904 the Canadian Pacific established its first direct passenger service with the European continent in Antwerp, the Belgian port became a principal route to Canada for emigrants from Central and Eastern Europe. By the early 1920s the Red Star Line, which since 1873 had been shipping millions of passengers from Antwerp to New York and Philadelphia, operated a regular line between the Belgian Port and Halifax, also reflecting the changes in transatlantic migration patterns in the wake of the US quota system discussed in this volume as well.

---

1 For more information see the website of the museum at www.redstarline.be.

Fueled by the activities of the Canadian Emigration Office, the railway and shipping companies, posters appeared in the Belgian streets, shops, and taverns, advertising Canada as a vast and rich land, ready to be cultivated. In that period, all third-class passengers on their way to Canada and passing through Antwerp were inspected in the departure halls of the Red Star Line, close to the Rhine Quay, where the ships departed for their transatlantic crossing. In this chapter I discuss the rise of Antwerp as an emigration port from the 1840s to the 1930s, with an emphasis on emigration to Canada. In the second part I provide insights into the experiences of emigrants from Central and Eastern Europe on their way to and in the port of Antwerp, highlighting the determining (but often overlooked) role of shipping companies and the transport industry during their journey to the sea, and even on their decision to leave.

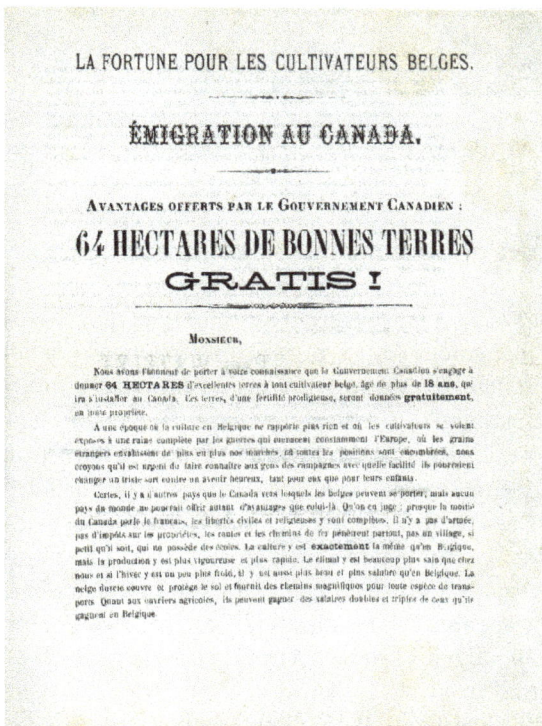

Figure 1: Information leaflet in French for Belgian emigrants to Canada[2]

Figure 2: Postcard of the Red Star Line[3]

Antwerp as a port of transatlantic emigration

As one of the great Western European urban centers of the early Modern Ages, and after centuries of stagnation, Antwerp came to prominence as an Atlantic port in the middle of the nineteenth century. On an equal footing with Rotterdam in the Netherlands and Hamburg in Germany, it had a large hinterland with early and excellent rail connections and inland navigation channels that ran deep into northern and central Europe (see Beelaert, "Have You Been to the Doctor Yet?" and Everaert). In 1863 a longstanding toll for the use of the mouth of the river Scheldt, which connects the city to the North Sea but lies in Dutch territory, was lifted and Antwerp harbor began to flourish. Amongst other things, grain and petroleum were imported from North America; coffee, animal skins, nitrates, guano, and cotton from Latin America; rice from British Colonial India; and wool from Australia (Hancké).

Emigrants started to arrive in Antwerp during the 1840s and 1850s, mostly from Germany and Switzerland. By that time, the first steamboats appeared on the Atlantic Ocean, making the crossing faster and more reliable. The authorities in Antwerp wanted to establish a passenger steam service with ships that departed regularly, but early attempts failed. Emigrants still had to cope with sail ships that were chartered by a shipping agent and departed irregularly. At the end of the 1850s

---

3 Collectie Stad Antwerpen, Red Star Line Museum. Available at: https://dams.antwerpen.be/asset/ K2RYOGVWbfeWVbaFeSRkOFUs/saeehMOPiPRUidVcmJ74Owxj

and throughout the 1860s emigrant traffic slowed down as a result of the American Civil War among others (Evaraert). Meanwhile, the conduct of several high-profile shipping agents in Antwerp also gave the city a bad name. Emigrants made the long journey to Antwerp only to find that they were ripped off, or they were led astray by malignant hoteliers or bar holders in port (see Evaraert and Spelkens for more information). Belgium had insufficient regulations to deal with this. Scandals and sensational stories were smeared out in the German press that rooted for the competing German ports Hamburg and Bremerhaven. But as the 1870s came along, crucial events would lead to decades of busy emigrant traffic to North America through the port of Antwerp.

LA VILLE D'ANVERS, VUE DU COTE DU PORT ET DES BASSINS

Figure 3: 1887 drawing of the Rhine Quay in Antwerp with a Red Star Line ship[4]

In 1872 the International Navigation Company from Philadelphia approached Jules von der Becke and Edouard Marsily, two Antwerp-based shipbrokers they knew through the Pennsylvanian oil export business (Vervoort and Beelaert 18-20). They wanted to bypass American protective maritime legislation and establish a European subsidiary that would allow them to build cheaper vessels on English wharves and

---

4 Collectie Stad Antwerpen, Vrienden van de Red Star Line vzw. Available at: https://dams. antwerpen.be/asset/U29l9bhVSwQgTRD8XIZyPBjH#id

hire cheaper crew overseas. Their plan was to export cargo on the eastbound journey and passengers on the westbound journey. The endeavor was bankrolled by the Pennsylvania Railroad Company that saw maritime trade and shipping routes as a natural extension of their railroad system on land (20).

Both the Belgian authorities and Antwerp City Government jumped at the opportunity. They exempted the new initiative from taxes and granted them the monopoly on the postal service to North America. At the end of 1872 the *Société Anonyme de Navigation Belgo-Américaine* (SANBA) was founded and its ships would sail under the name of Red Star Line. A red star against a white backdrop became the company flag. Its designers clearly drew inspiration from the emblem of the White Star Line (a white star against a red backdrop), which was at the time already a household name in the North Atlantic shipping trade. Weeks later, in January 1873, Red Star Line started its service to Philadelphia and one year later to New York (20).

Figure 4: Postcard showing passengers of the Red Star Line[5]

---

5 Collectie Stad Antwerpen, Red Star Line Museum. Available at: https://dams.antwerpen.be/asset/XjOO7gJ8YUQBECJLXR7CGQFi#id

Figure 5: Stereophoto of Red Star Line hangar with people waiting for embarkation[6]

Meanwhile, the authorities took steps towards the better protection of the emigrants passing through the city. In 1873 the Ministry of Foreign Affairs set up the Emigration Department to oversee the emigration flow. Three years later the Belgian government adopted a new and comprehensive emigration law, imposing more stringent and protective measures on shipping lines and their agents for the protection of emigrants. Among others, minimum food supplies on board of ships were required, agents had to have an official accreditation, emigration lodgings had to meet minimal hygienic standards. A commissioner was appointed to the Emigration Department that had to watch over the correct implementation of the emigration laws, serve as an information point for emigrants, and mediate in conflicts between shipping lines and its passengers. Additionally, a convention between the authorities and the shipping lines in 1874 stipulated that the latter had to provide waiting facilities in warehouses that were adjacent to their quays (for more information see Beelaert, "The Red Star Line" 51 and Spelkens 60-61).

This all led to a significant increase in transatlantic emigration from Antwerp. From the 1890s onwards Eastern Europe replaced Central Europe as the principal departure region and by 1906 Red Star Line transported 100,000 third-class passengers to the US. The busiest years of the company's existence were 1907 and 1913 with 119,000 and 117,000 passengers transported to and from North America, respectively. After a break during the German occupation of World War I, Red Star Line resumed its activities but never reached the numbers before the war. 1920 and 1921 averaged 60,000 passengers a year, but the next year the number was reduced

---

6 Collectie Stad Antwerpen, Red Star Line Museum. Available at: https://dams.antwerpen.be/asset/ K2RYOGVWbfeWVbaFeSRkOFUs/J16linEved9hUYXVhWQwyth4

to half due to the American immigration quotas (for an overview of US immigration regulation see the chapter by Venkovits). The depression from 1929 onwards all but halted transatlantic traffic to North America until after World War II and meant the end of the Red Star Line Company, which was liquidated at the beginning of 1935 (Vervoort and Beelaert 26-29).

Canada: The Last Best West

The US served as the primary destination for the majority of passengers during the period of New Immigration, but not everybody leaving Antwerp was going to the US. Ships from the Norddeutscher Lloyd called on Antwerp on route from Bremerhaven to ports in South America, to take on additional passengers. And in 1870, the Canadian Government founded its first emigration office in Antwerp, diffusing propaganda about Canada as a destination country (Journée, "De Canadese uitdaging" 148-66; Journée, Go West 29-45; Jaumain 108-23). The US federal government refrained from immigrant recruitment and left all advertising in the hands of the shipping companies. They advertised with their ships, promising a safe and comfortable passage, also for third class. The Canadian government, however, was actively involved (although also working with railroad companies) and much of the publicity was about the land. The government propaganda, and sometimes subsidies, was aimed at emigrants from desired countries such as Great Britain and Belgium, but nevertheless, in the countries of Central and Eastern Europe, where emigration to the US was high, a smaller but steady flow of passengers to Canada started. As opposed to the US, there was no direct connection yet from Antwerp. People going to Canada could buy their tickets from British companies such as the Allan Line and White Star Line but would have to take a smaller ship towards the UK before they could start their actual ocean crossing.

This changed in 1904 when the Canadian Pacific moved its European service from Bristol to London and Antwerp. The company now could pick up emigrants straight from the European continent, transport them overseas by ship, move them inland by rail, and sell them lands on the prairie (Musk 25). The ships of the company started their eastbound journey in Montréal. In steerage, livestock was transported to London, which was offloaded at the Deptfore cattle market on the banks of the River Thames. There, the stables were dismantled and the steerage compartments received a thorough cleaning. The next stop was Antwerp, where emigrants boarded the ships for the westbound journey back to Montréal (25).

Canadian Pacific made agreements with the German Hamburg America Line, diverting traffic to Canada from Hamburg to Antwerp, and the Red Star Line, which besides being a shipping company was also an emigrant agency accredited by the government that sold tickets for the transatlantic crossing. Red Star Line became the agent for Canadian Pacific, which meant that the latter had access to the vast network of emigration agents that Red Star Line had built over the European continent throughout the years (Beelaert, "Have You Been to the Doctor Yet?"). These agencies were situated in the big cities and had subagents in the countryside. Business owners such as shopkeepers and hairdressers would sell tickets to supplement their income.

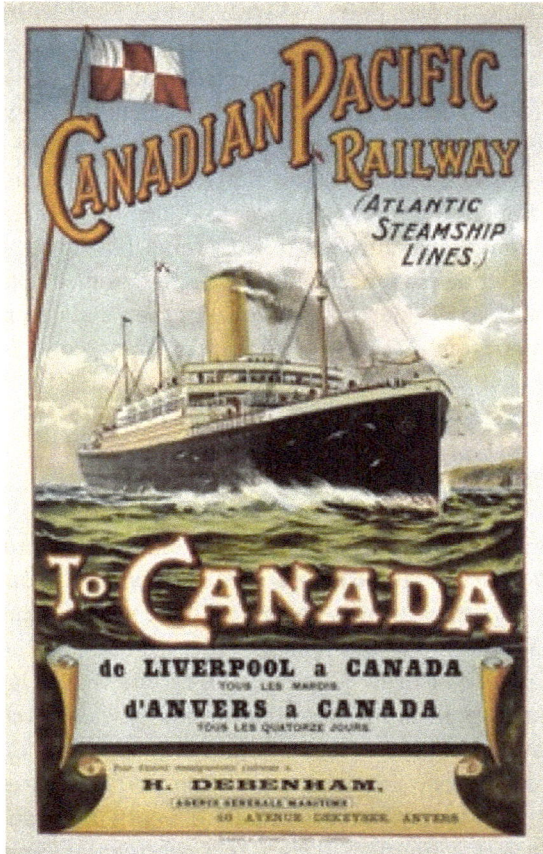

Figure 6: Canada Pacific Railway (Atlantic Steamship Lines poster)[7]

In 1908 Canadian Pacific received a concession in Austria-Hungary. Up until 1912, when the company opened a service in Trieste, it would ship its customers to the new world exclusively through the port of Antwerp. In 1913 Canadian Pacific had 36 agencies in Galicia and Bukovina alone, amongst others in Krakau, Lemberg, Brody,

---

7   Collectie Stad Antwerpen, Letterenhuis. Available at: https://dams.antwerpen.be/asset/ggGwCNGLBSTec8QYBsZNj7j3#id

and Oświęcim (Kowalski 159-66). Canadian Pacific conducted fierce propaganda with brochures, pamphlets, and the screening of movies. They even sold tickets through Catholic and Orthodox priests. Between 1904 and 1914 Canadian Pacific transported 188,000 emigrants from Antwerp to Canada in the third class of one of its five operational ships. Not all passengers were immigrants to Canada. A lot of immigrants to the US came in via Canadian ports and went to the US border by train. A famous example is the late Israeli Prime Minister Golda Meir, who took the ship from Antwerp to Quebec City with her family in 1908, only to travel on to Milwaukee in the US (see Meir and Verheyen 42). For Canadian Pacific, the summer port was Montréal, the winter port Saint John.

After World War I Red Star Line also started to sail to Canada, using Halifax as its arrival port. Emigration to the US never fully picked up after the war and the American immigration quotas introduced in 1921 and 1924 dealt a firm blow to all revenue from transatlantic passenger traffic. Therefore, the company experimented with new markets such as the tourism and cruise markets and new routes such as the connection to Canada. From 1922 to 1934 Red Star Line transported 30,000 passengers to Canada, with an apex in 1928.[8]

A guided process

So how did emigrants make their way from Central and Eastern Europe to Antwerp? It is impossible to do justice to all the different experiences European emigrants at the end of the nineteenth century and the beginning of the twentieth must have had, but we can try by using some telling and representative testimonies, thus reconstructing a typical route. That the so-called "push and pull factors" have played a crucial role in migration dynamics both in the past and present is widely known. But equally important in sustaining migration is the availability of migration routes that are perceived as reasonably easy to navigate and transportation means that are seen as reliable, safe, and relatively comfortable. By the end of the nineteenth century, when a railroad network connected all corners of continental Europe, and the bows of steamships plowed through the waves of the Atlantic with unparalleled speed, this applied to most European overseas emigration.

Transatlantic migration had become a guided process because of this transport revolution both on land and sea and because of the growth of a very competitive transatlantic passenger shipping industry which resulted in better amenities even for third-class passengers. Agents of the shipping lines were also active on land to guide their clientele as smoothly as possible from their departure zones to the ports of embarkation and onto the ships. In doing so they had to negotiate government

---

8 Gemeentearchief Rotterdam, collectie Holland America Lijn, 318.04. passage A, 579.

regulations both in Europe and North America. In countries such as Austria-Hungary and Russia, emigrants had to meet various requirements and were faced with a daunting bureaucracy. In transit countries, regulations were there to protect emigrants from maltreatment, but also to prevent them from straying too far from their transit route and ensure that they eventually left the countries they were passing through on the way to port. Lastly, immigration regulations of both the US and Canada became tighter towards the end of the nineteenth century and as the twentieth century progressed.

The shipping companies played a central role in implementing these regulations, as governments outsourced important aspects of their migration policies to them. From the 1890s onwards the United States government, followed by the Canadian authorities, made the shipping lines responsible for the deportation of those passengers who were denied access to those countries. As a result of this policy of "remote control" the shipping lines installed inspections of their third-class passengers in the ports of embarkation. They supplemented the inspections that were often already installed by the local authorities to prevent the outbreak of disease on the ships. This private-public cooperation extended throughout the European continent.

Leaving everything behind

As already mentioned, both Red Star Line and Canadian Pacific had agencies and subagents working for them throughout the Central European departure areas. They sustained and capitalized on the "emigration fever" that raged in the main emigration regions, as people were relatively well-informed by letters from friends and family who had already emigrated and by pamphlets being spread by emigrant aid societies. They tried to make the journey as easy as possible, selling door-to-door tickets with the train fare to the port of embarkation, from the arrival port to the final destination included. They also made a first selection. Clients had to fill in a questionnaire with the same questions they were to be asked upon arrival in America.

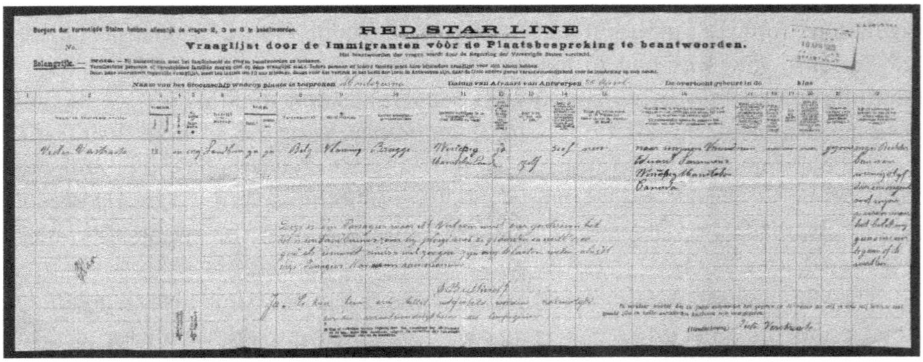
RED STAR LINE

Vraaglijst door de Immigranten vóór de Plaatsbespreking te beantwoorden.

Figure 7: A completed Red Star Line questionnaire[9]

The testimony, recorded in 1971 of an unnamed emigrant from West-Galicia, district Brzesko, who left for Canada and spent the rest of his life in Saskatchewan, shows the extent to which emigrants could base their decisions on information from the grapevine. It ranged, it appears, from big decisions such as the final destination to smaller ones such as what food to eat before you get on the train.

> In the meantime, our entire family was emigrating one by one to the US, so my mother and sister decided to send me to Canada, because they thought I could keep my faith there. In 1902, at the end of April, I went to the mayor to get a workbook because in America, I had heard, they would not let you in. Then I went to the district administration for the signature, which I also received on the same day. Then a travel agent gave me my ship card and a timetable when the steamboats left for Canada, and after several days I was ready for the trip.
>
> My mother gave me a dozen hard-boiled eggs on the way and some bread in a bundle. That was my only travel luggage. I let a pair of high boots hang over my shoulder, took the bundle and left with my mother, who accompanied me to the edge of the village. We said goodbye to each other there and I still remember very well how I walked towards Biadolin after crying for a long time, constantly looking back to see if I could still see my mother and my village. Eventually I reached Biadolin, not without fear about how to get it all done. After all I had never been to a station and I had never traveled by train. I bought a ticket to Krakow and got on the train. Even before I reached Krakow, I got rid of my luggage by eating the bread and eggs right away. And the eggs were, as I said, hard-boiled, with the blissful consequence that I didn't have to look for a toilet. My mum had assured me that she had cooked the eggs specially because there was no toilet on the train. (Qtd. in *Pamiętniki emigrantów: Kanada* 283-84)

In that same year eleven-year-old Anastasia Turner left her native village Rozsec ad Kunstátem in Bohemia. Two of her half-brothers and one half-sister, children from a previous marriage of her father, had already emigrated and wrote home about nice

9 Collectie Stad Antwerpen, Red Star Line Museum. Available at: https://dams.antwerpen.be/asset/L2SkmQEfJnCIJRTUSTtW3tw9#id ASmGD2WITm#id

living conditions and the richness of the natural resources in their new home, Tacoma in Washington, United States. Her father, Josef, was worried about the political situation in Europe at the time and decided to leave as well. They went to an agent in Brno, who sold them a ticket from the Brno station to Tacoma, including the train fares and an ocean passage from Antwerp on *de SS Vaderland* of the Red Star Line. Years later Anastasia, who became known as "Annie," gave an interview to the Ellis Island National Immigration Museum about her experiences.

> We had to sell everything. Some of it we gave to relatives because they wanted remembrance of us. . . . We all wrote it down on paper until we had enough. We had animals, a field, it was enough to come across. My father, mother, [older brother] Anton and [older sister] Agnes had to have a full ticket, the rest of us [small children] went on a half ticket. We didn't have to hire horses.[10]

Annie's father was well loved in the village. When the Mensik family left, the whole village came out to say goodbye.

> People didn't want us to go away. They wanted us to stay. And they donated a horse. The band played for us, everybody cried, but we were happy because we were going someplace, us kids. But father and mother weren't quite so enthused as the rest of us.

At the border

Agents of the shipping lines often operated on the border of the illegal. Archives of the Austrian emigration police in Galicia mention the Antwerp shipping agencies of Canon and Freudberg selling illegal tickets without a concession. Also, agents from the Red Star Line and the Canadian Pacific were not above selling tickets to potential customers who were not allowed to leave the country, such as conscripts. They assisted emigrants to leave the country illegally (Kowalski 62).

Between January 1911 and August 1913 3,319 men from 21 to 23 years were arrested at the Krakow Central station and forcibly sent back to their homes. They were en route to America, had no legitimate emigration documents, and were trying to leave the country while they were of conscription age.[11] To avoid detection, agents gave their clients directions to leave Austria-Hungary under the radar, such as in this letter, found in the archives of the emigration police:

---

10 Transcription of the interview with Annie Mensik Turner by Nancy Dallett of the Ellis Island National Immigration Museum, 14.4.1989, DP-22/TURNER.
11 Report of the Krakow police to the governor of Galicia in Lemberg, 29.8.1913, Archiwum Państwowe w Krakowie. C. k. Starostwo Powiatowe w Chrzanowie, 124, nrs. 327-28, consulted and translated for the Red Star Line Museum by Dr. Vladimir Ronin, 2009.

During the journey through Galicia, until you arrive in Myslowitz, you must not confess to anyone that you are going to America or Canada. Do not start a conversation with anyone and if you are approached, do not answer! If someone asks you where you are going, you answer: I follow my nose! You must resolutely chase away all persons who would ask you if you are going to America or Canada—and bite them that it does not concern them. Be brave! Don't be frightened by some gentleman who threatens you or promises you something. Because such a person just wants to earn from you and he will make you fall into misery and lose money. And if someone from the authorities stops you and starts asking where you are going, then under no circumstances should you admit that you are on your way to America or Canada, but say you are going to Prussia to work, to Myslowitz, where you will sign a contract for some work in a job placement agency. If they ask for your passport, feel free to say that those who go to Prussia do not need a passport, but that you have a work or service booklet or a certificate from the village administration. According to the law, one of those documents is sufficient for those who go to Prussia or Saxony to work. If you do not state that you are going by sea, no one will be able to prove that if you do not have a ship card and a large sum of money with you—and they will have to let you go. Only after your arrival in Myslowitz, where you are already completely safe, you can and must tell where you are actually going.[12]

The fact that documents such as these can be found in the archives is the result of the fierce competition between the agents on the borders of the Austrian-Hungarian Empire. Notifying the authorities with well- or not-so-well-founded accusations of breaking the emigration law was a way to eliminating competition. Also, between January 1911 and August 1913, 117 emigrant agents in the vicinity of Oświęcim at the border of Austria-Hungary, Russia, and Germany were reported to the district government. 32 were reprimanded, amongst whom 7 agents were from the Canadian Pacific Railway and 4 employees of the popular Zofia Biesiadecka agency that forwarded clients to Antwerp.[13]

Into Germany

Transit migrants on their way through Germany had to present a certain amount of money and a ship ticket to prove that they could sustain themselves during their stay, and that they were effectively planning to leave the country. Also, in the 1890s the exploitation of the control and disinfection stations on the Eastern Prussian borders was outsourced to the German shipping lines. Stricter immigration procedures in the US had strengthened the tendency of the German government to control the transit

---

12 Letter from Piotr Kikla to Stanislaw Kowalski, Antwerp, 3.10.1912, intercepted by the Galician authorities, Archiwum Państwowe w Krakowie. C. k. Starostwo Powiatowe w Chrzanowie, 127, nr. 63/12, consulted and translated for the Red Star Line Museum by Dr. Vladimir Ronin, 2009.
13 Report of the Krakow police to the governor of Galicia in Lemberg, 29.8.1913, Archiwum Państwowe w Krakowie. C. k. Starostwo Powiatowe w Chrzanowie, 124, nrs. 327-28, consulted and translated for the Red Star Line Museum by Dr. Vladimir Ronin, 2009.

movement of Eastern European emigrants on their way to the Atlantic ports. German shipping lines such as the Norddeutscher Lloyd operating from Bremerhaven and HAPAG from Hamburg used their position as gatekeepers at the German border as leverage in disputes, for example, over ticket prices, with the other shipping lines. Emigrants that were able to leave Russia or Austria-Hungary had to pass the control stations at the German border as already mentioned. An unnamed female laborer who passed through them in 1907 with her older brothers, still remembered this ordeal when she wrote down her memories in 1977:

> The treatment of the passengers completely outraged me. Like cattle, we were herded into one fenced place, except the women were kept separate. There we were forced to undress completely, they took our clothes to steam through and sent ourselves to a bathhouse. While we were still naked, we were examined by a doctor. I was 14 years old at the time and almost went through the ground with embarrassment. (*Pamiętniki emigrantów: Stany Zjednoczone* 504-05)

Jan Dziura, 26, a Polish farmer's son from West Galicia, bought his ticket to America from the travel agency of Ms. Biesiadecka in 1906. His account, written in 1977, gives an impression of the train journey that followed after the border controls.

> After we collected our ship charts in Oświęcim, they put us in fourth-class carriages and we took the train to the Belgian port of Antwerp. We were on the road for about two days and two nights. In the wagons the benches were only along the walls and the people were crammed in like herrings in a barrel. For most, there were no seats at all. People sat on the floor, on their trunks and bundles, in short, wherever and whenever they could. A number of women held small children in their arms. They had it the worst: they had nowhere to put their children, nor could they give them food or drink. Some, like me, did not take any food with them and on the second day hunger also began to torment us. (227-30)

Antwerp

When the trains arrived in the Antwerp Central Station after such an arduous trip, a lot of passengers were tired and confused. In the days of laissez-faire, they were beleaguered by all sorts of people from the moment they set foot on the platform. But since the emigration law of 1876 was in force, only accredited agents from the companies or the Belgian emigration service were allowed on the platform. They took the new arrivals under their wings immediately. First they had to pass a check of the Belgian emigration service in the station, and then they were transferred to their hotels.

These hotels were owned by the shipping companies and were exploited by people from and often named after the region where a lot of passengers came from. Based on the emigration law, they were also held to certain standards of cleanliness and to an occupation quota per facility. But in busy times, authorities turned a blind eye as they did not want to hinder business. This resulted in uncomfortable lodgings for the emigrants and irritation with their Antwerpian neighbors for the nuisance in their street.

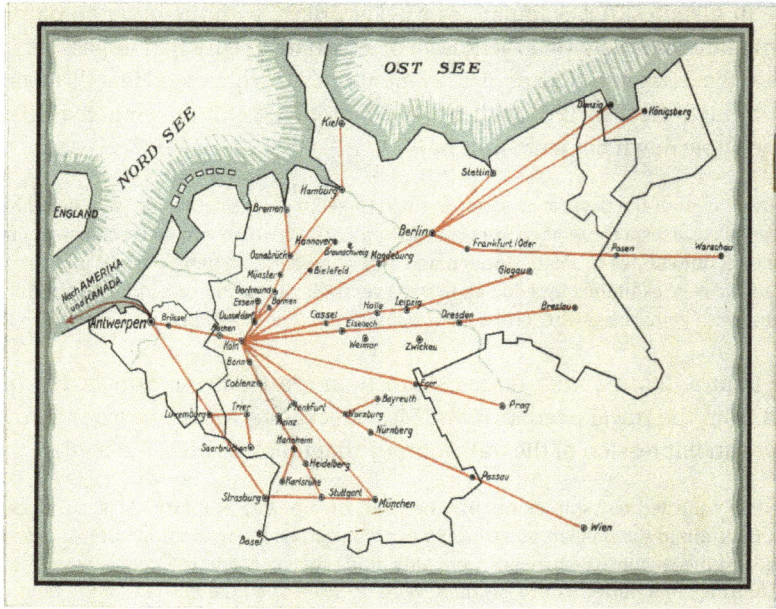

Figure 8: Reaching Antwerp: From a German-language Red Star Line brochure for third class crossings[14]

The hotels were dispersed throughout the city. Unlike Bremerhaven or Hamburg, Antwerp never had one central emigrant facility, despite efforts to build one. This means that the emigrants were highly visible. Any given week in 1913 there were 3,000 emigrants in the city. Antwerp writers and artists were inspired, in the depictions and descriptions a tone of compassion prevails, and a lot of attention goes to the exotic appearance of the strangers. Emmanuel de Bom wrote in 1918:

> Suddenly, at the end of the street, a dull rumor rose. It was getting closer and closer. A considerable heap of people, pressed against each other like herds of cattle, came driven . . . . Emigrants! There were over a hundred of them, mostly all bent under the load of packs. In front a man in a cap and uniform, surely a servant of the transatlantic steam company, who led them from the station to the harbor, where the boat was waiting. . . . They rushed, like souls in distress, their wretched goods on their shoulders dragging. (qtd. in Verheyen, "Zeit gezoent" 131-32)

---

14 Collectie Stad Antwerpen, Red Star Line Museum. Available at: https://dams.antwerpen.be/asset/y24EJPgfVaLBeLCXNRvNZo75#id

Figure 9: Eugeen van Mieghem: *Embarkation for the New World*, 1907-1917[15]

In 1958, Belgian writer Marnix Gijsen remembered scenes from Antwerp a couple of decades earlier:

> In my youth it was a strange and fascinating scene, to see emigrants passing through Antwerp on their way to the harbor, or lingering about timidly around their so called "hotels". . . . They gave the impression of great haste, as if the angels of vengeance were at their heels . . . . They were also notable for their strange clothes, they wore heavy high boots and short sheepskin coats, and their manners were primitive rural. . . . They corresponded perfectly to the description Emma Lazarus gave of the emigrants in the sonnet on the Statue of Liberty in the New York harbor: "the wretched refuge of your teeming shores." Hundreds of thousands of future Americans and Canadians have been washed through Antwerp. (qtd. in Verheyen, "Zeit gezoent" 131-32)

When word came from a departure country about dangerous epidemics such as cholera, quarantine hotels were installed. Emigrants who came from that country were taken to that hotel and were not allowed to leave it until they were disinfected

---

15 Collectie Stad Antwerpen, Museum Plantin-Moretus. Available at: https://dams.antwerpen.be/asset/VTugIbLnXFCbd7mdbKu5cStT#id

and physicians were certain that they were not contaminated. This sometimes lasted for weeks.

Before boarding the ship, emigrants had to shower, get their belongings disinfected and undergo a medical examination. These procedures were adopted under pressure from the American and Canadian governments. First, this happened on the quays, but after a lot of complaints, in 1893 Red Star Line built facilities for their passengers going to the US. When Canadian pacific started its service in 1904, they too held their checks on the quays where their ships were moored. Nonetheless, this also resulted in outrage. According to complaints in the archives of the Belgian emigration service, women were inspected in open air (Beelaert, "Have You Been to the Doctor Yet?" 17-19). The screen that was put up for their privacy was not high enough to prevent men wandering around in the harbor from looking over. Canadian Pacific started collaborating with Red Star Line and passengers for Canada were also checked in the latter's facilities.

Figure 10: The *SS Finland* before departure[16]

16 Collectie Stad Antwerpen, Vrienden van de Red Star Line vzw. Available at: https://dams. antwerpen.be/asset/G1RfHTTeJjEdUWljTcJXl6ZO#id

Interbellum

As already mentioned, emigration through Antwerp picked up once again after the end of World War I. The ports of Hamburg and Bremerhaven stayed closed until 1921. English companies such as Cunard Line and White Star Line came to Antwerp in the wake of the Red Star Line and Canadian Pacific (Caestecker 61). But at the same time, partly as a consequence of the war, immigration rules in the United States became tighter. The US adopted its quota laws in 1921 and 1924, aimed to curtail the "new" immigration from Central and Eastern Europe. Canada's very restrictive immigration policy from just after the war relaxed somewhat as the 1920s progressed, but here also immigrants from this region were regarded as non-preferred and needed a special permit to get into the country (Kelley and Trebilcock 186-92).

The stricter immigration procedures in North America after World War I resulted in more elaborate procedures in Antwerp as more and more immigrants were deported back to the city. These stranded emigrants had several options. They could go to one of the emigrant aid organizations that were active in Antwerp, including the Jewish aid organization Ezra or the Catholic St. Raphaels Verein. These could sponsor a return to where they came from, or provide shelter if people wanted to attempt the voyage later. If emigrants had a curable disease, they would search for treatment in one of the institutions of the city (for more information see Caestecker; Vloeberghs, and De Vroey). They could also appeal to the Belgian Emigration commissioner if they felt that they were treated unfairly, or if they could prove that the shipping agent had sold them a ticket knowing that they were not eligible to get into the US or Canada. Especially in the 1920s, the archives of the Belgian Emigration service house some telling files of Central European emigrants who filed a complaint. They provide insights into how emigrants could get lost in the regulations, procedures, and administrative burden that accompanied international migration more and more as the twentieth century progressed. Also, they reveal a tense relationship between the Belgian government, which was afraid of too many emigrants getting stuck in Antwerp and thus becoming a public charge; American and Canadian authorities, who enforced their policy of "remote control"; and the shipping lines, who wanted everything to go as smoothly as possible for their clients (Beelaert, "The Red Star Line").

For example, On February 15, 1921 two Polish emigrants named Katana and Rozek procured their passports in Cologne, Germany. As a result, they were also allowed to buy their tickets for a ship of the Canadian Pacific Railway Company departing from Antwerp. But in Antwerp, officers of the Canadian Pacific prevented them from boarding their vessel because they needed passports from their country of origin, not Germany. Katana and Rozek wanted their money back, and the Belgian emigration commissariat found them to be in the right. Canadian Pacific was forced to reimburse Katana and Rozek, but they referred the Polish passengers back to their office in Cologne where the tickets were bought. The wife of Rozek traveled back to Cologne to collect the money they were owed, but to no avail. The affair dragged on until May, and in the meantime the families Rozek and Katana were stuck in Antwerp.[17]

At the end of 1921 Belgian emigration commissioner Venesoen complained about the high number of refusals of emigrants by the Canadian authorities, in his view without consistent argument, who were sent back to Antwerp from the Canadian Pacific Railway Steamer *SS Scandinavian*.[18] These people included Nuchim Febrak and his wife, who were Romanian. According to the commissioner, they had passports from the Canadian Immigration services. Dionisios Formos, travelling with a prepaid ticket after receiving permission from the Canadian Immigration Service to leave for Canada, was rejected in Quebec. Jozef Profis, from Romania, also had permission but was eventually denied because he had come to the country on a non-continuous journey.

When Jozef Miasnik, travelling on an unknown ship, was also rejected, the commissioner questioned Mr. Percy Reid, Inspector of the Canadian Immigration Service in Antwerp and at the same time director of the Cunard Line in that city. He claimed never to have blocked the departure of Miasnik, but apparently there were differences of opinions between the Belgian and Canadian branches of the Immigration Service. Lastly, some Romanian passengers from the *SS Corsican* were mentioned: Paul Staub with wife and three children as well as Heinrich Schwager and wife. They left Antwerp on November 8, 1921 with approved visa, yet their entrance was eventually denied.[19]

---

17 Correspondence between Emigration commissioner Venesoen, the Provincial Governor of Antwerp, Canadian Pacific Railway Services, and the Belgian Minister of Foreign Affairs, Archives of the Emigration service, bundle 59, Provincial Archives Antwerp, consulted for the Red Star Line Museum by Erica De Coster.
18 Report of the judicial attaché of the Emigration service to commissioner Venesoen, 13.1.1922, Archives of the Emigration service, bundle 94, Provincial Archives Antwerp, consulted for the Red Star Line Museum by Erica De Coster.
19 Ibid.

Figure 11: The Red Star Line buildings[20]

Red Star Line

In 1921 the Red Star Line added a two-story wing to their buildings, still believing that transatlantic passenger transport was worth investing in. Third-class passengers from all shipping lines offering voyages to North America (both US and Canada) were inspected and bathed. Emigrants could leave their luggage to be disinfected under steam in giant autoclaves when they themselves had to take a shower. When they were in the shower their clothes were taken away to be disinfected along with the luggage. After an hour they got their clothes back in a sterile central zone in the building. Next, they went to the first floor where several doctors awaited them. There were doctors from the destination countries (US and Canada), a doctor from the Belgian emigration service, and sometimes officials from the consulates of the departure countries such as Poland. Their physical condition was checked, as well as their mental state, and it was determined if they had any contagious diseases (Beelaert, "Have You Been to the Doctor Yet?" 17-19; Beelaert, "The Red Star Line" 58-59).

---

20 Collectie Stad Antwerpen, Vrienden van de Red Star Line vzw. Available at: https://dams. antwerpen.be/asset/j2UjobEU9rPpdhrOlYrtQoBV#id.

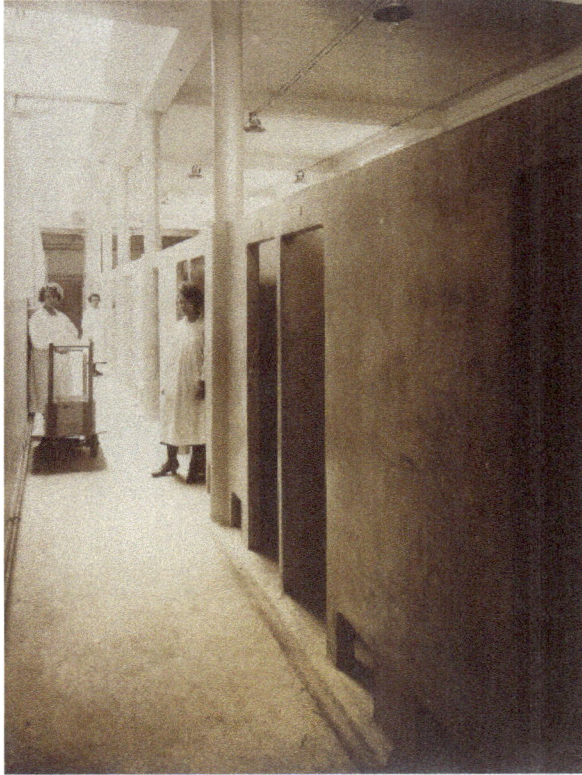

Figure 12: Bathing rooms for women[21]

These procedures were not without controversy. Already in November 1920, when checks were held in makeshift facilities of the new Red Star Line building, the Polish consulate organized an investigation into the emigrant procedures in Antwerp. There had been several complaints from young female Polish passengers who felt violated during the procedures.[22] This was an especially sensitive matter, as women and children constituted the lion share of emigrants passing through Antwerp as transatlantic emigration had become largely a follow-on migration. Of the estimated 75,000 Jewish immigrants to the US in 1920, 92% were on their way to join immediate family. Women and children made up 75% of those immigrants (Caestecker 61). Representative K. Downarowitz visited the facilities of the Red Star Line before departure and interviewed several officials from both the involved governments and

---

21 Collectie Stad Antwerpen, Vrienden van de Red Star Line vzw. Available at: https://dams. antwerpen.be/asset/K2RYOGVWbfeWVbaFeSRkOFUs/EDhPKdSfOhNV6WPMUewd8Zue.
22 Report of the Polish repatriation bureau to the Consul-General of Poland in Antwerp, 12.12.1920, Archiwum Akt Nowych w Warszawie. Ministerstwo Spraw Zagranicznych, 12538.

emigrant aid organizations. In his report, Downarowitz cited at length the testimony of Mrs. Wilkin of the local branch of the YMCA, lauding her as one of the most authoritative voices in the matter:

> Mrs. Wilkin told us the following details. During the check, apart from the doctors, all the male staff were removed; this regulation is strictly adhered to. The female emigrants are examined by different doctors: they are usually a number of Belgian doctors, a doctor appointed by the American government and possibly also two Canadian ones. Nurses are present during the investigation, while the formalities associated with travel documents are completed by a female employee of the shipping company. As a rule, Mrs. Wilkin is also present at the check. In view of the composition of the group present in the room and the presence in the next room of the Belgian authorities in the person of the Commissioner for Emigration and his assistants, any offense against the decency of the women must have caused immediate intervention.

> Another thing is, emphasizes Mrs. Wilkin, that such a check is in itself an extremely unpleasant experience for the women, which indeed makes them very nervous and often cry. Mrs. Wilkin even stated that if it were herself, she probably would have refrained from going to America if she had to undergo that kind of scrutiny. However, it is not an abuse by the shipping company, but a requirement of the American sanitary authorities . . . .[23]

In other words, according to Downarowitz's report, the shipping companies implemented the procedures correctly and as humanely as possible. However, the procedures as imposed by the destination countries in themselves were very stressful, echoing those on the German Border before the world war. Also, the fact that some emigrants were not allowed to go on board caused anxiety and resentment amongst everyone.[24]

A declaration from 1928, made by an interpreter who was present during the interrogations in the Red Star Line building, gives a detailed depiction of the inspection the Canadian doctor, also mentioning the tensions that often arose between the concerned parties.[25] Men had to undress above the waist, and do some physical exercises. They were weighed and their measurements were taken. After that, a majority had to drop their pants as well and were checked for venereal diseases, among others. This could take up to 20 minutes or more. Those who looked nervous (according to the report, around 50%) had to go to another room to pass a second examination of about the same length. Heart, lungs, and stomach were examined again. According to the interpreter, the Canadian doctor was notoriously strict with women. They also had to undress above the waist and undergo the same procedures

---

23 Report of the Polish repatriation bureau to the Consul-General of Poland in Antwerp, 12.12.1920, Archiwum Akt Nowych w Warszawie. Ministerstwo Spraw Zagranicznych, 12538, 3-6.
24 Ibid.
25 Report to emigration commissioner De Coster, 27.1.1928, 2.669 bis X Emigration – Questions Sanitaires et Service Médical, 2953 I-V: rapports – propagande – engagements, Archives of the Belgian Ministry of Foreign Affairs.

more rigorously, which could take up to one and a half hours. A woman was told she had bad sight and was forced to buy glasses in order to be able to travel on to Canada, while there was good reason to believe that she was not able to read. The Canadian Railway Company forwarded the declaration to the Belgian Emigration Commisioner De Coster, complaining that the behavior of the doctor caused unnecessary delays and difficulties.[26]

However, a lot of passengers experienced little of all this and made it on their ship without incident. After a short but tense stay from a couple of hours to a couple of days in Antwerp, it would take them on the Atlantic towards a new future. When they saw the city of Antwerp disappear on the horizon, they had only been on the ship for a few moments. But they had been under the care, guidance, and sometimes perhaps coercion of the shipping companies who had to navigate continuously between their business interests and the laws and regulations of both the departure and destination countries, from the moment the travelers had bought their tickets in Galicia or other regions of Central and Eastern Europe.

Conclusion

Transatlantic passenger traffic through Antwerp steadily declined throughout the 1920s and during the depression era. Red Star Line was liquidated in 1935, never to be replaced again by a major transatlantic passenger service out of Antwerp. The millions of emigrants who passed through Antwerp on their way to a new life left their mark on the city and found their way into the collective memory of Antwerpians today. The Red Star Line Museum revives their experiences in the original departure halls of the Red Star Line company at the quays where their ships left for the US and Canada. Yet, when reading immigrant biographies and memoires, or interviewing the last witnesses, places of transit such as the port of Antwerp are barely mentioned. Key topics in those testimonies usually involve nostalgia and sometimes mourning for the lost life in the country of origin, traumas experienced before, during or after the journey, the ocean crossing, and the arrival in and first impressions of the new country.

However, as I argue in this essay focusing on the European part of the immigrant experience, the shipping business also had a crucial role in the migration process. From the moment their passengers bought their shipping tickets in their hometown, up until the arrival in the new country, shipping companies and their agents shaped the migrant experience. By the end of the nineteenth century, it facilitated a relatively easy and reliable journey in comparison with a few decades earlier. But at the same time it played a crucial role in the selection process between wanted and unwanted

---

26 Ibid.

newcomers, as destination countries such as Canada adopted a policy of "remote control" and strove to organize the selection process as far from their borders as possible.

Works Cited

Beelaert, Bram. "Have You Been to the Doctor Yet? Het Red Star Line Hygiëne- en controlestation voor emigranten als plek van herinnering" [The Red Star Line Hygiene and Control Station for Emigrants as a Place of Remembrance]. *Brood en Rozen* 3 (2010): 5-23.

---. "The Red Star Line and the Medical Examination of Emigrants in Antwerp." Beelaert, ed. *Red Star Line* 50-60.

---, ed. *Red Star Line–Antwerp*. Leuven: Davidsfonds, 2013.

Brinkmann, Tobias. "Travelling with Ballin: The Impact of American Immigration Policies on Jewish Transmigration within Central Europe, 1880-1914." *IRSH* 53 (2008): 459-84.

Caestecker, Frank. "A Lasting Transit in Antwerp: Eastern European Jewish Migrants on Their Way to the New World, 1900-1925." *Tales of Transit: Narrative Migrant Spaces in Atlantic Perspective 1850-1950*. Ed. Michael Boyden, Hans Krabbendam, and Liselotte Vandenbusscheby. Amsterdam: Amsterdam University Press, 2013. 59-80.

Everaert, John. "Landverhuizers op doortocht: Antwerpen en de trans-Atlantische migratie 1843-1914" [Migrants in Transit: Antwerp and Transatlantic Migration, 1843-1914]. *Landverhuizers: Antwerpen als kruispunt van komen en gaan* [Emigrants: Antwerp as a Crossroads of Comings and Goings]. Ed. Rita Jalon. Antwerp: Uitgeverij Pandora, 2002. 9-17.

Feys, Torsten. "Trans-Atlantic Migration at Full Steam Ahead: A Flourishing and Well-Oiled Multinational Enterprise." Beelaert, ed. *Red Star Line* 32-44.

Hancké, Lode. "De omstreden opgang van een wereldhaven: De Antwerpse haven in de 19de eeuw tot 1914" [The Controversial Rise of a World Port: The Port of Antwerp in the 19th Century until 1914]. *Stroomversnelling: De Antwerpse haven tussen 1880 en nu* [Maelstrom: The Port of Antwerp between 1880 and Now]. Ed. Mandy Nauwelaerts. Antwerpen: Uitgeverij Pandora, 2002. 13-33.

Jaumain, Serge. "De Belgen in Canada: In de watten gelegde inwijkelingen" [The Belgians in Canada: Pampered Immigrants]. *Belgische emigranten*. Ed. Anne Morelli. Berchem: EPO,1999. 108-23.

Journée, Mark. *Go West: Een verhaal van vlaamse emigranten naar Canada* [Go West: A Story of Flemish Emigrants to Canada]. n.p.: Uitgeverij Snoeck, 2006.

---. "De Canadese uitdaging, 1888-1952 [The Canadian Challenge, 1888-1952]. *Boer vindt land: Vlaamse migranten en Noord-Amerika* [Farmer Finds Land: Flemish Migrants and North America]. Ed. Andreas Stynen. Leuven: Davidsfonds, 2014. 148-63.

Kelley, Ninette, and Michael Trebilcock. *The Making of the Mosaic: A History of Canadian Immigration Policy*. Toronto: University of Toronto Press, 2000.

Kowalski, Gregorz Maria. *Przestępstwa emigracyjne w Galicji 1897-1918* [Emigration Crimes in Galicia 1897-1918]. Krakow: Wydawnictwo Uniwersytetu Jagiellońskiego, 2003.

Meir, Golda. *My Life*. London: Weidenfeld and Nicolson, 1975.

Musk, George. *Canadian Pacific: The Story of the Famous Shipping Line*. London: David and Charles, 1989.

Pamiętniki emigrantów: Kanada [Memoirs of Emigrants: Canada]. Warsaw: Instytut Gospodarstwa Społecznego, 1971.

Pamiętniki emigrantów: Stany Zjednoczone [Memoirs of Emigrants: The United States]. Warsaw: Instytut Gospodarstwa Społecznego, 1977.

Ronin, Vladimir. *Eindverslag Researchopdracht Red Star Line*. Unpublished report. 2009.

Spelkens, Eric. *Antwerp as a Port of Emigration, 1842-1913*. Brussels: Center for American Studies, 1976.

Vervoort, Robert, and Bram Beelaert. "Star Boats: The Red Star Line in Antwerp." Beelaert, ed. *Red Star Line* 18-28.

Vloeberghs, Lien, and Linde De Vroey. "Antwerp 1913: Stay and Pathways of Emigrants in the City." Beelaert, ed. *Red Star Line* 82-92.

Verheyen, Luc. "Zeit gezoent, Antwerpen!" [To Your Health, Antwerp!]. *One Foot in America: De Joodse migranten van de Red Star Line en Eugeen Van Mieghem* [One Foot in America: The Jewish Migrants of the Red Star Line and Eugeen Van Mieghem]. Antwerpen: BAI, 2009. 125-54.

Zollberg, Aristide. *A Nation by Design*. New York: Russell Sage Foundation, 2006.

Balázs Venkovits

From Non-Preferred to Unlawful: Illegal Hungarian Immigration on the US-Canada Border in the 1920s

Introduction

Hungarians wishing to emigrate in the years following World War I found themselves in a completely novel regulatory environment compared to the pre-war era, which fundamentally restructured the available migration trajectories and opportunities.[1] This is true primarily because of changes in US immigration policy and related restrictions, which effectively closed the doors to mass immigration to the United States, a prime destination before the Great War. However, social and economic reasons and the consequences of the dismemberment of Hungary, which resulted in many Hungarians now residing outside the mother country, still prompted many to emigrate, and those wishing to leave sought alternative options. Stressing the need for the settlement of its western provinces and encouraging immigration in the second half of the 1920s, in parallel with the US restrictions, Canada opened up and became one of the main emigration destinations with nearly three times as many Hungarians arriving in the country in just five or six years as in the entire pre-world war period. Although this process was cut short by the Great Depression, it was one of the most intense and fascinating periods in the history of Hungarian-Canadian relations and Hungarian emigration, with many details still requiring further scholarly attention.

Iván Hordósy, the head of the Canadian Hungarian Immigrant Protection Office, in *Külföldi Magyarság* [Hungarians Abroad], similarly highlighted Canada's changing role in the 1920s:

> Let's admit it: before the war, we were not very interested in Canada and Canadian Hungarians. The only thing that made this distant country in the north attractive for us was the onset of emigration. In this regard the American continent for us used to equal the United States. . . . But now that the United States closed its doors we had to prepare, with a sad heart, for a significant loss of blood due to emigration as a result of the depressing economic conditions and Duca's policy on the occupied territories; thus we began to talk more and more about two countries [sic] in mutilated Hungary: South America and Canada.[2]

1 The research was funded by the Ministry of Culture and Innovation with support from the National Research, Development, and Innovation Fund under grant no. FK 143388.
2 "Csonkamagyarország és a kanadai kivándorlás" [A Maimed Hungary and the Emigration to Canada]. *Külföldi Magyarság*. LAC RG76-I-A-1, vol. no.: 145, microfilm reel no.: C-7302, file no.: 34274, image 100. Unless otherwise noted, all translations of Hungarian sources are mine.

As emigration (re)started, Canada received increasing attention, and both the perception of Canada in Hungary and the image of Hungarians in Canada changed; meanwhile, the unforeseen wave of immigration had significant impact on the Canadian-Hungarian community as well.[3] This era provides an opportunity to examine the inter-American and transatlantic effects of US restrictions, the activities of Canadian railway companies and agents (in Hungary), and the success of settlement campaigns, among other issues. In this chapter, I explore a topic that has received less scholarly attention so far: many of the Hungarians who arrived in Canada during the period under scrutiny did not see the country as a final destination but as a springboard to the United States and tried to cross the border illegally. The number of such attempts was high enough for the subject to appear in the contemporary press (not only in general, but also with specific Hungarian implications), in politics, books, consular documents, and even in Hungarian regulations. Examining this topic in more depth, this paper sheds light on the history of illegal Hungarian migration 100 years ago in the context of international migration policies of the 1920s and examines this period and region in more detail from the perspective of illegal Hungarian migration, specifically to assess the extent to which this phenomenon played a role in the history of Hungarian emigration and how it influenced the image of Canada in Hungary.

Changes in North American immigration policies and Hungarian emigration

In order to understand Hungarian emigration trends in the 1920s and to contextualize the emergence of illegal migration as an option, a brief inter-American and transatlantic overview is necessary, since the simultaneous transformation of American, Canadian, and Hungarian migration policies created the international environment that for many people could present illegal immigration as an attractive alternative. These trends illustrate the impact of measures restricting or encouraging immigration not only on the countries that adopt them, but also on neighboring nations, while also highlighting that the debates about (illegal) immigration, restriction, and tighter border control today have roots going back at least a hundred years.

One of the most important periods in Hungarian migration history is the era of mass emigration between the 1870s and World War I, when more than a million people left Hungary and emigrated mainly to the United States (Puskás, Tezla). Already during this period, the need for the stricter screening and selection of immigrants (including from Central and Eastern Europe) and restrictions on immigration were repeatedly raised (see Daniels and Venkovits, "Záródó kapuk"). As early as 1894 the

---

3 See, for example, Dreisziger, *Struggle and Hope*; Patrias, *Hungarians in Canada* and *Patriots and Proletarians*; Paizs, *Hungarians in Canada*.

Immigration Restriction League was formed to press for such regulations as a literacy test, but the adoption of their proposal had to wait until 1917, when a law was passed in the United States denying entry to any alien over the age of 16 who could not read 30 to 40 words in his or her native language. With such restrictions in place, more and more people demanded even stricter regulations, which were finally enacted in the early 1920s, ending a period of free immigration to the United States, and closing the doors of the US almost completely to Hungarians (similarly to other "undesirable" immigrants).

In 1921, the first law quantitatively regulating the number of immigrants was passed, setting quotas for each country (3% of the number of residents from that country living in the United States, according to the 1910 census). This in itself was a significant restriction, but the quota was further reduced in the following years. The Immigration Act of 1924 capped the total annual limit at 153,700 and set the quota per country at 2% of the population as recorded in the 1890 census. This meant that the quota for groups arriving in large numbers after 1890 was significantly reduced, while those from countries in the Western Hemisphere were not subject to the quota. The door was almost completely closed to arrivals from Central and Eastern Europe: whereas in the peak year of 1907 almost 200,000 people from Hungary alone arrived in the United States, under the quota this number was limited to 473 per year.[4]

It is less often emphasized, but alongside the introduction of quotas (and not insignificantly for the purposes of this study), border patrol also received increasing attention. As Ashley Johnson Bavery notes, in 1924 one million dollars were set aside to create the federal Border Patrol, one of the main purposes of which was to prevent illegal immigration and combat smuggling, initially focusing mainly on the country's northern border, where, in addition to the illegal alcohol trade, the smuggling of immigrants was becoming more prominent (Johnson Bavery 39, 42). The tightening of border control is illustrated by the increase in the number of immigration inspectors (of particular importance in this respect) in Detroit: while in 1894 there was only one such person working in the Detroit region, by 1913 this number slowly rose to 18, and by 1931 there were 115 inspectors supervising the movement of people between the two countries (Klug 79).

At the same time, the deportation rules also changed, as the yearbook of the *Amerikai Magyar Népszava* [American Hungarian People's Voice] informed its readers:

> As far as the deportation regulations are concerned, the law makes a strong distinction between those who entered illegally after July 1, 1924, and those who had entered in some way before that date. Those who entered illegally after July 1, 1924 and those who have abused the temporary residence permit issued since then and have remained here may be deported at any time and

---

4 "Immigration Quota-s—A Proclamation by the President of the United States of America" (Washington: G.P.O, 1924), HLCC. Available online: https://curiosity.lib.harvard.edu/immigration-to-the-united-states-1789-1930/catalog/39-990070752250203941.

there is no time limit as to when this provision will expire. However, those who entered illegally before July 1, 1924 may be deported only within five years.[5]

This provision is of crucial importance, and the report also indicates that Hungarian-Americans were concerned about the issue of illegal immigration and the threat of deportation. The same document mentions that for the period between July 1, 1925 and July 1, 1926 the US deported 902 persons on the grounds that they had entered the country illegally.

The Hungarian government reacted to all these changes, and the Ministry of the Interior pointed out in a 1923 circular that since the new regulations would allow only a very small number of Hungarians to enter the US (which would be reduced even further later on), the number of Hungarians going to Canada was expected to be very high, since in the same year Canada abolished its restrictions on Hungarian immigration.[6] This expectation of the Hungarian leadership proved to be correct, as Canada opened its doors practically simultaneously with the US restrictions, which led to major changes: before World War I, only a fraction of Hungarians had arrived in Canada compared to the US: according to Kósa, fewer than 10,000 Hungarians lived in Canada before 1911 (4). (Bődy's figures show that only 8,000 Hungarians emigrated to Canada before World War I [28]). However, this number rose to 13,181 by 1921 (based on more reliable census data) and to 40,582 by 1931, thanks in large part to the arrival of new immigrants in the 1920s (Kósa 5).

At the turn of the century, there was also a growing call for restrictions in Canada, and this was reflected in the Immigration Act of 1906 (which greatly expanded the definition of "undesirable" immigrants, strengthened control of the US-Canadian border, and increased the government's relevant powers [Knowles 107-10]). The Immigration Act of 1910 allowed for immigration to be regulated on the basis of ethnicity or occupation, while other measures sought to reduce the number of immigrants from Central and Eastern Europe (110-12). However, while Asian immigration was successfully reduced, Central and Eastern European immigration was not (123). Here, too, World War I brought further restrictions, as immigration from enemy countries was banned in 1914, and the Immigration Act of 1919 introduced even more restrictions, thereby widening the list of inadmissible immigrants and specifically excluding immigration from countries that fought against Canada in the war. Under the regulations, immigration could be prohibited for individuals of any nationality, race, class, or occupation who were thought to be unsuitable to the "climatic, industrial, social and educational, labour or other conditions or requirements of Canada," because of their "peculiar customs, habits, modes of life

---

5 "Mikor deportálhatók a törvénytelenül érkezett bevándorlók?" [When Can Illegal Immigrants Be Deported?], *Az Amerikai Magyar Népszava képes naptára az 1926-27-es évre*, 182.
6 "Royal Hungarian Ministry of the Interior—Circular Order No. 130.000/1923. XII. B. M." LAC RG76-I-A-1, vol. no.: 145, microfilm reel no.: C-7302, file no: 34274, Image 8.

and methods of holding property and because of their probable inability to become readily assimilated."[7]

Although Minister of Immigration and Colonization James Robb divided Europe into "preferred" and "non-preferred" countries (Johnson Bavery 34), with Hungary included in the latter category, the growing demand for labor opened up the possibility of immigration to Canada from 1923 (just as the US was tightening up), as the ban on immigration from previous enemy countries was lifted in that year, even if it was limited to certain categories of immigrants, including farmers with enough money to buy land, farm workers with employment guarantees, female domestic workers, and close relatives of Canadian residents. In addition, they had to meet a number of requirements: they had to be in good physical and mental condition, be able to read, have a valid passport, and have a train ticket to their final destination in Canada (to avoid being stranded in eastern cities).[8]

In 1925, in order to secure a sufficient agricultural labor force through immigration, the Canadian government made an agreement with the Canadian Pacific Railway and Canadian National Railway (called the "Railway Agreement") for the recruitment of European agricultural workers (including from non-preferred countries), giving the two railways (and their agents) a prominent role in the management of Canadian immigration policy (Machildin 59-129), and in effect the two railways and the shipping companies they worked with oversaw and operated the Canadian immigration selection system in Europe (Vineberg 14).

Canadian archival documents show that there was interest in immigration from Hungary to Canada as early as 1922 (probably initially due to false information in Hungarian newspapers), but at that time, Hungarians were reminded that they were not allowed to immigrate to the country, citing existing regulations.[9] Already at the end of this year, a Canadian immigration official pointed out the unfairness of the decision, for example, that Hungarians living in Romania could emigrate while Hungarians in Hungary could not, and argued that Hungarian farmers were of a very high quality and would be a good target for Canadian settlement efforts.[10] All of this is to anticipate the possibility that the previous strict restriction could be altered. By the time the ban was actually lifted, reports of Hungarian immigrants were increasing, and in March 1924 the first large group of 160 Hungarians left Antwerp (Dreisziger, *Struggle and Hope* 99).

---

7 A collection of Canadian immigration regulations and laws can be found online on the website of the Canadian Immigration Museum. Available at: https://pier21.ca/research/immigration-history/canadian-immigration-acts-and-legislation.

8 On the regulations concerning Hungarian immigrants, see, for example, "Canadian Immigration Office, May 19th, 1923," LAC RG76-I-A-1, vol. no.: 145, microfilm reel no.: C-7301, file no: 34274, image 1615, and footnote 18.

9 LAC RG76-I-A-1, vol. no.: 145, microfilm reel no.: C-7301, file no.: 34274, images 1525-26;

10 LAC RG76-I-A-1, vol. no.: 145, microfilm reel no.: C-7301, file no.: 34274, image 1557.

Dreisziger and Kósa both mention that it is difficult to give exact figures of the Hungarians living and arriving in Canada at that time since Hungarians also came from the successor states (according to Bakó, 4,000 people came from Romania, Yugoslavia, Czechoslovakia, but claimed to be Hungarians [35]) and from the USA (Canadian statistics show that nearly 100 people a year moved to Canada from the southern neighbor[11]), and those arriving from Hungary were not always Hungarian (Dreisziger, *Struggle and Hope* 100). We also do not know exactly how many returned home, or how many continued to the US, maybe even illegally (see below). The statistics show that about 28,000 Hungarians (the statistical tables do not include "Hungarian" but "Magyar") arrived in the country between 1923 and 1930, a significant jump from the earlier period, and only after 1956 did more Hungarians arrive in Canada in a short period of time (more than 37,000 people as discussed in the chapter by Trimble). The Great Depression and the resulting immigration laws (protecting the Canadian workforce) put an end to this rapidly rising trend, with only 2,041 Hungarians arriving in 1930-31.[12] Although this seems a minuscule number compared to the Hungarians who settled in the United States during the period of New Immigration, the environment had changed considerably and it is worth noting that Hungarians represented one of the largest groups: between 1925 and 1929 (apart from the British), only German (46,225), Polish (24,042), and Ruthenian immigrants (39,953) arrived in larger numbers.[13]

The changing role of Canada is also illustrated by the shift in the proportion of emigrants to the country. Previously only less than 2% of Hungarian emigrants chose Canada as a destination, rising to 20% from the 1920s (Dreisziger, *Struggle and Hope* 28-29) and this could, of course, be much higher locally. For example, according to a 1927 statement of emigration from the Derecske district (in Hajdú Bihar County), all of the six emigrants went to Canada.[14] However, it seems that many could see the country not as a final destination but as a springboard and were determined to go to the United States, even if illegally.

What represented an opportunity for Canada was a threat for Hungary, however, as the loss of a large number of (young male) emigrants provided economic, social, and military (security) challenges. The attitude of the Hungarian government followed the principles already established at the beginning of the 20th century: it stressed that migration should not (and could not) be prohibited but needed to be regulated or even restricted in certain cases (in the interest of the country and the emigrants); that the propagation, encouragement of emigration should be prevented (for example, by

---

11 LAC RG 26, vol. 7. Fiscal Year Statement 1925-26, 1926-27, 1929-30. In 1925-26 75, in 1926-27 77, and in 1929-30 99 Hungarians arrived in Canada from the United States (no data for the other years are available).
12 LAC RG 26, vol. 7. Fiscal Year Statement 1930-31.
13 LAC RG 26, vol 7. Fiscal Year Statement 1928-29.
14 MNL HBML, "Kimutatás a folyó évben a derecskei járás területéről kivándoroltakról" [Report on Emigrants from the Derecske District in the Current Year], Documents of the vice comes, 3168/927.

agents as seen in the previous chapter), the activities of shipping companies and their agents should be strictly controlled, and that those wishing to emigrate should be properly informed.[15]

This kind of attitude was already present in the 1909 Emigration Act with its strict regulation of emigration propaganda,[16] but the large number of Canadian emigrants meant that a similar attitude was also prevalent in the 1920s. In 1922, in order to provide adequate protection and information, the Office for the Protection of Emigrants and Returning Emigrants was set up to help both those leaving and those returning to Hungary and to protect Hungarians from fraudulent agents who even offered to circumvent immigration rules and get emigrants to their final destination (Dreisziger, *Struggle and Hope* 99). Study tours and reports were conducted to assess the situation of Hungarians in Canada, and the Canadian Hungarian Immigrant Protection Office was established in Winnipeg. In addition to banning propaganda, the Hungarian government also sought to restrict the railway companies. A letter written by the Canadian National Railways in 1927 points out that while Romania, Yugoslavia, Czechoslovakia and Austria had no problem with the operation of the Railway Agreement, the main difficulty with Hungary was that the Hungarian government believed that the posting of immigration officers to Hungary by the railway companies went contrary to the law prohibiting anyone from carrying out colonization activities in Hungary.[17] Part of the information provided to emigrants included the issue of illegal immigration and, as we shall see, there were many attempts to dissuade Hungarians from such a decision.

Illegal immigration at the Canada-US border

Canada was an attractive destination for emigrants in its own right, and the reports of railway and shipping agents and Hungarians who had already settled there all conveyed a positive image of the country (even if both sources were often exaggerated) and the conditions and opportunities awaiting immigrants.[18] This positive image was countered by the Hungarian government, and even in Canada there was criticism of immigration propaganda that often concealed difficult conditions (see, for example, the United Farmers of Canada's publication "On Immigration," which specifically criticizes the often misleading communication). At the same time, Canada appeared

---

15 For an overview see, for instance, Venkovits, *Magyar kivándorlás Észak-Amerikába.*

16 See the Explanatory notes to Act II of 1909 on Emigration. Available at: https://net.jogtar.hu/ezer-ev-torveny?docid=90900002.TVI&searchUrl=/ezer-ev-torvenyei%3Fpagenum%3D46.

17 LAC RG 25, G-1, vol. 1501, file 911, Dec. 7, 1927: 2.

18 See, for example, Venkovits, *The New Mecca of Immigrants*; Patrias, *Patriots and Proletarians* 49-75.

to be an appealing destination because of its proximity to the United States, offering the possibility of entering the country that many considered even more attractive. A longer way of doing so would be to take advantage of the provisions of the quota act and resettle legally in the United States as non-quota immigrants after five years of residence in Canada (Sadowski-Smith 789). According to Mae M. Ngai, this was a popular strategy, as the proportion of lawful admissions from Canada of persons not born in Canada rose from 20 percent in 1925 to more than 50 percent by the 1930s (84).

A shorter, but increasingly risky, alternative after immigrating to Canada in compliance with immigration rules was to try to cross to the United States illegally, where they hoped for even better conditions. Thus, some immigrants may have participated in agricultural programs in Canada's western provinces only in order to cross illegally into the United States after arrival (Sadowski-Smith 789). There is ample direct and indirect evidence that illegal immigration was a real opportunity for many Hungarians as well.

On March 6, 1924, an article in *Az Est* [The Evening] (an English translation of which reached Canada) reported that Canada was taking special care to ensure that Canadian immigration permits could not be used to enter the United States illegally, and that anyone found to be doing so would be deported.[19] In 1928, János Németh, a Hungarian immigrant living in Saskatchewan, wrote a letter to the Hungarian consul in Winnipeg requesting that his passport be extended to the United States. In his reply, the consul asked Németh to send the usual photographs and documents (including the US permit required for entry), but also warned the Hungarian to "cross the U.S. border only legally or you will be fined heavily" and emphasized that he should be careful to avoid fraudulent agents.[20] A year later a Hungarian Ministry of the Interior decree on the extension of passports to the United States appears in the files of the Consulate General in Montréal, stating that "passports to the United States may be obtained only with the preliminary approval of the Hungarian Royal Ministry of the Interior and this is mainly intended to prevent emigration to Canada of those who leave their native country with the intention of going over to the United States with time." The decree also adds:

> Finally, warn the emigrants that it is now almost impossible to cross from Canada into the United States, as the border controls are so perfect that even the smugglers, who have hitherto been operating in large numbers, are gradually giving up their business, because it no longer pays, and that it also endangers their lives, because the border guards at the American border have the right to use arms. Even those who have entered the United States in an unauthorized manner in the past are now being vigorously investigated and deported. Those who have been deported are never again admitted to the United States.[21]

---

19 LAC RG76-I-A-1, vol. no.: 145, microfilm reel no.: C-7302, file no.: 34274, image 65-66.
20 HU-MNL-OL-K 139. Records of the Winnipeg Consulate, 1927-1941. 3339/1928. Aug. 22, 1928.
21 *Külügyi Közlöny* [Foreign Affairs Gazette] 9 (21 Aug. 1929), EN-MNL-OL-K 128. Documents of the Consulate General in Montréal, 1924-1941.

The consulate tried to point out that the extension of passports may have been requested for many other reasons, but together with the other sources presented below, this shows that illegal crossing of the US-Canadian border and collaboration with smugglers was part of the Hungarian emigration experience in the 1920s in the wake of US quotas.

From 1924 onwards a growing number of newspaper articles appeared in the world press, and in Hungary as well, stating that during the prohibition period more and more people became involved not only in the smuggling of alcohol but also that of people.[22] According to Johnson Bavery, international concerns increased further when such groups expanded their activities abroad and sought to recruit potential (illegal) immigrants in Europe. Major gangs were active in Hamburg, Brussels, Paris, Prague, and Naples (Johnson Bavery 46). All this was not without precedent, of course, as since the 1882 Chinese Exclusion Act, many Asian immigrants tried to enter the United States in similar ways: it is estimated that at least 17,300 Chinese immigrants entered the United States illegally from Canada and Mexico between 1882 and 1920 (Lee 55).

In the 1920s, following the establishment of quotas, southern/eastern/central Europeans joined this group and illegal immigration reached mass proportions, making deportation a central element of immigration policy and measures (Ngai 70). Exactly how many people were affected is difficult (if not impossible) to determine, since they entered the country illegally and could be deported at any time under the new rules, thus they obviously tried to avoid being exposed. For all these reasons, the figures vary widely in this respect: according to Johnson Bavery's research, between 1927 and 1929 Detroit smugglers were bringing around 2,000 Europeans into the US every month, with southern and eastern Europeans making up the bulk of the total. The number of undocumented immigrants in the United States has been estimated by some to be over a million, which is high even if we know that such figures could often be exaggerated (Johnson Bavery 8, 40, 46, 48). Although deportation statistics are not always reliable, they do highlight the extent to which the number of illegal immigrants soared during this period. Ngai points out that the number of aliens deported from the US rose from 2,762 in 1920 to 9,495 in 1925 and jumped to 38,795 by 1930. Of course, immigrants were deported for many other reasons (and even the use of categories did not always reflect reality), but aliens without proper visas made up the largest group, accounting for more than half of all formal deportations (77). In 1928, for example, the Hungarian *Nyírvidék* [Nyír region] reported that "in the past year no fewer than 19,000 people were apprehended by border guards at the Canadian and Mexican borders and on the coast of Florida when they attempted to enter the United States without a permit. Authorities estimate that 170,000 people entered the United States through

22 "Newspaper clippings," LAC RG76-I-A-1, vol. no.: 167, microfilm reel no.: C-7323, file no.: 48185, image 1520, 1532, 1533; see also LAC RG76-I-A-1, vol. no.: 81, microfilm reel no.: C-4748, file no.: 8051.

smuggling routes in the past year. . . . Legions of smuggling agents operate in Canada, Mexico, and Cuba."[23]

The number of illegal immigrants from Hungary is perhaps even more difficult to determine, partly because they may have included people from successor states, while the categories used are not always clear, and the numbers reported in the press are often contradictory. Many sources refer simply to "many" such immigrants or deportees, while others report the number as insignificant. As early as 1924 it is stated outright that "the vast majority of emigrants attempt to reach America illegally."[24] *Bácsmegyei Napló* [Bács County Journal] mentions in connection with the 674 Hungarians who emigrated from Yugoslavia in 1927 that "in the same period 1,898 people returned from overseas countries, including one hundred and four Hungarians. Many were deported for trying to cross illegally from Canada or southern states to the north."[25] In 1928, however, József Moldásy, Ministerial Advisor and head of the Emigration Department of the Ministry of the Interior, wrote in response to an inquiry from *Esti Kurir* [Evening Courier]: "I have read in the American newspapers about the activities of the cruel smugglers and I am aware of specific cases also. However, I must point out that such a threat to Hungarians is very rare." He adds, "I would like to stress that I know of only one specific case related to Hungarians and that is also from Cuba, where many Hungarians are settled and from where some ventured to America illegally and who were thrown overboard to escape from the authorities and then fished out by the coast guard. Among them were some Hungarians who, however, crossed to America not from Hungary but from Cuba."[26] Such contradictory reports make it difficult to determine the number of Hungarians affected by illegal immigration, while it should also be taken into account that such estimates (whether they are trivialized or exaggerated) may have varied depending on the purpose of the various reports.

Taking all this into account, it is likely that between 1924 and 1930 hundreds, even thousands, of Hungarians may have attempted to cross the Canadian-American border illegally, but what we can say for sure is that their numbers reached a level that prompted politicians and the press to take up the issue; thus illegal immigration appears in consular files and at the level of regulations, while the contemporary press also reported on the subject (both inside and outside Hungary, in Hungarian-language articles), both in general and in relation to specific Hungarian cases.

---

23 "Amerika megszigorítja a bevándorlást" [America Takes Stronger Measures to Restrict Immigration], *Nyírvidék* 3 Jan. 1928: 3.

24 "A külföldi hajóstársaságok közös irodát akarnak" [Foreign Shipping Companies Want to Set Up a Joint Office], *Uj Nemzedék* [New Generation] 3 July 1924: 9.

25 "674 jugoszláviai magyar vándorolt ki az év első felében a tengerentúlra" [674 Hungarians from Yugoslavia Emigrated to Overseas in the First Half-Year], *Bácsmegyei Napló* 22 Nov. 1927: 4.

26 "Amerika szigorú vizsgálatot indít a lelketlen embercsempészet megakadályozására" [America Undertakes a Severe Investigation to Hinder Barbarous Human Trafficking], *Esti Kurir* 4 Jan. 1928: 6.

The perception of illegal immigration in the Hungarian press

As a result of the wave of emigration just described, interest in Canada increased in Hungary in the 1920s, as the Hordósy article cited in the introduction shows. Ödön Paizs in his book *Magyarok Kanadában* [Hungarians in Canada], published in 1928, claims that it is the first account of this kind, but within a few years the question of emigration and Hungarians in Canada was to appear in several other volumes (see the books of Sámuel Zágonyi, Győző Drozdy, Pál Wéber). Newspaper articles were also increasingly devoted to the country, often presenting two contrasting images: a positive one supporting immigration and the other emphasizing the hazards and negative aspects of emigration. The former can often be linked to the activities of the railway and shipping companies, while in the case of the latter, we may suppose that the Hungarian government and the Office for the Protection of Emigrants sought to highlight the threats. Either way, the issue of emigration became an integral part of the image of Canada in Hungary at the time. The importance of illegal immigration is shown by the reports on Canada, in which we often find references to the shared border with the United States and the issue of illegal immigration.

Samuel Zágonyi is one of the best examples of how Hungary tried to counteract the propaganda encouraging Canadian immigration. In his book published in 1926, he clearly focused on the difficulties awaiting immigrants in Canada and he also went on a lecture tour to dissuade those who wanted to emigrate from going to Canada. Zágonyi makes a clear link between the boom in Canadian emigration and US restrictions: "Most of those who want to come to America cannot get a permission to enter the United States because of immigration restriction. But because they have already decided to emigrate, and reportedly more have received positive news from Canada, confidence and the prospect of immigration are driving them to Canada" (70-71). However, he adds that "for many, Canada is—in their minds—just a stopover from which they will take forbidden routes to the United States." In fact, Zágonyi devotes a subsection of his report to the subject, titled: "Getting from Canada to the United States without a permit is pointless daydreaming" (73-75). The author describes the impact of the US immigration quotas, the human trafficking already known from Cuba, and the extent of the Canada-US border (3,000 kilometers of common border without any natural barriers), which "makes people who want to enter the US without a permit think of trying to get there through Canada by forbidden routes, because they have no prospect of obtaining a permit due to the restrictions" (Zágonyi 74). At the same time, Zágonyi describes such an undertaking as not only difficult (due to the strict border control and technological advances), but also downright dangerous:

> Not to mention the frequent murders, where the gullible immigrants are often abandoned to their uncertain fate by soulless soul-suckers who will get the transit fees and then strip them of their last penny. Most of them fall into the hands of the Border Patrol once in the border zone and are condemned by the US authorities to detention and deportation. . . . The same fate befalls those

who manage to cross the border and get a job, but later it turns out that they do not have entry or residence permits. To discover this, all it takes is the denunciation of a resentful or dismissed employee, not to mention the periodic searches carried out by the authorities for this purpose. (75)

Since Zágonyi's clear aim is to dissuade Hungarians from emigrating to Canada, he may (also) be exaggerating somewhat in this regard and trying to paint a picture that is more gloomy than reality, but what is certain is that he is reporting on an existing phenomenon that is consistent with the news that appeared in the print media.

Newspaper articles published in the second half of the 1920s repeatedly address this aspect of illegal immigration and the issue of human smuggling at the Canada-US border. They do this by providing translations of articles published abroad, but increasingly Hungarian-related news also appeared, often in a way that resembles the migration discourse of today. As early as 1924, the same news item appeared in several newspapers, drawing attention to the emergence of smuggling and its dangers. Both *Nyírvidék* and *Prágai Magyar Hírlap* [Hungarian Newspaper of Prague] published a report from New York:

> . . . the border prisons are crowded with arrested people who tried to enter the United States without permission and above the quota, but their attempt was thwarted by the vigilance of the authorities. The illegals are overwhelmingly of the undesirable stock. Those caught are locked up in prison and transported handcuffed in pairs to Ellis Island. These adventurers are then deported to Europe on the next ship. Along the border, inspectors report that there are well-organized Canadian and American smuggling rings offering smuggling services for between $75 and $150. But the smugglers' work is yielding fewer and fewer results because border officers are so vigilant that it has become almost impossible to smuggle people.[27]

Both papers were published in the area affected by emigration—their purpose might have been to curtail such intentions, to raise awareness—which, as we have seen, is also in line with the basic principles of Hungarian emigration policy at the time.

The Canadian-US border appears in the news as a trafficking site. In 1924 *Bácsmegyei Napló* published a report titled "Human Smuggling on a Submarine": "[S]ince the quota act came into effect a new industry has emerged in America: human smuggling. Businessmen smuggle immigrants from Canada and Mexico sporadically, as part of individual operations, including some Canadian Hungarians who have recently been arrested."[28] In the same year, *Új Kelet* [New East] reported that "this type of immigrant comes mainly from South American countries, Canada, and Mexico. According to the minister's findings, an average of 1,000 immigrants cross

---

27 "Az amerikai hatóságok erélyesen védekeznek az embercsempészek ellen" [The American Authorities Defend Vigorously Against Human Traffickers], *Prágai Magyar Hírlap* 9 Nov. 1924: 6; *Nyírvidék* 9 Nov. 1924: 10.
28 "Embercsempészet tengeralattjárón" [Human Trafficking on Submarines], *Bácsmegyei Napló* 27 Sept. 1924: 3.

the Canadian and Mexican borders illegally into the United States every month. . . . They are now also using airplanes."[29] *Amerikai Magyar Népszava* also dealt with the phenomenon in various ways, writing in 1930 about the extensive activities of the smuggling gangs in an article titled "Alcohol and People Smuggled from Canada by Airplane":

> It has also been found, however, that not only alcohol but also aliens without passports and visas were being transported en masse from Canadian territory in the 30 airplanes used to carry out the large-scale smuggling operation. The smuggling gang's operations were almost exclusively limited to Detroit and the surrounding area, but detectives found that they sometimes traveled farther away and smuggled liquor and aliens into Indiana and Illinois.[30]

The above-mentioned *Esti Kurir* article reports similarly:

> Over time, human smuggling has emerged near the American border, with smuggling companies being set up to traffic immigrants for horrendous sums. However, the US authorities guard the border extremely strictly, so that smuggling is not only risky, but also life-threatening. It is precisely this circumstance that is exploited by unscrupulous smugglers, partly to blackmail emigrants and partly to sacrifice them in case they run into trouble at the American border.[31]

Such reports tend to highlight the dangers, and like Zagonyi, news about smuggling are mostly aimed at discouraging potential emigrants from making such decisions. The prospect of illegal immigration, the crossing itself, the traffickers, and the period afterwards are all represented as serious threats, which probably also gave a true picture of the circumstances and consequences. However, it is also likely that, as with negative news in general, potential emigrants ignored such warnings, and were more likely to listen to villagers telling exaggerated stories rather than to information that focused on the dangers and could be simply classified as government propaganda (even if it did highlight real challenges). As Tibor Glant noted about emigration to the US: "people tended to disbelieve their government, although it was telling the truth, and accepted at face value what their relatives and fellow villagers told them about the New World, although these accounts were blatantly one-sided" (Glant 176). Patrias also gives clear examples of this and shows how the emigrants selected from the information they received and completely ignored information and warnings that did not fit their positive image of America/Canada (for example, during Zagonyi's lecture tour) (Patrias, *Patriots* 58-59).

---

29 "Enyhítenek az amerikai bevándorlási kvótatörvényen" [The American Immigrant Quota Law Is to Be Mitigated], *Új kelet* 6 Dec. 1924: 3.
30 "Repülőgépen csempészték az italt és embert Canadából" [Alcohol and People Were Smuggled from Canada on Airplanes], *Amerikai Magyar Népszava* 20 Nov. 1930: 3.
31 "Amerika szigorú vizsgálatot indít a lelketlen embercsempészet megakadályozására," *Esti Kurir* 4 Jan. 1928: 6.

The low Hungarian involvement cited by the Ministerial Advisor mentioned earlier seems to be contradicted by several other occasions when newspapers report on specific cases where Hungarians were clearly involved in illegal border crossing. In 1926, *Új Kelet* reported that "a Canadian airship was intercepted in Detroit attempting to smuggle four Hungarian emigrants to America. The airship, which landed near Detroit, was confiscated by the United States and the four Hungarian emigrants that they tried to smuggle into the country were detained. The official report dealing with this case has not yet released the names of the four Hungarian emigrants for various reasons."[32] According to the August 10, 1930 issue of *Magyarság*, "Smugglers attempted to take six Hungarians by boat to the United States, but were intercepted by the coast guard. The six Hungarians were imprisoned for a year of forced labor each, only to be deported. A few weeks ago, two Hungarians from Nyíradony were deported. They paid $155 each for a passport that turned out to had been forged."[33] In 1932 *Amerikai Magyar Népszava* illustrated the negative consequences of human smuggling through a specific Hungarian example, but the newspaper claimed the same situation occurred in hundreds of cases:

> György Sztancs writes in his letter that life forced him to Canada in 1927, where he worked hard for years without luck. When he had a few dollars saved up, he found himself faced with unemployment, which quickly ate up what little savings he had. . . . some Hungarian men came to him, who promised all the good things and finally agreed to smuggle ten Canadian Hungarians across the border one night for 100 dollars. . . . they were reported by the same people who had brought them across the border for $1,000. But we receive many such letters from Hungarian victims, and so we know that the cruel smugglers are just waiting for the people they traffic to get a job and a few dollars to earn so that they can start a further extortion campaign against them. This extortion is never-ending. And the victim, fearing deportation, is forced to give everything he has to these people. And if he finally loses patience and refuses to pay further fees, he is denounced to the immigration authorities without remorse in order to intimidate the other victims.

The author also adds, "We know from the letters we receive asking for advice that there are hundreds, thousands of unfortunate Hungarians in this country who have fallen victim to this kind of abuse and who are still being blackmailed by traffickers for years to come."[34] Even if it is possible that these reports are exaggerated (since they could be written to discourage illegal immigration), they show that we are not dealing with a few isolated Hungarian cases.

---

32 "Hárommillió illegális bevándorló él Amerikában, akiket sem deportálni, sem naturalizálni nem lehet" [Three Million Illegal Immigrants Live in America Who Can Be Neither Deported Nor Naturalized], *Új Kelet* 13 Nov. 1926: 5.

33 "Magyarok a nagyvilágban" [Hungarians in the Wide World], *Magyarság* 10 Aug. 1930: 28.

34 "Rosszabbak az útonállóknál" [Worse than Highwaymen], *Amerikai Magyar Népszava* 5 Jan. 1932: 4.

Amerikai Magyar Népszava covered the issue in several other cases, and illegal immigration not only appears in the context of reports on human smuggling, but articles also indirectly show that the issue affected Hungarians (and Hungarian-Americans) to a greater extent. In 1926 the newspaper ran an advertisement in its pages for a publication titled "Immigration and Citizenship Counselor," which advertised itself as offering help to readers (in English and Hungarian) with questions such as: "How can one come from Hungary to Canada, and how can one come from Canada and Cuba to America? What happens to Hungarians who are here illegally? Is it possible to legalize the stay of an illegal immigrant? When can illegal immigrants be deported?" The advertising text tries to target the people concerned: "Order now, because you may need it anytime."[35] The fact that the issue of illegal immigration and deportation was worth addressing in such a publication also suggests the more extensive involvement of Hungarians.

The issue of illegal border crossing from Canada to the United States was also raised in the newspaper's "Editorial Messages" section with specific cases, including in the form of questions and answers:

QUESTION: 1. The person has entered Canada illegally and now wants to travel to the old country but is afraid to get his passport for fear of being caught. What should he do?
2. Before the war he came out legally, then went home and after the war came illegally. He would like to go home, but he would not apply for a passport to come back here but would come out on the basis of his first arrival. Is it possible? N. N. Trenton.
RESPONSE: You can only travel home with a Hungarian passport, which you must obtain at the Hungarian consulate. No harm can come to you here. But you can't come back to the US because you can't get a return permit, or even apply for one, because they will find out you are here illegally, in which case you would certainly be deported.[36]

QUESTION: My brother entered illegally in 1927. He would like to get his first papers after 5 years. Could this cause him any inconvenience? Old reader, Akron.
RESPONSE: He cannot get his first papers and can be deported at any time.

QUESTION: I arrived from Canada illegally. Can I register without any problems? Miner, W. Va.
RESPONSE: It is unlikely that compulsory registration would be introduced. Don't worry about it.

QUESTION: I came to the United States illegally from Canada before June 1, 1924. On the way I was arrested and placed under bond for $500, from which I escaped. Am I deportable?
RESPONSE: This is an extremely rare case. In our opinion, it is not deportable. Only the court can decide this case.[37]

---

35 "A bevándorlási és polgárosodási tanácsadó most 50 cent" [You Can Get the Immigration and Citizenship Counselor for 50 Cents Now], *Amerikai Magyar Népszava* 18 June 1927: 3.
36 "Szerkesztői üzenetek" [Editor's Messages], *Amerikai Magyar Népszava* 27 Aug. 1928: 4.
37 "Szerkesztői üzenetek" [Editor's Messages], *Amerikai Magyar Népszava* 31 March 1930: 4.

These questions and answers provide an excellent insight into the ways in which illegal immigration affected Hungarian-Americans and the ways and contexts in which the consequences of illegal border crossing came back to haunt them, even years later. It draws a sharp line between the two groups of Hungarians who immigrated to America in 1924, not only because of quotas but also because of the changed deportation rules. Although we cannot accurately determine the number of Hungarians arriving illegally on the basis of these documents, it seems clear that the phenomenon was visible in the US, Canada, and Hungary and had longer-term consequences.

All this suggests that illegal border crossing by Hungarians between Canada and the United States took place in a similar manner to that of immigrants from other countries and reached a rate that attracted the attention of Hungarian politicians and the press. Based on unofficial figures published in the press, this could have involved hundreds or thousands of Hungarians. However, illegal immigration, similarly to Canadian emigration in general, is cut short by the Great Depression and the resulting restrictions, as in 1931 Canada closed its doors to continental Europeans, including Hungarian emigrants. In 1930, the *Keleti Újság* [Eastern Newspaper] already gave an adequate summary of this in its article "Canada is No Eldorado":

> The vast majority of those who left for Canada did not emigrate to Canada with the intention of staying there, but to cross to the United States at the first chance. This was not too difficult, as there were groups engaged in quite a business of smuggling. . . . Nowadays, however, people are not escaping to the United States but from America to Canada. . . . Since the police have even started giving a financial reward to the informers, hundreds of people are being reported every day. The only option for those who haven't been caught is to sneak back to Canada. But due to the high unemployment rate, the Canadian Border Patrol is also more vigilant. And if a caught delinquent has been in the US illegally for more than a year, Canada will deport them back to Europe. Montréal, meanwhile, is full of people who have fled back to Canada in fear of being rounded up, but seeing the misery here, they voluntarily come forward and are happy when the authorities say the words, "back to Europe." And it is typical that people can even rejoice at being deported.[38]

Emigration made up an integral part of the image of Canada in Hungary in the 1920s, involving constant comparisons with the United States, which seems to have included illegal border crossing. In these cases, the United States is portrayed in a more positive light, which may have been a way of preventing an even larger wave of Canadian emigration from Hungary, minimizing the perception of illegal immigration as an opportunity and making Canada appear less attractive. Such a goal is clear in Zágonyi's case, which is also in line with the Hungarian government's principles on emigration. The issue of illegal immigration illustrates the inter-American and transatlantic impact of US immigration policy, how restrictions contributed to the

---

38 "Kanada sem Eldorádó" [Canada Is No Eldorado], *Keleti Újság* 4 Oct. 1930: 4.

increase in illegal border crossings and consequent deportations, and how they created an international environment (in parallel with changes in Canadian migration policy) in which illegal immigration, with all its difficulties and risks, emerged as a possible alternative.

Works Cited

Archival sources

Library and Archives Canada, Ottawa, Canada (LAC)
Hungarian National Archives, Budapest (MNL-OL)
Hungarian National Archives, Hajdú Bihar County Archives, Debrecen (MNL HBML)

Online databases

Arcanum Digital Library
Harvard Library, *CURIOSity Digital Collections*, "Immigration to the United States, 1789-1930" (HLCC)
Héritage Canadiana
Hungaricana: Public Collections Portal

Primary sources

Drozdy, Győző. *Amerika*. Budapest: Magyar Ugar Kiadóvállalat, 1924.
Paizs, Ödön. *Magyarok Kanadában: Egy most készülő országról* [Hungarians in Canada: A Country in the Making]. Budapest: Athenaeum, 1928.
United Farmers of Canada. *On Immigration*. Saskatoon: Publicity and Research Dept., 1929.
Wéber, Pál. *Feljegyzések: Róma, Amerika, Kanada* [Notes: Rome, America, Canada]. Veszprém: Egyházmegyei Könyvkereskedés, 1928.
Zágonyi, Sámuel. *Kanada egy európai bevándorló megvilágításában* [Canada Through the Eyes of a European Immigrant]. Budapest/Bridgeport: n.p., 1926.

Newspapers

Amerikai Magyar Népszava (1927-32)
Bácsmegyei Napló (1924-27)
Budapesti Hírlap (1926)
Esti Kurir (1928)
Keleti Újság (1930)
Külföldi Magyarság (1925)
Magyarság (1930)
Nyírvidék (1928)
Prágai Magyar Hírlap (1924)
Uj kelet (1924-26)
Uj Nemzedék (1924)

Secondary sources

Bakó, Ferenc. *Kanadai magyarok* [Canadian Hungarians]. Budapest: Gondolat, 1988.

Bődy, Paul. *Emigration from Hungary, 1880-1956*. Dreisziger, et al. 27-60.

Daniels, Roger. *Coming to America: A History of Immigration and Ethnicity in American Life*. New York: Perennial, 2002.

Dojcsák, Győző. *A kanadai Esterházy története* [The History of the Canadian Esterházy]. Budapest: Magvető, 1981.

Dreisziger, Nándor F. "Rose-Gardens on Ice-Floes: A Century of the Hungarian Diaspora in Canada." *Hungarian Journal of English and American Studies* 6.2 (2000): 239-58.

---, M. L. Kovacs, Paul Bődy, and Bennett Kovrig, eds. *Struggle and Hope: The Hungarian-Canadian Experience*. Toronto: McClelland, 1982.

Glant, Tibor. "Travel Writing as a Substitute for American Studies in Hungary." *Hungarian Journal of English and American Studies* 16.1-2 (2010): 171-84.

Johnson Bavery, Ashley. *Bootlegged Aliens: Immigration Politics on America's Northern Border*. Philadelphia: University of Pennsylvania Press, 2020.

Klug, Thomas A. "Residents by Day, Visitors by Night: The Origins of the Alien Commuter on the U.S.-Canadian Border during the 1920s." *Michigan Historical Review* 34.2 (2008): 75-98.

Kosa, John. *The Land of Choice: Hungarians in Canada*. Toronto: Toronto University Press, 1957.

Kovacs, Martin Louis. *Esterhazy and Early Hungarian Immigration to Canada*. Regina: Canadian Plains Research Centre, 1974.

Knowles, Valeria. *Strangers at Our Gates: Canadian Immigration and Immigration Policy, 1540-2006*. Toronto: Dundurn Press, 2007.

Lee, Erika. "Enforcing the Borders: Chinese Exclusion along the U.S. Borders with Canada and Mexico, 1882-1924." *The Journal of American History* 89.1 (2002): 54-86.

Marchildon, Gregory P. *Immigration and Settlement, 1870-1939*. Regina: Canadian Plains Research Center, 2009.

Ngai, Mae M. "The Strange Career of the Illegal Alien: Immigration Restriction and Deportation Policy in the United States, 1921-1965." *Law and History Review* 21.1 (2003): 69-107.

Patrias, Carmela. *The Hungarians in Canada*. Ottawa: The Canadian Historical Association, 1999.

---. *Patriots and Proletarians: Politicizing Hungarian Immigrants in Interwar Canada*. Montréal: McGill-Queen's University Press, 1994.

Puskás, Julianna. *From Hungary to the United States (1880-1914)*. Budapest: Akadémiai Kiadó, 1982.

---. *Kivándorló Magyarok az Egyesült Államokban, 1880-1940*. Budapest: Akadémiai Kiadó, 1982.

---. *Ties That Bind, Ties That Divide: 100 Years of Hungarian Experience in the United States*. New York: Homes and Meir, 2000.

Sadowski-Smith, Claudia. "Unskilled Labor Migration and the Illegality Spiral: Chinese, European, and Mexican Indocumentados in the United States, 1882-2007." *American Quarterly* 60.3 (2008): 779-804.

Szente-Varga, Mónika. *A gólya és a kolibri: Magyarország és Mexikó kapcsolatai a XIX. századtól napjainkig* [The Stork and the Hummingbird: Relations between Hungary and Mexico from the 19th Century to the Present Day]. Budapest, Áron Kiadó, 2012.

---. *Migración húngara a México entre 1901 y 1950* [Hungarian Migration to Mexico between 1901 and 1950]. Puebla, Mexico: Instituto de Ciencias Sociales y Humanidades, 2007.

Tezla, Albert. *"Egy szívvel két hazában": Az amerikás magyarok, 1895-1920* ["With One Heart in Two Countries": The Hungarian Americans, 1895-1920]. Budapest: Corvina, 2005.

---. *The Hazardous Quest: Hungarian Immigrants in the United States, 1895-1920*. Budapest: Corvina, 1993.

Thirring, Gusztáv. *A magyarországi kivándorlás és a külföldi magyarság* [Emigration from Hungary and Hungarians Abroad]. Budapest: Fritz Armin, 1904.

Torbágyi, Péter: *Magyarok Latin-Amerikában* [Hungarians in Latin America]. Budapest: Magyar Nyelv és Kultúra Nemzetközi Társasága, 2004.

Várdy, Steven Béla: *The Hungarian-Americans*. Boston: Twayne, 1985.

Venkovits, Balázs. "Csempészett idegenek: Dél- és kelet-európai illegális bevándorlók a kanadai-amerikai határon a két világháború között" [Smuggled Aliens: Illegal Immigrants from Southern and Eastern Europe on the Canada-US Border between the Two World Wars]. *Klió* 32.1 (2023): 28-33.

---. *Magyar kivándorlás Észak-Amerikába: Transzatlanti és Amerika-közi áttekintés a nemzetközi migrációs politika alakulásáról, 1870-1929* [Hungarian Emigration to North America: A Transatlantic and Inter-American Overview of International Migration Policy, 1870-1929]. *Migráció tegnap és ma* [Migration Past and Present]. Ed. Bozzay Réka and Pete László. Debrecen: Debreceni Egyetemi Kiadó, 2021. 139-157.

---. "The New Mecca of Immigrants": Hungarian Emigration to Canada and the Role of Immigration Propaganda." *Minorities in Canada: Intercultural Investigations*. Budapest: L'Harmattan, 2021. 99-121.

---. "Záródó kapuk, új lehetőségek: Magyar kivándorlás Észak-Amerikába a 20. század elején" [Closing Doors, New Opportunities: Hungarian Emigration to North America in the Early 20th Century]. *Aetas* 33.1 (2018): 131-43.

Vineberg, Robert. *Responding to Immigrants' Settlement Needs: The Canadian Experience*. Dordrecht: Springer, 2012.

Lukáš Perutka

Czechoslovak Resistance in Canada During World War II

On the eve of World War II, the Czechoslovak community in Canada was the second largest outside of Europe, preceded only by the one in the United States of America.[1] It grew especially in the interwar period thanks to the restrictive policies of the US government that introduced the quota system with the Immigration Act of 1924 (as discussed in the previous chapter). The Czechoslovak emigrants wanted, at first, to overcome the new reality by settling in Canada or Mexico and then move on to the US in line with the regulations. However, many eventually decided to stay in Canada as the government, the shipping companies, and other organizations established a dignified environment for them.[2] It was thanks to their effort that even the Czechoslovak government, reluctant to let its citizens emigrate and skeptical about the colonization possibilities across the Atlantic, eventually recommended Canada as one of the endorsed destinations for those willing to leave the country (Gellner and Smerek).

This trend can be observed in two interwar censuses. The one in 1921 shows 8,840 Czechoslovaks living in Canada, principally in Saskatchewan, Alberta, Ontario, British Columbia, and Manitoba (Sixth Census of Canada, vol. 1, 356-57). There were probably more but they identified themselves as Austrians because their passports were issued before Czechoslovak independence. In the census of 1931, the number of Czechoslovaks was significantly higher. The 30,401 people labeled Czechoslovaks based on their "racial" origin[3] lived predominantly in Ontario, Alberta, Saskatchewan, and Quebec (Seventh Census of Canada, vol. 2, 294-95). However, there were more people from Czechoslovakia, as it represented a multi-ethnic and multilingual country at the time. When we look at the language information, we find that there were 25,099 Slovaks and 6,414 Bohemians[4] for a total of 31,513 people (812-14). This number exceeds the previous one, so it is obvious that some naturalized Canadians still spoke the language

1 The funding for the present publication was provided by the Czech Ministry of Education, Youth, and Sports for specific research (IGA_FF_2023_011).
2 In the 1920s, Czechoslovaks were considered good settlers: perceived as healthy, able-bodied, hardworking, and honest by the Canadian authorities, and were refused only under specific circumstances. Canada welcomed either farming families, agriculture workers, single women (housemaids) with prearranged jobs, and the wives or children of immigrants already established in Canada. This policy changed in the 1930s due to the Great Depression and only farming families with enough capital were allowed into Canada. See Kelley and Trebilcock 139-88.
3 This is the archaic term/category used in the census. Today we would use ethnicity.
4 This was the term probably used for Czech speakers in the census. It does not say if the Moravians are also part of this group as they did not come from Bohemia.

of their parents. At the same time, we cannot identify the other minorities that came from Czechoslovakia because they are included within the groups of Jews, Ukrainians (Rusyns), Hungarians (Magyar), or Germans (812-14). Also, we do not know whether the Moravians were counted as Bohemians in this case or were among other Slavic groups coming from Austria.[5] Irrespective of these questions and the difficulty of categorizing Central and Eastern European immigrants adequately in the censuses, we can observe the rise in the number of Slovaks in Canada, which corresponds to the shift in emigration trends after World War I. The number of Bohemians, and to a certain level Moravians, dropped and those of Slovaks and Rusyns, that is, people from the most economically and socially underdeveloped parts of Czechoslovakia, rose (Vaculík 255-57). This trend was partly altered during World War II. We lack accurate census information from 1941 because the number of Bohemians is questionable but overall the number of Czechoslovaks grew to 42,912, based on their "racial" origin, and so did the number of Slovak speakers to 37,804 (Eighth Census of Canada, vol. 2, 271). Yet, the number of Bohemians fell to just 3,445 (752, 754) due to their enemy status and harassment by the local authorities.[6] We must thus consider the census of 1941 inaccurate and rely on the estimates from other sources that put the number of Czechoslovaks (of all ethnicities) between 50,000[7] and 60,000 with a growing share of exiles from Bohemia, Moravia, Ruthenia (including Jews and Germans) rather than Slovaks.[8]

Nevertheless, even this substantial number of compatriots and their activities during World War II have evaded the attention of scholars, both Czech and Canadian.[9] Some authors presented Czechoslovak-Canadians only within studies of overall migration (Vaculík). Recognized Czech historian of migration to the Americas Josef Polišenský decided, in his most prominent work, to focus inexplicably on the expatriates in the US and Latin America (*Úvod do studia*). It is especially surprising because he was the author of a book on Czechoslovak-Canadian relations published

---

5 There is confusing information in the census. The number of Austrians by "race" is 48,639, but in the language section there are just 6,842, and these are placed among Slavic language speakers, while the note tells us that they were *probably* German speaking, which does not make sense as Germans have their own language category both individually and as a group. See Seventh Census of Canada 294 and 814.

6 In 1941 Bohemia and Moravia were part of Hitler's Germany as a protectorate. It was the territory organized after the Nazi occupation in March 1939, and the Sudetenland had been an integral part of Germany since the Munich Agreement in September 1938. Slovaks had an independent state that declared war on the United Kingdom only in December 1941. Czechoslovak nationals were recognized as citizens of the allied country by Order in Council of April 10, 1941. See Gellner and Smerek 106.

7 Czechoslovak National Alliance in Canada (CNAC) to Mackenzie King, June 28, 1939, ACASA.

8 *Kronika československé vojenské mise v Kanadě* [Chronicle of the Czechoslovak Military Mission in Canada], 20, box 1, collection Československé vojenské mise Kanada, Vojenský historický archiv-Vojenský ústřední archiv (ČSVMK, VHA-VHÚ).

9 It is even more staggering when we realize that the list of archival collections to study this issue has been published already in 2007. See Zaoral 121-32.

to commemorate the Expo in Montréal in 1967. Even here, however, he dedicates only three paragraphs to World War II (*Le Canada*). We can find other studies of Czechoslovaks in Canada with a similar scope (Gellner and Smek 82-84 and 105-08; Hanzlík 121-22), while sometimes the topic was approached from the perspective of family history (Stolarik). Only Josef Čermák decided to write more about the organizations of Czechoslovaks in Canada (154-81). It, however, provides only a rather encyclopedic summary of the book *Památník československé Kanady* [Memorial of Czechoslovak Canada] that was written in the middle of World War II (Buzek et al).

The only exceptions in current scholarship about Czechoslovaks in Canada during World War II present the topic of the Czechoslovak military mission there, mentioning it either as a part of the effort of the Czechoslovak government in exile in London (Zudová Lešková 10-91) or in a more superficial way by Július Baláž (234-45). He and Tomáš Jiránek even prepared very similar editions with short commentaries of the *Chronicle of the Czechoslovak Mission in Canada* written by Rudolf Nekola (Jiránek, "Kronika československé" 205-38; Baláž, "Kronika Československé" 93-139). Jiránek then continued to examine the topic in his two articles about the groundwork of the mission ("Československá vojenská mise předhistorie" 163-76), its activities, and results ("činnost a výsledky" 247-78). However, he does not follow the story of the military organization in Canada after the mission was suspended, and he uses mainly the perspective of the Czechoslovak government in exile and presents the expatriate community only briefly.

The main aim of this chapter is to complement the current state of research on the period that has concentrated principally on the Czechoslovak military mission in Canada. It will thus focus on the other, so far, neglected actors and assess their roles and contributions to the renewal of the independent Czechoslovak state in Central Europe. It is based on the historical analysis (content and thematical) of archival material housed in the United States and the Czech Republic and so far not researched adequately. The Czechoslovak National Council in America (CNCA) documents are the most valuable collection in the Archives of Czechs and Slovaks Abroad (ACASA) housed in the University of Chicago Library. The council was operating from Chicago, but it was responsible for communicating with the Czechoslovak expatriate communities aiding their war effort in all American states, including Canada. The Czech archives offer valuable information as well. The Archive of the Ministry of Foreign Affairs of the Czech Republic houses the collection of the Czechoslovak government in exile in London.[10] It contains material on diplomatic relations, state visits, and compatriot organizations in Canada. In the Central Military Archives of the Czech Republic we can find information mainly on the Czechoslovak military mission in Canada; however, as its work also comprised of communication with expatriates' organizations in Canada, we can extract valuable information from their correspondence.

---

10 It is divided into two collections: general and confidential.

Czechoslovak diplomacy negotiating Canadian support

With the outbreak of World War II in September 1939, there were four principal problems and questions the Czechoslovak government in exile had to address in its relations with Canada. First, its recognition as the proper representative of the Czechoslovak people, both at home and abroad. Second, the establishment of a military mission to recruit soldiers for the Czechoslovak army in England. Third, change the status of the Czechoslovaks in Canada from hostile aliens that needed registration. Fourth, disapproval of the Munich Agreement.

The Czechoslovak situation was complicated in 1938 in North America. When the Munich Agreement was signed, the governments of Mexico, the United States, and Canada acted similarly. They celebrated the fact that regions with a German majority in Czechoslovakia were annexed by Germany. Influenced by the British policy of appeasement, they saw it as a necessary sacrifice on the part of Czechoslovakia to preserve peace in Europe. Historian Tony McCulloch even claims that the Canadian liberal prime minister William Lyon Mackenzie King influenced his American counterpart Franklin Delano Roosevelt on the matter, who was in private cautious about the agreement (McCulloch). However, the opinions in America changed quickly. In March 1939, Czechoslovakia was dissolved by Hitler, Slovakia became a German satellite, and Bohemia and Moravia were organized into a protectorate, *de facto* part of the Third Reich. Both Roosevelt and Mackenzie King immediately rejected this act of aggression that violated the spirit of the Munich Agreement.[11]

Canadian refusal of the Protectorate was important for the Czechoslovak consul general in Montréal who was pressured by the Germans (and by the former Czechoslovak Foreign Minister František Chvalkovský) to hand over his office. The consul František Pavlásek refused, and the Canadian government still recognized him as the Czechoslovak representative.[12] In September 1939 he observed as the Canadian Parliament decided unanimously to support the British war effort. Nevertheless, the declaration of war on Germany complicated the Czechoslovak situation, as the inhabitants of Bohemia and Moravia were considered Germans, *ergo* as enemy. Pavlásek, together with the expatriates, started a lengthy process of reversing this decision. The first step was the provisional recognition of the Czechoslovak government in exile in the United Kingdom on October 12, 1940.[13]

---

11 House of Commons Debates, June 3, 1943 (Ottawa: Edmond Clouthier, 1943) 3399.

12 Czechoslovak National Council in America (CNCA) press service, *Čsl. Národní rada děkuje Kanadě* [Czechoslovak National Council Thanks Canada]. October 23, 1940. b. 49. Archive of the Czechs and Slovaks Abroad (ACASA).

13 Massey to Ripka. Nov. 20, 1940. b. 81, c. Londýnský archiv – důvěrný, 1939-1945 (LA-D), Archiv ministerstva zahraničních věcí (AMZV).

This first diplomatic victory led directly to the decision to organize a military mission in Canada. The Czechoslovaks opted for Canada instead of the US for two reasons. The US did not enter the war yet and the expatriate community that had ties to the old country was more numerous than in the United States, and it was close enough to attract Czechoslovaks from the US anyway. The officials assumed they could get as many as 3,000 volunteers,[14] even though their goal was only 600 from both countries (Jiránek, "Československá vojenská mise předhistorie" 169). They predicted that many others would join the Canadian army instead.[15] The Czechoslovak military mission reached Montréal on July 4, 1941, and their arrival was not only publicized but also massively welcomed by the local Czechoslovak community and its leader, Štefan Rudinský. They settled down in the city because there was the consulate (the only diplomatic office at the time), and it was home to the second-largest expatriate community in Canada.[16] The officers came at the right moment; in April, Mackenzie King rejected the German occupation of Czechoslovakia and declared the Czechoslovaks in Canada members of the Allied nation.[17]

Figure 1: Poster for a meeting to help the Czechoslovak war effort. Organized by Czechoslovak Military Mission in Canada and Senator Vojta Beneš. Drumheller Valley, Alberta, no date. Source: VHA-VHÚ, collection: Československé vojenské mise: Kanada, box 7.

14 "Czech 'Aliens' to Enlist War Legion in Canada," *The Globe and Mail* 21 Dec. 1939.
15 Hutník to Španiel, April 17, 1942. 400-Vel/42, Annex A, b. 1, c. ČSVMK, VHA-VHÚ.
16 *Kronika československé vojenské mise v Kanadě*, 1, 7, b. 1, c. ČSVMK, VHA-VHÚ.
17 Karel Buzek, "Počátky a rozvoj čs. Kanady," *Čechoslovák* 26 March 1943: 5.

The mission had seven members; its commander was Čeněk Kudláček, who used his alias Hutník. Other members included lieutenant Rudolf Nekola, responsible for propaganda, and Ján Ambruš, liaison of the air force.[18] Their main goal included the recruitment of volunteers, at first Czechoslovaks, but since December 1941 also Canadians of Czechoslovak descent. There were several limitations to this, however. Canadian officials could exclude those who were essential for the economy. The officers also refused those who were unfit, too old,[19] or those with families, because the Czechoslovak government could not provide for them. Other aims of the mission included intelligence and counterintelligence services against enemy propaganda.

The evaluation of the mission is difficult. Its activity had its benefits, but the principal aim was not accomplished. By the end of 1942 there were 611 volunteers (41 from the US), but only 147 were sent to England.[20] A similar situation was visible in the air force. By the end of 1942 only 45 volunteered (15 from the US). Just 22 of them were accepted as pilots and had to undergo schooling and training.[21] Commander Hutník tried to explain in his dispatches the reasons for this lukewarm enlistment. He blamed the activities of the Slovak League (see below) against the mission, the vastness of Canada that prevented more personal contacts with Czechoslovak communities, and the decision of the Canadian government to proclaim conscription "if necessary" in 1942.[22] Other problems included communist propaganda, its influence on the youth, and the lack of propagandistic support. Hutník wanted a specialized information office but was refused by his superiors.[23]

At the same time, the mission was the most successful when comparing it with other Allies (for instance, Poles, Belgians, Yugoslavs, Dutch, Belgians, Norwegians, and the French), some with bigger communities in Canada.[24] Also, thanks to the members' several trips across Canada, even to western provinces like Alberta and British Columbia, the soldiers helped to raise awareness and sympathies for the Czechoslovak resistance. Particularly the CNAC benefited from this activity. Nevertheless, the Czechoslovak ministry of defense decided to terminate the mission.

---

18 *Kronika československé vojenské mise v Kanadě*, 2, b. 1, c. ČSVMK, VHA-VHÚ.

19 The limit varied between 40 and 45 years.

20 The numbers come from *Kronika československé vojenské mise v Kanadě* 39-40. B. 1, c. ČSVMK, VHA-VHÚ, and Jiránek, "Činnost a výsledky" 272-73.

21 *Kronika československé vojenské mise v Kanadě*, 40, b. 1, c. ČSVMK, VHA-VHÚ.

22 The decision came from a non-binding plebiscite in 1942. The English-speaking Canadians voted for conscription, but Quebec voted "no." The Canadian prime minister King had to consider both results, so he decided to issue the conscription only if necessary. It became necessary only in late 1944. For Czechoslovaks it meant they could choose between the Canadian and Czechoslovak armies in 1942. Many volunteers opted for the former.

23 *Zpráva o příčinách našeho dosavadního neúspěchu v Montréalu* [An Account of the Causes of Our Failure in Montréal], Sept. 15, 1941. B. 1, c. ČSVMK, VHA-VHÚ.

24 *Kronika československé vojenské mise v Kanadě*, 20. b. 1, c. ČSVMK, VHA-VHÚ.

The officials considered it too expensive, and the number of volunteers was depleted. On March 3, 1943, the mission was shut down and its commander, Hutník, was transferred to Latin America, first to Montevideo and then to Brazil.[25]

The tide of war was slowly turning, and the Czechoslovak government decided to rely more on diplomatic efforts from 1942. In July, the Canadian officials decided to fully recognize the Czechoslovak government in exile[26] and the next month established official diplomatic ties with it when František Pavlásek was accepted as minister of the Czechoslovak legation in Ottawa (*Příručka o navázání diplomatických*). Jaroslav Gardavský took over the consulate in Montréal, and Horace Hume Van Wart became the Czechoslovak honorary consul in Toronto (*Konzulární zastoupení Československa*). As Vojta Beneš put it, they were a small group but of great importance and great labor.[27]

We can divide their work and aims into several categories. First, they invited important Czechoslovak people and connected them with Canadian politicians. Pavlásek invited the Czechoslovak Foreign Minister Jan Masaryk in the winter of 1941-1942. The son of the founder of the Czechoslovak independent state was welcomed by the Czechoslovak community and, according to their representatives, he strengthened their determination everywhere he went.[28] In 1943 Pavlásek hosted Vojta Beneš and Štefan Rudinský to meet dignitaries in Ottawa[29] to prepare for the most important visit of the Czechoslovak president. Edvard Beneš visited Canada between June 2 and 5, 1943, as part of a longer trip to the United States of America. His stay was truly important for the expatriate community and Czechoslovak-Canadian relations. Surprisingly, it is mentioned only briefly in his memoirs (Beneš 275-76) or by his biographers (Dejmek 392-93),[30] often overshadowed by his stay in Washington. Beneš spoke with Prime Minister Mackenzie King, and before the parliament. He was assured of Canadian support and the acknowledgement of the legal continuity of Czechoslovakia since 1918 and within its original borders.[31] The prime minister then repeated that the Munich Agreement ". . . was not recognized and is not recognized today."[32] As Canada was not a signatory party, it did not need to be nullified. Beneš was satisfied with his reception and the Canadian declarations. The president

---

25 *Kronika československé vojenské mise v Kanadě*, 37. 41, b. 1, c. ČSVMK, VHA-VHÚ.

26 House of Commons Debates, June 3, 1943 (Ottawa: Edmond Clouthier, 1943) 3399.

27 Vojta Beneš, "Drahým krajanům kanadským," *Památník československé Kanady*, ed. Buzek et al. 18.

28 Karel Buzek, "Počátky a rozvoj čs. Kanady," *Čechoslovák* 26 March 1943: 6.

29 Pavlásek to Ministry of Foreign Affairs of Czechoslovakia (MFAC), Jan. 31, 1945. 193/45, b. 152, c. Londýnský archiv – obyčejný, 1939-1945 (LAO), AMZV.

30 The historian looked for the information in box 444/1, c. LAO, AMZV. There is a folder of Beneš's state visits but only one document about Canada, the summary of mainly positive press reaction to his stay.

31 Pavlásek to Bydžovský, May 9, 1943. 15/43, b. 81, c. LAD, AMZV.

32 House of Commons Debates. June 3, 1943. 3395.

expressed his gratitude in his speech in parliament: "The sympathy of the Canadian government and people for Czechoslovakia, expressed in words and deeds during the past four years has been an encouragement and inspiration in this darkest period of modern Czechoslovak history."[33]

The work of Pavlásek was highly appraised by the president and by Mackenzie King, who considered him a friend. The personal relations between Czechoslovak diplomats and Canadian politicians were crucial, especially the cordial one between Pavlásek and Mackenzie King, as illustrated by mutual correspondence. When the prime minister celebrated his 70th birthday, the minister gave him a grand silver tray and passed on greetings from Edvard Beneš.[34] In January 1945 the Pavláseks organized a ceremonial dinner where Mackenzie King asked about the Czechoslovak president and recollected their meetings. In the subsequent thank you letter, he emphasized his feelings towards Pavlásek and his wife: "While I recognized, of course, that the honor paid me was a tribute on the part of Czechoslovakia to Canada, I felt even more strongly what it meant to each of our countries that we are such close friends; and what it means to me, personally, to possess such true friends."[35]

The Czechoslovak diplomats did not focus only on politicians but also on the general public. They intended to present Czechoslovakia as a sovereign nation with its own history and culture. They organized many cultural events, such as concerts, folklore presentations, movies, and exhibitions, and promoted them in the Canadian press. The concert of piano virtuoso Rudolf Firkušný in 1943 in Ottawa and the exhibition of Czechoslovak paintings and sculptures in the Canadian National Gallery in Ottawa in October 1943 were the most successful. The latter was presented as a commemoration of 25 years of Czechoslovakia, and the Canadian prime minister gave the introductory address.[36] Also important was the organization of bazaars to collect money for the war effort.

The compatriots were another focus of Czechoslovak diplomacy. The minister and consuls focused not just on organization; they used their resources to pay some of the most prominent members of the CNAC such as the secretary Karel Buzek. They contributed to the Czechoslovak Canadian press, especially the weekly *Nová vlast*,[37] and even organized the special Canadian issue of *Čechoslovák*, the weekly of the Czechoslovak ministry of foreign affairs in London.[38] Minister Pavlásek intended to establish a Czechoslovak information service in Canada, but it never materialized. Therefore, he used other opportunities for propagandistic purposes to raise support

33 Ibid, 3397.
34 Pavlásek to MFAC, Dec. 30, 1944. 3339/44, b. 152, c. LAO, AMZV.
35 Mackenzie King to Mrs. Pavlásek, Jan. 14, 1945. b. 4, c. LAD, AMZV.
36 Pavlásek to MFAC, Apr. 23, 1945. 762/45, b. 152, c. LAO, AMZV.
37 Pavlásek to MFAC, March 20, 1944. 1041/44, b. 152, c. LAO, AMZV.
38 *Čechoslovák* 26 March 1943.

of the expatriates often focusing on the trinity: Tomáš Garrigue Masaryk, Edvard Beneš, and Milan Rastislav Štefánik, the founding fathers of the unified Czechoslovak nation. Such was the program to commemorate the 95th anniversary of the birth of the president-liberator Masaryk. It was aired by the Canadian Broadcasting Corporation on March 7, 1945. It started with the Czechoslovak national anthem, continued with Pavlásek's speech on Masaryk, and ended with the music of the famous Czechoslovak composer Josef Suk.[39]

Pavlásek and his activities were generally praised by expatriates and both Canadian and Czechoslovak authorities. The only problem he had was with the military attaché Ján Ambruš. The former member of the Czechoslovak military mission stayed in Canada to cooperate with the minister and to look after the volunteers and the air force students.[40] Pavlásek described Ambruš as a problematic and ambitious man who intervened in Czechoslovak foreign relations without any authority and who borrowed money from Czechoslovak compatriots.[41] Ambruš, on the other hand, complained about the ambitious Pavlásek, who wanted to overshadow him and even refused to invite him to meet the president Edvard Beneš.[42] The ministry of defense started to investigate the matter, and it was resolved by Oldřich Španiel, who knew both men. He stood by Pavlásek, describing him as a responsible co-worker. In his eyes, it was Ambruš and his psychical and health condition that caused this unpleasant relationship, which luckily did not affect the Czechoslovak war effort much.[43]

Figure 2: Army week in Regina, Saskatchewan, 1942.
Source: VHA-VHÚ, collection: Československé vojenské mise: Kanada, box 8.

---

39 Pavlásek to MFAC, March 26, 1945. 591/45, b. 152, c. LAO, AMZV.
40 Ministry of National Defense of Czechoslovakia (MNDC) to MFAC, Dec. 31, 1942. 4914-dův, /2.odděl.1942, b. 99/100, c. LAO, AMZV.
41 Pavlásek to MFAC, Jan. 11, 1944. 70/44, b. 221, c. LAD, AMZV.
42 Ripka to Pavlásek, Dec. 8, 1943. 8792/dův/43, b. 221, c. LAD, AMZV.
43 Španiel to MNDC, Nov. 9, 1943. box 221, c. LAD, AMZV.

The Czechoslovak National Alliance in Canada

Similarly to World War I, the effort of Czechoslovak compatriots in North America was essential to the resistance. The Munich Agreement caused some demonstrations, but it was the dissolution of Czechoslovakia in March 1939 that activated the Czechoslovak community in Canada. One month later they sent their delegates, Karel Buzek and Gustav Přístupa, to Chicago where they met with Beneš and participated in the creation of the Czechoslovak National Council of America, the unified and central organization of Czechoslovaks in the United States.[44] When they got back to Canada, they initiated a meeting between the two biggest Czechoslovak communities in Toronto and Montréal. It was decided to organize a congress in June to create a similar unified front in Canada.[45] They met in Toronto on June 24, 1939, were supported by the consul general František Pavlásek, and received a greeting and approval letter from Edvard Beneš.[46] The created organization took the name National Alliance of Slovaks,[47] Czechs, and Rusyns in Canada. The chairman was Štefan Rudinský, the honorary chairman was consul Pavlásek, and Karel Břečka was elected secretary.[48]

The first year of the organization was, however, complicated, and it had to overcome the divisions between communities in Montréal and Toronto, communists and liberals, and Czechs and Slovaks.[49] A radical change was needed, and it came in April 1940. The association changed its name to Czechoslovak National Alliance in Canada and got rid of its divisive elements: the communists, and the secretary Karel Břečka, who sided with them and the separatist Slovaks. They raised money, so Buzek could quit his job and become the new secretary.[50] Nevertheless, the second congress of the CNAC in August 1940 reflected its low point, the number of participating regional organizations dropped to 54, and therefore Rudinský sent Buzek to the West to agitate there among their countrymen.[51] This campaign was repeated in subsequent years with the help of the Czechoslovak military mission. The association found its balance in 1942 and decided to organize congresses just every two years because there was no need to take immediate action as there was during the first war years.

44 Karel Buzek, "Počátky a rozvoj čs. Kanady," *Čechoslovák* 26 March 1943: 5.
45 They decided not to take part in CNCA but closely cooperate with it. They reasoned that Canada was a British dominion and was more likely to enter the war than the US.
46 CNCA, *Kanadští Čechoslováci a Karpatorusové do osvobozeneckého zápasu* [Canadian Czechoslovaks and Rusyns into the Resistance], June 6, 1939. b. 49, ACASA.
47 The Slovaks were in the first place, confirming their majority in Canada.
48 Zmrhal to Pail, Sept. 21, 1939. b. 49, ACASA.
49 Pavlásek to CNCA, Aug. 21, 1939. 2505/39, b. 49, ACASA.
50 Zmrhal to Vajdík, May 2, 1940. b. 49, ACASA.
51 Karel Buzek, "Počátky a rozvoj čs. Kanady," *Čechoslovák* 26 March 1943: 5.

Figure 3: Delegates of the 2ⁿᵈ Annual Convention of the Czechoslovak National Alliance in Canada.
Toronto, 1940.
Source: VHA-VHÚ, collection: Československé vojenské mise: Kanada, box 8.

During the conflict, the CNAC had about 6,500 members (Gellner and Smerek 106) distributed around Canada in 88 branches.[52] The Czech majority (including Germans), both among leaders and members, managed 46 of them. The rest were led by the Slovaks. Although the ethnic division was even, the spatial redistribution of the branches was not. Half of them were in the Province of Ontario. Its capital, Toronto, thus became the center of the Alliance. All the congresses were held there and, in 1944, the organization bought a building near downtown and renamed it Masaryk Hall. The Czechoslovak companies such as Baťa or Prenco contributed to the purchase and operation. Masaryk Hall then could be offered for free to compatriots' meetings or events.[53]

The goals of the CNAC were diverse. The first was to raise money to help the Allied war effort and to liberate and rebuild Czechoslovakia. Second was to build cooperation with Canadian politicians and citizens. Third was to unify all the Czechoslovaks in Canada, so their organization could exert more influence. Fourth was to organize military committees for the recruitment of volunteers. Since the latter two were not as successful (as seen in other subchapters), I will focus on the former two.

The Alliance had two principal sources of financing. There were contributions of members (1 dollar per year), but this money was used just to support the organization as costs amounted to 3,266 dollars in 1943, and 3,314 dollars in 1944.[54] Donations represented the other source collected principally in the Czechoslovak War Charities Fund. It was organized as soon as the Czechoslovaks were officially recognized as an Allied nation and collected large amounts of money. In 1943 this amounted to

---

52 The number of branches changed over time, as new organizations joined CNAC, and others stopped communicating. There were 91 in 1943, but only 88 of them were active. Compare Karel Buzek, "Počátky a rozvoj čs. Kanady," *Čechoslovák* 26 March 1943: 6.

53 CNAC, Masarykov Dom (Masaryk House). 1945. b. 49, ACASA.

54 *Zpráva ústředního tajemníka K. Buzka* [Report of Secretary K. Buzek], Nov. 25, 1944. b. 49, ACASA.

68,000 dollars, a year later 84,000 dollars.[55] In the course of the war, the overall sum was 331,000 dollars (Gellner and Smerek 106). Also, the Czechoslovaks in Canada contributed three-fourths to the amount of 450,000 dollars that the Canadian government sent to Czechoslovakia after the war for rebuilding (Rovná 378-79).

The funds for CNAC were raised in various ways. The organization held collections (of money, or items that could be sold), trips and excursions, lectures, and talks of members or invited guests. Even weddings or christening parties were used to raise money. Concerts of famous Czech composers Antonín Dvořák's and Bedřich Smetana's compositions were also very common, as the organization rightfully believed that music represented the universal language around the world. The special occasions were celebrations of the important historical events of Czechoslovak history: Masaryk's birthday, Independence Day, and so on. Lastly, CNAC also published its own newspaper *Nová vlast*, which was never profitable but raised awareness and highlighted important events to raise funds.[56] Women's support was also invaluable, even though they organized themselves as part of the CNAC branches later, thanks to efforts of the wife of the commander of the Czechoslovak military mission, Milada Kudláčková. They organized the same activities as men (trips, concerts), but also produced clothing and food for the celebrations.[57] Women and children helped with growing garden produce, which was sold in bazaars.[58] They were successful, for instance, in Montréal, with a bazaar aimed at collecting 1,000 dollars but received twice as much.[59] The money they collected was used for social purposes, such as providing help to the incoming refugees. They also supported the soldiers with cigarettes and chocolate. With the help of the Czechoslovak Red Cross,[60] they sent products abroad. In 1942 they sent Christmas gifts to Czechoslovak soldiers and pilots in England, the Middle East, Jerusalem, and the Soviet Union, or to their wives and children abroad.[61]

---

55 Ibid.

56 CNAC reports. 1942. b. 6, c. ČSVMK, VÚA-VHA.

57 CNAC, *Naše ženy na poloostrově vancouverském se činí* [Our Women on the Vancouver Peninsula are Making Themselves], Oct. 1942, box 6, VHU. CNAC, *Roční zpráva Žen. Odboru ve Fort Erie* [Annual Report of the Women's Department in Fort Erie], Jan. 1943. b. 6, c. ČSVMK, VÚA-VHA.

58 F. Bildová, *Československá žena v odboji* [Czechoslovak Women in Resistance], concept article, no date, b. 49, ACASA.

59 CNCA, *Československý bazar v Montréalu ve prospěch naší armády ve Velké Británii* [Czechoslovak Bazaar in Montréal to Aid Czechoslovak Army in Great Britain], no date, b. 49, ACASA.

60 The activities of the Czechoslovak Red Cross are also worth mentioning. The archival material from World War II is fragmented, but we know they organized their collections. In Montréal they held a concert with Dvořák's music, and they received support from the Lieutenant Governor of Quebec, Eugène Fiset, and other members of Quebec politics. It was a very successful event that was quickly sold out. See *Koncert Dvořákovy hudby v Montréalu* [A Concert of Dvořák's Music in Montréal], Feb. 14, 1942, b. 2, c. ČSVMK, VÚA-VHA.

61 CNAC, Report from headquarters, Dec. 1942. b. 6, c. ČSVMK, VÚA-VHA.

The main aim of the CNAC regarding the Canadian authorities was to achieve a change of status to an Allied nation, which was attained in April 1941. However, they also cooperated with the Canadian Friends of Czechoslovakia. Together, they intended to inform the Canadian public about Czechoslovaks and their fight for freedom and democracy, which they did through culture, arts, and the promotion of democratic and civic institutions.[62] Canadian Friends had 5,000 members; their chairman was J. McIntosh and the secretary J. Arthur Wistraw. Other initiatives were not so successful. The Lidice massacre, the reprisal for the assassination of Reich Protector Reinhard Heydrich, raised great support for the Czechoslovakian cause all over the world. In the Americas, for example, some countries decided to rename cities to "Lidice." The Premier of Quebec, Adélard Godbout, tried the same initiative. However, citizens of the selected town, Frelighsburg, refused to follow the proposal.[63]

The entrepreneurs

The Czechoslovak private companies that moved to Canada because of Munich and World War II may be seen as other actors in the resistance. They established good relations with the Canadian government by helping the war industry, employed refugees, and, thanks to that, organized resistance in their vicinity. Canada owed the "refugee" industry for its independence in several sectors: medical instruments, aerospace industry, and optical glass.[64] The best example was that of Tomáš Baťa, Jr., who moved part of his famous shoe company, established by his father, to the site of future Batawa in Ontario. The importance of Batawa for the Czechoslovak community is also clear from archival material and other sources. We can show a certain microcosm of resistance in the example of Baťa's new home.

The Baťa company planned an expansion into the Americas already in the 1930s. After the Great Depression, Jan Antonín Baťa[65] wanted to overcome the protective measures of the countries there. He decided to build a small enterprise in Canada, but it never developed. The rapid change came in September 1938, when the Munich Agreement was signed. Tomáš Baťa was sent by his uncle to Canada to find a suitable plot to build a new company town. The Quebec authorities offered him several possibilities, but Baťa decided to start over in the English-speaking part of Canada. He thought the French language could cause problems for his Czechoslovak employees. Eventually, he found an ideal spot in Ontario, near the village of Frankford in the

---

62 Resolution Passed by the Executive Committee of the Canadian Friends of Czechoslovakia, July 24, 1940. b. 49, ACASA.

63 Kudláček to Pavlásek, Nov. 21, 1942. 5464/42, b. 4, c. ČSVMK, VÚA-VHA.

64 Hanč to MFAC, March 1, 1944. 799/44, b. 233, c. LAO, AMZV.

65 Half-brother of the founder Tomáš Baťa and uncle to Tomáš Baťa junior.

Trent River valley with power supply, railway, highway, and a navigable river nearby (Baťa and Sinclairová 42, 47-48).

The next year presented a great challenge to Baťa's Canadian plan. The country received only farmers at the time, so the government allowed the entrepreneur to bring with him just 100 instead of 250 families. The others came later when World War II commenced. The machinery was brought on a German merchant ship, and when the captain realized what cargo he was carrying, he decided to sail back to Europe and had to be stopped by the Canadian authorities (Baťa and Sinclairová 43-51; Cekota 21, 43). The coming of World War II made things even more difficult for Tomáš Baťa, and the idea of building an ideal industrial city in Canada had to be abandoned.

> The first street of this new Ontario township of the future—still without a name—was laid out according to a plan which envisaged the development of an industrial community of some thousand people. . . . The hell which gaped open in Europe during the fall of 1939 swallowed all the great plans for a new model industrial town in Canada. Instead of a town, only a small village sprang up around a middle-sized rather than full-sized plant. (Cekota 58-59)

The area was called Batawa and its development was slow and full of hardships. Baťa was lucky that his employees were hard-working and skilled people. In 1939, he decided to muster support for the Canadian government when he offered a part of the plant capacity to the war industry. For instance, he made shoes for the Canadian army[66] and other military components and armaments such as the scarce gyroscopes for torpedoes (Baťa and Sinclairová 60-61). Unlike his uncle, Jan Antonín Baťa, who was clumsy in negotiating with the allied governments, Tomáš, Jr. skillfully ran his factory and invested in his employees. In subsequent years Batawa had lined the boulevard with stores, offices, and public buildings on both sides. The factory was a 5-storey building; nearby was also the Bata Hotel suitable to accommodate single workers, and the Recreational Hall used by residents as a theatre, cinema, and indoor sports gymnasium.[67] The employees received a small but cozy house as their nearby dwelling. They were also provided life, health, workers', and family insurance (Cekota 60-61, 118-119).

There were two main Czechoslovak organizations in Batawa, the gymnastic and cultural association Sokol and the branch of the CNAC. Both collaborated on various events that were meant for the Czechoslovak cause. Sokol was the smaller of the two because its members had the obligation to exercise regularly, so the participation was time consuming. It had 85 male and 39 female members as well as a children's class, with an annual budget of around 1,000 dollars. Their main income was represented by individual contributions and admission fees from various events: New Year's Eve parties, theatres, balls, or special events like the United Nations Day. Most of

---

66 Hanč to MFAC, March 1, 1944. 799/44, b. 233, c. LAO, AMZV.
67 *Bata Bugle* July 1944.

the expenditures were used for the war effort, donations to the Czechoslovak Red Cross or the nearby aviation school in Belleville. Their gymnastic exercises took place in the Recreation Hall until a new Community Hall was inaugurated. According to documents, the only problem was attendance, but that was understandable during the war. The people in Batawa volunteered after work hours; the women, for instance, helped with ammunition production.[68]

The CNAC branch had more than 180 members in 1942 and 1943. Its budget was four times higher than Sokol's. Its major income was the memorial fund of František Muška,[69] founder of the Czechoslovak War Charities Fund, who lived in Batawa. In 1942 the members contributed 2,709 dollars, which was supplemented by a donation from Bata Shoe Company and sent to the Czechoslovak Red Cross in London.[70] Other expenditures went to resistance media: the newspaper *Nová vlast* and radio station St. Catharines. The members also supported the Czechoslovak army in the Soviet Union and donated Christmas gifts to Czechoslovak soldiers in Canada and England. These 137 packages[71] were prepared for them by the women's department of CNAC.[72] In 1942 the leadership decided to put Jan Navrátil in charge of the cigarettes (later cigarettes and chocolate) fund. He was very successful and thanks to his effort, Batawa could support the Czechoslovak soldiers in yet another way.[73]

Similarly to Sokol, various events contributed to the major source of income of CNAC Batawa. Some were traditional and repeated every year: the Neighbourhood Ball, Slavic February carnival, the birthday of former president Tomáš Garrigue Masaryk (March 6), Mothers' Day, and remembrance of Milan Rastislav Štefánik, a Wine Festival, Czechoslovak Independence Day (October 28), Feast of Saint Nicholas, and the New Year's Eve party. Other events were organized ad hoc. In 1943 lectures were presented by Vojta Beneš, former senator and brother of the Czechoslovak president, and by the Czechoslovak airmen from the Royal Air Force, Captains Karel Kuttelwascher and Josef Jaške.[74]

The most successful event, perhaps in all of Czechoslovak Canada, was the United Nations Day in 1942, organized by citizens of Batawa. It was attended by 4,500 visitors that contributed to the resistance. Tomáš Baťa, Jr. was part of the organizational

---

68 *Tělovýchovná jednota Sokol Batawa, Ontario. Výroční zpráva 1942* [Sokol Batawa annual report]. b. 49, ACASA.

69 Later renamed to Czechoslovak War Charities Fund.

70 Report from Batawa-Frankford, Sept. 1942. b. 6, c. ČSVMK, VHA-VHÚ.

71 There were gloves, towels, socks, handkerchiefs, and chocolate in the packages. See Report from Batawa-Frankford, Oct. 1942. b. 6, c. ČSVMK, VHA-VHÚ.

72 Československé národní sdružení Batawa, Ontario. Výroční zpráva 1942 [CNA Batawa annual report], b. 49, ACASA.

73 S. Kvarda. Report from Batawa-Frankford, Aug. 1942. b. 6, c. ČSVMK, VHA-VHÚ.

74 Československé národní sdružení Batawa, Ontario. Výroční zpráva 1943 [CNA Batawa annual report]. b. 49, ACASA.

committee, and as an important figure of Czechoslovak Canada, he was able to approach famous people from the Allied camp. The UN Day welcomed compatriot guests from Chicago, Cleveland, Toronto, and Montréal, but also delegates from Poland, Norway, France, and the Soviet Union. Baťa even attracted two Canadian cabinet ministers. Thomas Crerar oversaw immigration and was welcomed warmly because the inhabitants were thankful for his intervention on their behalf. The second dignitary was Colin William George Gibson, the minister of national revenue. Both witnessed how Tomáš Baťa was promoted to lieutenant JG[75] of the Canadian reserve army.[76]

As mentioned above, Baťa was not the only Czechoslovak entrepreneur in Canada. Brothers Koerner from Hodonín established themselves in New Westminster, near Vancouver, in British Columbia. They were experts in wood production and had to leave their sawmill and chemical plant in Europe when they migrated to Canada during the autumn of 1938. In New Westminster, they started their business anew and processed the western hemlock (*Tsuga heterophylla*). It was an underused wood in Canada but thanks to innovative processing the Koerner brothers found success.[77] They also understood the problematic social situation in Canada, so they employed principally its citizens and only brought six employees from Czechoslovakia. They offered important social benefits to their workers, too, like group life insurance, health insurance, up to 26 sick days pay, and even provided doctors.[78]

Another example of a Czechoslovak company is the Toronto-based enterprise Prenco, which produced parts for munition manufacture[79] and supported the local Sokol club in its resistance efforts.[80] Louis Fischl and his wife were glovemakers from Carlsbad and fled to Prescott, Ontario. They remodeled an old brewery and brought machinery from Europe and the US as well as Czechoslovak refugees. They also opened a large goat farm nearby that was the source of hides and cheese.[81] Hesky Flax products in Seaforth, Ontario, was the major producer and processor of flax in Canada. All these companies presented a success story of how to establish themselves from scratch and help the refugees and the Canadian war effort. In fact, their accomplishment was so great that the government of Mackenzie King intended to keep them in Canada after the war.[82]

---

75 When the war was over, Tomáš Baťa, Jr. was already a captain.

76 Tělovýchovná jednota Sokol Batawa, Ontario. Výroční zpráva 1942 [Sokol Batawa annual report]. b. 49, ACASA.

77 Report from New Westminster visit, no date, probably 1941, b. 6, c. ČSVMK, VHA-VHÚ.

78 "Czechoslovakian enterprises in Canada," *Čechoslovák* 26 March 1943: 16.

79 Ibid.

80 Article *Vítaná návštěva* [Welcomed Visit], Oct. 1942. b. 6, c. ČSVMK, VHA-VHÚ.

81 "Czechoslovakian enterprises in Canada," *Čechoslovák* 26 March 1943: 16.

82 Hanč to MFRC, March 1, 1944. 799/44, b. 233, c. LAO, AMZV.

The minorities[83]

As mentioned before, Czechoslovakia was still a multinational state at the time of World War II. The majority was made up by the Czechoslovaks (8.8 million). It was an "artificial" nationality composed of Bohemians, Moravians, and Slovaks, united, above all, for a practical reason of leverage against the Germans (3.1 mil.) living mainly in the border areas called Sudetenland. The other minorities were not that numerous, but they had local importance. Rusyns (0.5 mil.) in Carpathian Ruthenia, Hungarians (0.8 mil.) in Slovakia, Jews (0.2 mil)[84] mostly in Bohemia, and Poles (70,000) in Silesia.[85] The minorities were traditionally ignored in the historical works about the second Czechoslovak resistance. Jan Křen recognized this problem already in 1969, when he pointed out that the resistance is mainly depicted as Czechoslovak only and other nationalities are ignored; he especially talked about the Rusyns (Křen 342). Recently, the topic of minorities in the Czechoslovak resistance received at least some attention. The scholar Radko Maršálek presented the participation of Rusyns and Jews in the army but not from a Canadian perspective (Maršálek 385-442). Tomáš Jiránek dedicated at least some paragraphs to other minorities, this time from Canada (Jiránek, "činnost a výsledky" 260-63). The emphasis on Rusyns and Jews is obvious, as they, like Czechoslovaks, were the principal victims of Hitler's occupation of Czechoslovakia. However, the issue of Germans and Hungarians that opposed the Nazis still awaits thorough research. The present subchapter might shed some light on this problem, at least from a Canadian perspective.

The Slovaks in Canada were split at the beginning of World War II. There were those loyal to Czechoslovakia and their organizations were part of the CNAC. For instance, the members of the First Slovak Benevolent Society (*Prvý Slovenský Podporujúcí Spolok*) supported the Czechoslovak resistance. Their organizations, like the one in Coleman, Alberta, bought war bonds for 1,000 dollars, organized cultural events to support the war effort, and in their publications emphasized the role of Milan Rastislav Štefánik, Slovakian founding father of independent Czechoslovakia.[86] Similarly, part of the Slovaks in Fort William joined the Alliance and even organized the recruitment for the army.[87]

---

83 The system of minorities in Czechoslovakia was a bit complicated as there existed two categories: nationality and citizenship. For instance, German speakers had German nationality but Czechoslovak citizenship and passport. For more details see Tóth, Novotný, and Stehlík 185-288. In English, the situation is briefly explained in Pánek et al., *History of the Czech Lands* 437-44.

84 The Jews could choose their nationality, but only about half of them did so. Others maintained their nationality according to the region they were born into.

85 The numbers are from 1921 and are presented in a useful overview of this issue in a recent book on Czech history, Pánek et al., *Dějiny Českých zemí* 409-15.

86 *Zpravodaj našej mládeže*, May 1943.

87 Petrovič to Nekola, Aug. 24, 1941. 4164, b. 1, c. ČSVMK, VHA-VHÚ.

The other part of Slovaks in Canada was united in the Slovak League and presented a challenge to the Czechoslovak government. The organization was established in 1907 in Cleveland, Ohio and supported the idea of a Czechoslovak state during World War I. Its Canadian branch was founded in 1926 in Winnipeg and its members were disillusioned with the situation of Slovaks in Czechoslovakia. When the independent Slovak state was created in March 1939, they supported it and celebrated the dissolution of Czechoslovakia. During the first years of World War II, they actively fought the united Czechoslovak resistance in their press and even intervened with the Canadian authorities.[88] They found support among the Catholic organizations in the province of Quebec. František Jamnický, the accountant of the Czechoslovak consulate in Montréal, decided to join the League in March 1939, supported Josef Tiso, the president of the Slovak state, and actively defamed the Czechoslovak president Edvard Beneš. [89]

The attack on Pearl Harbor and the fact that the Slovak state declared war on the United States and the United Kingdom in December 1941 undermined the efforts of the Slovak League. Some of its members, organized around the newspaper *Slovenské bratrstvo* [Slovak Brotherhood],[90] decided to support the Czechoslovak National Alliance in exchange for their aid.[91] The Slovak League broke ties with the Slovak state and altered its rhetoric. Their foreign policy was aligned with the Allies, but they still actively fought the idea that Czechoslovakia would be restored with the pre-war political system that did not grant the Slovaks the autonomy they wanted.[92] The restructuring of the Slovak League to resistance also presented a new challenge to the CNAC, which feared it would attract the Slovaks among their ranks.[93] This never materialized, however, and the Slovak League still undermined the Czechoslovak war effort, and its members protested the activity of the Czechoslovak military mission in 1942[94] and rather joined the Canadian army.[95]

The Germans[96] from Czechoslovakia, now living in Canada, were divided in a similar fashion to the Slovaks, only the fault lines were clearer, and three branches

---

88 Some members of the League claimed they did want Czechoslovakia to be re-established, unless with Slovak autonomy. They were closely united with the former Czechoslovak prime minister Milan Hodža, who was in exile in the United States and tried to achieve federalization of Czechoslovakia.

89 Pavlásek to MFAC, Nov. 30, 1944. 3148/44, b. 4, c. LAD, AMZV.

90 Later renamed *Slovenský priekopník*.

91 *Kronika československé vojenské mise v Kanadě* 26-27, b. 1, c. ČSVMK, VHA-VHÚ.

92 Ibid, 23,

93 Pavlásek to CNCA, Jan. 16, 1942. 190/42, b. 49, ACASA.

94 *Kronika československé vojenské mise v Kanadě*, 14, b. 1, c. ČSVMK, VHA-VHÚ.

95 MFAC to MNDC, June 18, 1942. 2787/dův./42, b. 216, c. LAD, AMZV.

96 The same division is apparent also in the case of the Hungarians. We do not have much information about them from the archives; however, when they appear, they are associated with the Germans. See Frolka to Martínek, Feb. 3, 1943, b. 49, ACASA.

crystalized during World War II. The first group were the older migrants that supported, though not publicly, Hitler's Germany. When the Czechoslovak mission visited Minitonas in Manitoba, they found 350 German families there, and some were from the Sudetenland and even spoke Czech. They visited the lecture of the representatives; nevertheless, they left in the middle of the speech and some even wanted to disturb the meeting. The local Czechoslovaks prevented them from doing so, in the end.[97] The second group were the supporters of Wenzel Jaksch, leader of the German Social Democratic Workers Party in Czechoslovakia. They were first supportive of Beneš, but early in World War II, they developed the idea of reconstructing Czechoslovakia with more German autonomy. This put them close to Milan Hodža's Slovaks in the Americas but distanced them from the Czechoslovak resistance movement abroad.[98]

The third group of Sudeten Germans was the youngest generation that migrated because of their political beliefs (democratic or social democratic). They decided (or were forced) to move after the annexation of Sudeten by Germany.[99] These were present principally in four communities in Canada. The Germans in Tupper Creek, British Columbia appeared even in contemporary literature (Španiel 135). There were 18 families who fled after Munich to the Czechoslovak inland and then continued to Canada. They established a local branch of the CNAC, and all males volunteered for the Czechoslovak army.[100] Second, and the largest, was the younger generation of Germans in St. Walburg, Saskatchewan. They immigrated to Canada in 1939 and, according to their spokesman, Rudolf Helperle from Carlsbad, they were social democrats. Their 55 families lived together with older, more pro-German, neighbors.[101] Saskatchewan province hosted also the other two groups of Sudeten Germans that joined the CNAC. The first community in Goodsoil donated the embroidery of the greater coat of arms, after the Allied victory over Germany.[102] In Loon River, the 33 Sudeten families lived and all but three spoke Czech. They were supporters of social democracy, joined the CNAC, and demanded Czechoslovak propagandistic literature. Oskar Gregor even volunteered for the Czechoslovak army at 52, although he was not accepted, unlike his 19-year-old son who joined the air force.[103]

The admission of Czechoslovak Germans in Canada to the army was a complicated issue. Some were accepted until 1942. They had to be checked because the Czech and Slovak fellow combatants did not trust them, but it was politically advantageous to

---

97 Report from Minitonas visit, Sept. 28, 1941. b. 6, c. ČSVMK, VHA-VHÚ.

98 Dojáček to Martínek, Sept. 11, 1943. b. 49, ACASA.

99 Frolka to Martínek, Feb. 3, 1943. b. 49, ACASA.

100 CNA press service, *Sudetští Němci v Kanadě proti Hitlerovi* [Sudeten Germans in Canada against Hitler], no date, b. 49, ACASA.

101 Report from St. Walburg visit, no date, but probably 1941. b. 6, c. ČSVMK, VHA-VHÚ.

102 Gardavský to MFAC, June 2, 1945. 1102/45, b. 143, c. LAO, AMZV.

103 Report from Loon Lake and Loon River visit, no date, but probably 1941, b. 6, c. ČSVMK, VHA-VHÚ.

accept at least some. We know of 78 who volunteered but many were refused because they had families and were over 42 years old. Only five made it to England and three, who did not know Czech, were advised to join the Canadian army.[104] The five went in two convoys, on April 6 (one), and on August 20 (four), 1942 (Jiránek, "činnost a výsledky" 272). After 1943 the Germans could still apply but they were all refused. The Czechoslovak consulate only gave a certificate of loyal citizens to those who completed military service.[105] Early in 1945, the Czechoslovak ministry of defense decided to continue with this policy, but the ministry of commerce criticized this decision because the German members of the Czechoslovak resistance did not lose Czechoslovak citizenship and this decision was considered unfair. However, the war was ending, and the government did not change the policy because of the expected expulsion[106] after the conflict.[107]

The participation of Rusyns in Canada in the Czechoslovak resistance was also complicated. At first, they joined the CNAC but later, under the influence of the communists and the Carpathian Ruthenian Committee in New York, decided to form their own resistance movement. Their goal was to become united in the Americas and after the war present their demands, either to the Czechoslovak or the Soviet governments.[108] However, their individual contribution was not so influenced by the committee in New York. In Canada, they publicly criticized the attitude of the Slovak League, which activity they considered treacherous. They recognized the economic and social development sponsored by the Czechoslovaks during the Interwar period and thus were sympathetic to their cause.[109]

---

104 Bydžovský to Nosek, Feb. 22, 1943. 1167/dův/43, b. 514, c. LAD, AMZV.
105 Ingr to Ambruš, Aug. 19, 1943. 2886-dův.I/2.odděl.1943, b. 514, c. LAD, AMZV.
106 The Czechoslovak government, with support from Moscow, sought approval for their "final solution of the German question" already in 1943. Beneš and the exile government planned the expulsion of Germans from Czechoslovakia. The Allies agreed with this procedure at the conference in Potsdam on the condition that the move would be orderly and humane, which was not the case. It was part of the evacuations and deportations of Germans from Central and Eastern Europe after World War II.
107 Procházka to Ripka, Feb. 15, 1945.é b. 514, c. LAD, AMZV. And Majer to MND, Jan. 11, 1945, 10/45, b. 514, c. LAD, AMZV.
108 *Kronika československé vojenské mise v Kanadě* 25-26. b. 1, c. ČSVMK, VHA-VHÚ.
109 Interview between Rudol Nekola and Vasil Greňo, Feb. 17, 1942. b. 5, c. ČSVMK, VHA-VHÚ.

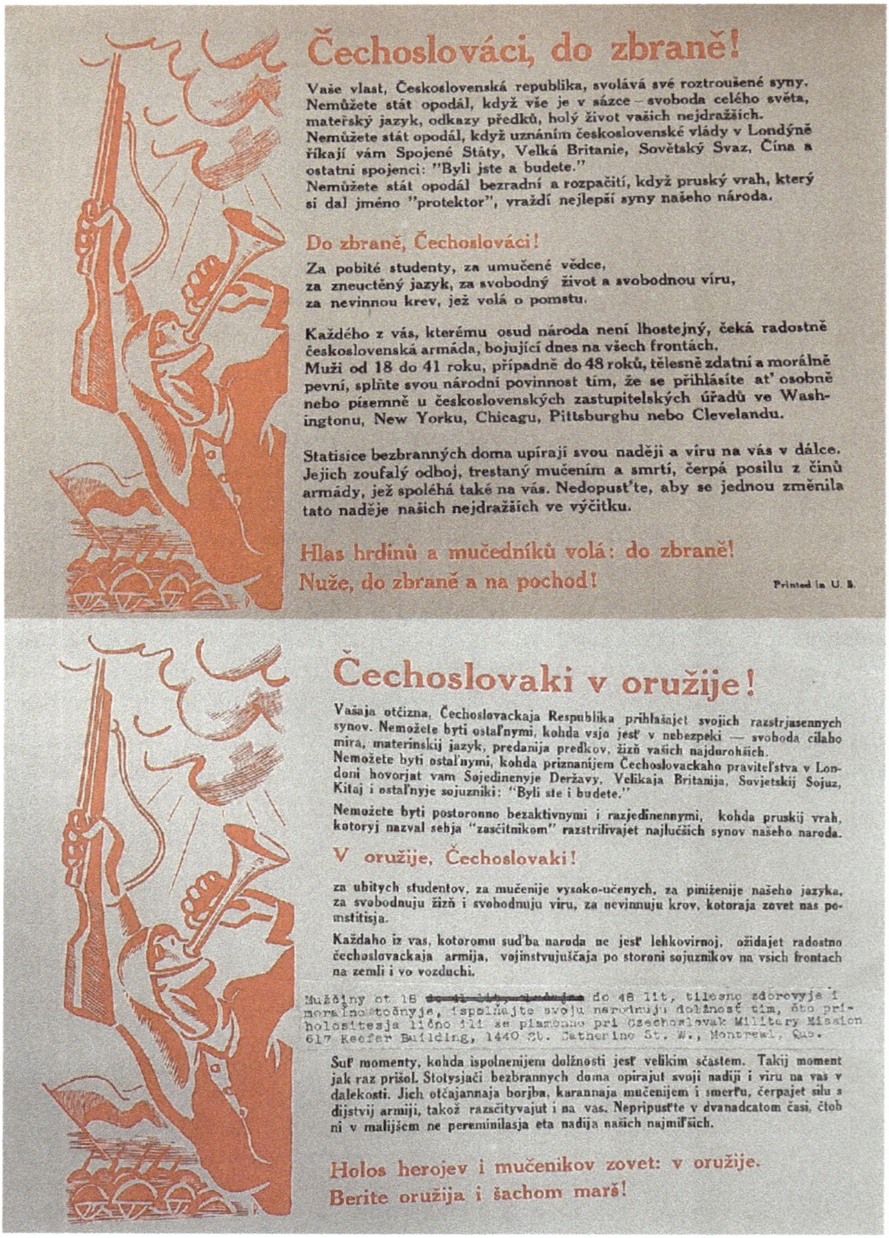

Figure 4: Recruitment posters for Czechoslovak army. Upper one in Czech, lower in Ruthenian. No date. Source: VHA-VHÚ, collection: Československé vojenské mise: Kanada, boxes 3 and 6.

In January 1942, the Ministry of Foreign Affairs of Czechoslovakia tried to persuade Pavel Cibere, the secretary for Carpathian Ruthenia in London, to go to Montréal and convince the Rusyns there to collaborate more with the Czechoslovak resistance. It was the largest organization with 200 members and with only a loose connection to the committee in New York.[110] This trip never materialized, but it did not prevent the Rusyns from participating and contributing.[111] The Czechoslovak military mission attended their meetings, they published leaflets in their language, and some eventually joined the Czechoslovak army. Others at least supported materially the guerrilla movement in Ruthenia that was in part organized by Czechoslovak officers.[112]

The last ethnic group of Czechoslovakia to be examined in this respect is the Jewish one (for Hungarians see note 96). We know that many decided to immigrate to the Americas in 1938 or 1939. However, their participation in the Czechoslovak resistance was not emphasized by the official documents and there are only a few specific mentions of them. They did not receive special attention because they also formed part of the other nationalities, either Czechoslovak, German, Hungarian, or Rusyn. Historian Tomáš Jiránek revealed that in the military statistics the Jews were identified principally according to their religion and not nationality (Jiránek, "činnost a výsledky" 260).

The Czechoslovak resistance, however, did not rely only on their compatriots. As in World War I, they tried to cooperate closely with other Slavic groups in the Americas. Already in 1941, the Czechoslovak National Council in America embraced this idea, and its executive secretary Josef Martínek recommended cooperation with Slovaks, Rusyns, Poles, Yugoslavs, Ukrainians, and non-communist Russians (Martínek). A year later, the American Slav Congress took place in Detroit. The attendance of 2,500 Slavs was respectable[113] but the results were questionable. The Congress did not introduce any statutes and its administrative body was very loose. The only outcomes were the manifestation of a common interest in defeating Hitler's Germany and an increase in the production of the war industry in the US and Canada.[114] In 1944, the meeting in Pittsburgh was similarly unfruitful and after World War II, the congress was split by the emergence of the Cold War (*Report on the American Slav Congress* 17-24). Local partnerships were more successful. The Czechoslovaks with Poles established a committee for mutual cooperation and organized several events to support their armies in England. In November 1942, they celebrated Polish National Independence

---

110 MFAC to Cibere, Jan. 26. 175/dův/42, b. 81, c. LAD, AMZV.

111 Frolka to Martínek, Feb. 3, 1943. b. 49, ACASA.

112 *Kronika československé vojenské mise v Kanadě*, 30. b. 1, c. ČSVMK, VHA-VHÚ.

113 CNCA press service. *Slovanský kongres v Detroitu se zdařil* [Slavic Congress in Detroit Was Successful], Apr. 28, 1942. b. 6, c. ČSVMK, VHA-VHÚ.

114 Zmrhal to Goda, May 15, 1942. b. 49, ACASA.

Day at the famous Massey Hall in Toronto.[115] Otherwise, the partnership proved useful during the fundraising campaign called Tag Day, a collection that raised almost 20,000 dollars.[116]

Conclusion

The motto of the Czechoslovak resistance in the Americas was "[u]nited we win." It had flaws in Canada, as only 6,500 compatriots out of 50 to 60,000 participated directly. At the same time, those active did stick together and helped the Czechoslovak cause. The diplomats led by František Pavlásek focused more on the Canadian public and politicians, and they achieved their goals, albeit some negotiations took longer than expected. The compatriots, including the entrepreneurs, were more active from the economic and social perspectives. They collected more money for Czechoslovak soldiers and refugees than anticipated. The minorities were more divided, but this chapter demonstrates that they should not be excluded from the resistance narrative. It is a paradox that Czech historiography has been interested, so far, mostly in the Czechoslovak military mission in Canada, which was probably the least important of the actors presented here as recruitment, their principal goal, brought only disappointing results. This chapter was written with the aim of providing a more nuanced understanding of this topic.

Works Cited

Archival sources

Archive of the Czechs and Slovaks Abroad (ACASA). Collection: Series 1. Czechoslovak National Coucil in Canada. Boxes 48 and 49.
Vojenský historický archiv-Vojenský ústřední archiv České republiky (VHA-VHÚ) [Military Historical Archive-Military Central Archive of the Czech Republic]. Collection: Československé vojenské mise: Kanada (ČSVMK) [Czechoslovak Military Missions: Canada]. Boxes 1-7.
Archiv ministerstva zahraničních věcí České republiky (AMZV) [Archive of the Ministry of Foreign Affairs of the Czech Republic]. Collection: Londýnský archiv – důvěrný, 1939-1945 (LA-D) [London Archive – Confidential, 1939-1945]. Boxes 4, 6, 26, 81, 177, 204, 216, 221, 514. Collection: Londýnský archiv – obyčejný, 1939-1945 (LAO) [London Archive – Ordinary, 1939-1945]. Boxes 99/100, 143, 152, 233, 443, 444/1, 505.

---

115 *Další podnik čsl.-polského výboru v Torontě* [Another Event of the Czechoslovak-Polish Committee in Toronto], Oct. 1942. b. 6, c. ČSVMK, VHA-VHÚ.
116 CNAC. *Skvělý úspěch čsl.-polského Tag Day* [Great Success of Czechoslovak-Polish Tag Day], Nov. 1942. b. 6, c. ČSVMK, VHA-VHÚ.

Newspapers

Bata Bugle (1944)
Čechoslovák (1943)
The Globe and Mail (1939)
Zpravodaj našej mládeže (1943)

Primary and Secondary Sources

Baláž, Július. "Československá vojenská mise v Kanadě (1941-1943) a Brazílii (1943-1945)" [The
Czechoslovak Military Mission in Canada (1941-1943) and Brazil (1943-1945)]. *Československá
vojenská zahraniční služba v letech 1939-1945* [Czechoslovak Military Foreign Service in the
Years 1939-1945]. Ed. Zlatica Zudová Lešková and Petr Hofman. Prague: Ústav pro soudobé
dějiny a Historický ústav Akademie věd České republiky, 2008. 234-45.
---. "Kronika Československé vojenské mise v Kanadě (1941-1943)" [Chronicle of the Czechoslovak
Military Mission in Canada (1941-1943)]. *Ročenka 2006* (2007): 93-139.
Baťa, Tomáš, and Soňa Sinclairová. *Švec pro celý svět* [Shoemaker for the Whole World]. Prague:
n.p., 1991.
Beneš, Edvard. *Paměti: Od Mnichova k nové válce a novému vítězství* [Memoirs: From Munich to a
New War and a New Victory]. Prague: Orbis, 1948.
Buzek, Karel, Lidmila Wauthierová, and Alica Haasová, eds. *Památník československé Kanady*
[Memorial of Czechoslovak Canada]. Toronto: Čs. národní sdružení, 1943.
Cekota, Antonín. *The Battle of Home: Some Problems of Industrial Community*. Toronto: MacMillan,
1944.
Čermák, Josef. *It All Started with Prince Rupert: The Story of Czechs and Slovaks in Canada*.
Luhačovice: Atelier IM, 2003.
Dejmek, Jindřich. *Edvard Beneš: Politická biografie českého demokrata* II [Edvard Benes: Political
Biography of a Czech Democrat II]. Prague: Karolinum, 2008.
Eighth Census of Canada, 1941, vol. 2. Population by Local Subdivisions. Ottawa: Edmond Cloutier,
1944.
Gellner, John, and John Smerek. *The Czechs and Slovaks in Canada*. Toronto: University of Toronto,
1968.
Hanzlík, František. *Krajané a československý zahraniční odboj 1938-1945* [Compatriots and
Czechoslovak Foreign Resistance 1938-1945]. Prague: Ministerstvo obrany České republiky,
2010.
House of Commons Debates. 3 June 1943. Ottawa: Edmond Clouthier, 1943.
Jiránek, Tomáš. "Československá vojenská mise v Kanadě: činnost a výsledky" [Czechoslovak
Military Mission in Canada: Activities and Results]. *Theatrum historiae* 8 (2011): 247-78.
Jiránek, Tomáš. "Československá vojenská mise v Kanadě za 2. světové války: předhistorie" [The
Czechoslovak Military Mission in Canada during World War II: Prehistory]. *Theatrum historiae* 6
(2010): 163-76.
Jiránek, Tomáš. "Kronika československé vojenské mise v Kanadě (1941-1943)" [Chronicle of the
Czechoslovak Military Mission in Canada (1941-1943)]. *Sborník vědeckých prací Univerzity
Pardubice: Série C* 9 (2003): 205-38.
Kelley, Ninette, and Michael Trebilcock. *The Making of the Mosaic: A History of Canadian
Immigration Policy*. Toronto: University of Toronto Press, 2010.
Konzulární zastoupení Československa v cizině a cizích zemí v Československu v letech 1918-1974
[Consular Representation of Czechoslovakia Abroad and Foreign Countries in Czechoslovakia in
the Years 1918-1974]. Prague: Archivně dokumentační odbor MZV, 1975.

Křen, Jan. *V emigraci: Západní zahraniční odboj 1939-1940* [In Emigration: Western Foreign Resistance 1939-1940]. Prague: Naše vojsko, 1969.

Maršálek, Zdenko. *"Česká," nebo "československá" armáda? Národnostní složení československých vojenských jednotek v zahraničí v letech 1939–1945* ["Czech" or "Czechoslovak" Army? National Composition of Czechoslovak Military Units Abroad in the Years 1939–1945]. Prague: Academia, 2017.

Martínek, Josef. *O slovanské vzájemnosti a naší spolupráci s Americkými Slovany* [About Slavic Reciprocity and Our Cooperation with the American Slavs]. Chicago: České národní sdružení v Americe, 1941.

McCulloch, Tony. "Mackenzie King and the North Atlantic Triangle in the Era of Munich, 1938–1939." *London Journal of Canadian Studies* 36.1 (2022): 1-23.

Pánek, Jaroslav, Oldřich Tůma, et al. *A History of the Czech Lands*. Prague: Karolinum, 2018.

Pánek, Jaroslav, Oldřich Tůma, et al. *Dějiny Českých zemí* [A History of the Czech Lands]. Prague: Karolinum, 2018.

Polišenský, Josef. *Le Canada et la Tchecoslovaquie*. Prague: Orbis, 1967.

Polišenský, Josef. *Úvod do studia dějin vystěhovalectví do Ameriky: 2, Češi a Amerika* [An Introduction to the Study of the History of Immigration to America: 2, Czechs and America]. Prague: Karolinum, 1996.

Příručka o navázání diplomatických styků a diplomatická zastoupení Československa v cizině a cizích zemí v Československu [Handbook on the Establishment of Diplomatic Relations and Diplomatic Representations of Czechoslovakia Abroad and Foreign Countries in Czechoslovakia]. Prague: Archivně dokumentační odbor MZV, 1987.

Report on the American Slav Congress and Associated Organizations, June 26, 1949. Washington: United States Government Printing Office, 1950.

Rovná, Lenka. *Dějiny Kanady* [A History of Canada]. Prague: Lidové noviny, 2001.

Seventh Census of Canada, 1931. Vol. 2: Population by Areas. Ottawa: J. O. Patenaude, 1933.

Sixth Census of Canada, 1921. Vol. 1: Population. Ottawa: F. A. Ackland, 1924.

Sixth Census of Canada, 1921. Vol. 2: Population. Ottawa: F. A. Ackland, 1925.

Stolarik, Mark. M. *Where is My Home? Slovak Immigration to North America, 1870-2010*. New York: Peter Lang, 2012.

Španiel, Oldřich. *Československá armáda druhého odboje* [Czechoslovak Army of the Second Resistance]. Chicago: Československá národní rada v Americe, 1941.

Tóth, Andrej, Lukáš Novotný, and Michal Stehlík. *Národnostní menšiny v Československu 1918-1938: od státu národního ke státu národnostnímu?* [National Minorities in Czechoslovakia 1918-1938: From a National State to a National State?]. Prague: Univerzita Karlova v Praze, Filozofická fakulta, 2012.

Vaculík, Jaroslav. *České menšiny v Evropě a ve světě* [Czech Minorities in Europe and the World]. Prague: Libri, 2009.

Zaoral, Roman. "Přehled archivních fondů k dějinám Čechů v Kanadě" [Overview of Archival Collections]. *České archivy a prameny k dějinám zahraničních Čechů. Sborník příspěvků z mezinárodního vědeckého sympózia konaného ve dnech 27.-28. června 2006 v Českých Budějovicích v rámci 23. světového kongresu Československé společnosti pro vědy a umění* [Czech Archives and Sources for the History of Czechs Abroad: Proceedings of the International Scientific Symposium Held on 27-28 June 2006 in České Budějovice as part of the 23rd World Congress of the Czechoslovak Society for Sciences and Arts]. Prague: Národní archiv, 2007.

Zudová Lešková, Zlatica. "Československá vojenská zahraniční služba 1939-1945: Úvod do problematiky" [Czechoslovak Military Foreign Service 1939-1945: Introduction to the Issue]. *Československá vojenská zahraniční služba v letech 1939-1945* [Czechoslovak Military Foreign Service in the Years 1939-1945]. Ed. Zlatica Zudová Lešková, Petr Hofman, 10-91. Prague: Ústav pro soudobé dějiny a Historický ústav Akademie věd České republiky, 2008.

Sheena Trimble

Shaping Destinies: Women and the Hungarian Refugee Movement to Canada (1956–1958)

Introduction

The Hungarian uprising in the fall of 1956 and the fate of some 200,000 refugees who fled the country following brutal suppression by Soviet forces captivated the attention of Canadian women along with the rest of the world. Canadian advocates of refugee relief found the Liberal government's initial response of simply giving priority to Hungarian immigration applications half-hearted. Those advocating more forceful action sparked a public outcry, taken up by the press and opposition parties. For days, the minister of citizenship and immigration, J. W. Pickersgill, adhered to his department's "gatekeeper" role before finally bowing to pressure (Dirks 193–99; Donaghy 264–67). On November 23, 1956 he sought Cabinet approval to simplify admission procedures and charter aircraft to bring refugees to Canada (DMCI[1], Pickersgill). The movement began in earnest five days later when Pickersgill announced that the Canadian government would bear the cost of transport. By the end of 1958 37,566 Hungarian refugees had been admitted, marking a watershed in Canada's refugee policy (Canada, Parliament, 28 Nov. 1956, 111; "Hungarian Refugee Movement" 1–2, 4). The Hungarians were the first group of refugees admitted in such large numbers in such a short period of time, facilitated by favorable government policies and widespread mobilization within Canadian society (Dreisziger, "Biggest Welcome" 42).

A rich historiography has examined this migration from a range of perspectives, but an analysis of women's actions and attitudes represents an uncharted approach. It has the potential to call into question stereotypical representations of 1950s Canadian women as being singularly preoccupied with domesticity, maternity, and consumerism (Strong-Boag 315–19). Indeed, archival research reveals that Canadian women expressed opinions and took on a variety of roles related to this remarkable migration. Examining those opinions and roles not only offers a novel perspective on Canada's response to the Hungarian refugee crisis, but it also provides insights into the evolving positioning of women in Canadian society.

The 1956 refugee movement replicated the male-female imbalance that had been typical of the smaller waves of Hungarian immigrants that arrived at the turn of the century, during the interwar period and as displaced persons following World War II (Patrias 4–7, 10–12, 20–21). By the 1951 census, the male-female ratio had finally

---

1 Deputy Minister of Citizenship and Immigration fonds.

been reduced to 1 female for every 1.2 males (Dominion Bureau of Statistics, table 32, 1). Still, the weight of intersectionality—the imbrication of two or more subaltern identities (Nakano Glenn 105), woman and ethnic minority in this case—often muted the voices of women of Hungarian origin when it came to expressing their opinions about the admission of the 1956 refugees. Among the refugees, women were clearly in the minority; in 1957 one female refugee was admitted to Canada for every 1.74 males (Kalbach 48). Yet women were accorded a symbolic power that played an important role in the movement.

Historians tend to chronicle the activism regarding Hungarian refugee admission in an anonymous way that provides little information about the individuals involved (Dirks 194–97; Patrias 23–24; Dreisziger, "Toward a Golden Age" 204). Passing references to women can be found in some works, but these provide only snippets of information on women's roles or attitudes. Susan M. Papp's 1986 article on "Hungarian Immigrant Women" reserves only two paragraphs for the 1956 refugees (44). The published autobiographies of four refugee women serve as important primary sources (Grossman; Kende; Romvary; Verrall). Oral history collections developed by the Multicultural History Society of Ontario and the Canadian Museum of Immigration at Pier 21 contribute additional testimonies of transition to life in Canada. By drawing upon these sources, as well as the archives of the Department of Citizenship and Immigration, welfare organizations and women's associations, this chapter provides insights into Canadian women's views on their country's response to the refugee crisis and their actions in support of, or in opposition to, refugee admission. Meanwhile, the accounts of Hungarian refugee women demonstrate that, despite their precarious situation, they found ways to exercise their agency to achieve their desired admission and settlement outcomes.

Facilitating admission, reception, and settlement

On November 6, 1956, just two days after Soviet tanks rolled into Budapest, the Catholic Women's League of Canada sent a letter to Prime Minister Louis St. Laurent expressing "deep admiration for the people of Hungary in their struggle for freedom against a foreign oppressor and urg[ing] that every possible aid be given to alleviate their sufferings" (PCO, Catholic Women's). The significant Catholic presence among earlier Hungarian immigrants and strong anti-communist sentiment undoubtedly impelled the league to action. Other women's associations may not have had the same sectarian motivations, but support for the refugees' rejection of communist tyranny was widespread. As the days and weeks passed, the Canadian Federation of University Women, the Women's Division of the United Nations Association of Canada, the Women's International League for Peace and Freedom, the National Council of Women of Canada, the Women's Missionary Society of the United Church of Canada, and individual women communicated their support for admitting Hungarian refugees

(McLean 3; Local Council of Women of Toronto 2; Department of External Affairs; Atkinson). The desire to help the refugees once they arrived was so profound that a plethora of voluntary organizations engaged in intense activity in many host cities (DMCI, Manion). The fact that countless women and women's associations involved themselves in the reception and settlement of Hungarian refugees would also have been interpreted by the federal government as endorsement of their admission.

The Department of Citizenship and Immigration was responsible, to a certain degree, for the multiplicity of actors involved in receiving the Hungarian refugees. It organized a meeting on November 27, 1956 with representatives of national voluntary agencies, Hungarian Canadian organizations, and the government of Ontario to ensure that the voluntary sector and the provinces would help shoulder the burden of refugee reception and settlement. According to the meeting's minutes (2–3, 9), civil society was to be tapped in unprecedented ways: "the Department . . . made it clear that it was willing to utilize the services of anyone . . . willing to receive and care for a refugee or a refugee family even if only for a short time." Among the thirty-four people present at the meeting only four were women, representing the Canadian Welfare Council (Marion Murphy), the Canadian Hungarian Relief Committee (Peggy Jennings), and the department's Citizenship Branch. Murphy and Jennings expressed concerns that the department's scenario would place a heavy financial burden on homes and voluntary agencies. The deputy minister, Laval Fortier, claimed that the department's limited funds meant that "[t]he only possible solution . . . was to recruit socially-minded persons in Canada to receive and care for the refugees." He responded in a similar vein to Murphy's query as to whether government funding would be made available to help hard-pressed social agencies hire additional staff to meet refugee needs. Fortier claimed that church groups could be used to "develop offers to receive and care for the refugees without the special establishment of a costly government agency" (6, 8).

Having agreed to pay for refugee transport, the department sought to save on all other budget lines. This implied relying heavily upon women's contributions, through their voluntary work and by opening their homes to refugees. Even professional women, a significant portion of the staff of social welfare agencies, were expected to take on extra work with little prospect of additional staff being hired to help with the increased workload. For Fortier, the solution lay in distributing the burden among multiple sources of voluntary assistance (2, 9). Government officials and non-profit representatives alike emphasized the need for coordination. Regional citizenship liaison officers would contact interested organizations at the local level to promote the establishment of "coordinating committees." Constance Hayward, a liaison officer based in Ottawa, was to oversee the work of the officers in the regions. Two other women, Charity Grant in Toronto and Françoise Marchand in Montréal, were among the regional citizenship liaison officers involved (4-5, 8).

A memorandum of 6 December 1956 (DMCI, McCarthy 2–3) outlined the framework for coordination between the department's citizenship and immigration branches while underscoring the preeminence of the latter. The Citizenship Branch was to encourage coordinating committees "to assist" officers of the Immigration Branch by meeting trains, finding accommodation, and distributing "creature comforts." The female liaison officers and the volunteer and professional women who became the backbone of the coordinating committees were thus cast in the role of helpmate to the almost exclusively male immigration officers, "self-made men" who had few qualms about expecting more highly-educated women liaison officers and social workers to follow their lead (Hawkins 337, 96–97).[2] The Catholic Women's League's 1957 annual report provided a typical list of the accessory and gendered tasks that voluntary women were to perform:

> Each Province [sic] reports meeting trains, work at clothing depots, assistance with housing, furnishing and employment and social assistance. Christmas parties, showers, entertainment and providing of wedding receptions with cake, outfitting of bride, etc. The spiritual side was not neglected. Religious articles were distributed, arrangements were made for special Masses, transportation to church provided. (Panaro 83)

The case of the Canadian Welfare Council's Committee on the Welfare of Immigrants

The role of the Canadian Welfare Council, a national, non-profit organization, in the Hungarian refugee movement is of particular interest because of the sizeable representation of women on its staff and advisory committees. Its Committee on the Welfare of Immigrants (CWI), created in 1954 to assemble national organizations with an interest in "the adjustment of immigrants," was no exception (CWI, "Committee," 17 March 1957). In early 1957, Phyllis Burns, an experienced social worker and educator (Harris and Beals 22), became the Director of Welfare Services for the council as well as secretary for the Committee on the Welfare of Immigrants. Burns quickly went to work organizing a special meeting between committee members and government representatives to discuss the Hungarian refugee crisis. Local welfare councils and social agencies had been conveying concerns about challenges at their level and it was thought the committee could facilitate "co-operation between public and private services" and seek "clarification on present policy or the development of new policies" (CWI, 14 Jan. 1957, 2). Burns's background information for the meeting (CWI, Burns, 10 Jan. 1957, 1–4) pinpointed the Department of Citizenship and Immigration policies considered unbefitting the needs and "dignity" of the refugees: housing them in private homes rather than government-financed hostels and providing financial

---

2 Hayward (Knowles 210), Grant (Armstrong-Reid and Murray 345), and Marchand (Bourbeau 101) all had two university degrees.

assistance in the form of vouchers rather than cash and only as a "last resort." Of the thirty-two participants in the meeting of January 14 fifteen were women, representing voluntary associations, welfare agencies, and government (Constance Hayward). Bessie Touzel of the Ontario Welfare Council argued that refugees should have the option of staying in hostels, but Fortier continued to assert that private homes were a better solution because they acclimated refugees to "the Canadian way of life" (5-6).

A second special meeting, scheduled for February 25, was preceded by a memorandum from Burns (CWI, Burns, 22 Jan. 1957, 1–2) outlining concerns raised during consultations with coordinating committees across the country: a diminishing supply of free housing, refugees arriving in communities with limited employment opportunities, and a need to clarify roles between "public officials" and "citizen groups." Of the twenty-nine representatives of social and voluntary agencies and local coordinating committees who attended the meeting, fifteen were women (CWI, 25 Jan. 1957, 1). The absence of government observers allowed for a freer exchange of views and frank criticism of the Department of Citizenship and Immigration's policies, including its miserly approach to providing financial assistance, its refusal to acknowledge the benefits of hostels, and its preoccupation with immediate employment rather than finding the "right job for the refugee" (3, 6, 8-9). Grace Hartman of Sudbury's Hungarian Relief Committee reported that several refugees sent to her city had left for Toronto as soon as they had made enough money. Refugee trepidations about life in small cities were matched by some vexation with the refugees themselves. Hartman referred to grumblings in Sudbury that presaged criticisms that slowly began to gain ground across Canada based on the idea that "too much [was] being provided for Hungarians giving them a false idea of their own responsibilities" (3, 7).

At the conclusion of the meeting, it was decided that a letter would be sent to Minister Pickersgill to seek clarification on certain policies. The committee also recommended that the minister be informed of "[t]he need for more direction and control in the treatment of Hungarians who [were] confused by the complete freedom . . . accorded to them in contrast to what they [had] been accustomed to" (11–12). Jean Henshaw, of the Montréal Travellers' Aid Society, undoubtedly played a role in making this recommendation as she expressed similar sentiments in a November letter (CWI, Henshaw). Citing her thirteen years of work with postwar immigrants, including thirty months in displaced persons camps, she felt well-qualified to offer this reductionist interpretation. Historian Nandor F. Dreisziger's assessment that the Hungarian refugees had grown accustomed to a system that placed them in jobs and housing, paid for vacations, and provided free education and medical treatment does, however, give some credence to her observations ("Refugee Experience" 72–73).

Joseph Kage, Jean-Baptiste Lanctot, Dorothy Gregg, Henshaw, and Burns prepared the letter for Minister Pickersgill and had it sent on March 12, 1957 (CWI, McCutcheon 1–6; CWI, 8 Apr. 1957, 2). His response revealed an unwillingness to adopt what the committee saw as best practices in social welfare when it came to providing adequate financial assistance, housing immigrants in hostels, or placing them in suitable employment (CWI, Pickersgill 1-7). Although disappointed with the minister's response, the committee concluded that government had at least recognized the value of a public-private partnership in the "field of immigration" (CWI, 8 Apr. 1957, 2, 5). Another decade would elapse, however, before the Department of Citizenship and Immigration would develop more openness to the advice of social welfare experts and the women who made up their ranks (Hawkins 170, 322).

Assessing women's roles in receiving the refugees

Although the Committee on the Welfare of Immigrants had limited success in convincing the Department of Citizenship and Immigration to adopt some of its recommended measures, it remained an important player in the relationship between government and non-profit actors. Using its access to senior government officials, the committee kept up the pressure to clarify roles between the two sectors and to implement best practices in social welfare. It also served as a conduit between coordinating committees and senior department officials, thus serving as an alternative source of information to front-line immigration officers. In functioning at almost complete parity, the committee provided an important national tribune for women involved in refugee reception and settlement. Traditional women activists—members of women's organizations—were among the initial members, but the Hungarian refugee movement brought more professional welfare workers onto the committee (CWI, 29 Oct. 1957, 1; CWI, "Expected Attendance 29 October 1957" n.d.). This mirrored what was happening at the local level where almost all the coordinating committees included the participation of welfare councils. Since women's longstanding predominance in the charitable welfare sector was matched by their predominance in its professional version, the welfare councils were usually represented by professional women (CWI, Address List, n.d. [1957] 1-2; CWI, Dyson 1-2). Phyllis Burns was perhaps the epitome of the new face of immigrant welfare services. As an experienced and respected social worker, she provided critical support and information for the Committee on the Welfare of Immigrants and interacted with senior immigration officials on a relatively equal footing. That she had gained the respect of the department was demonstrated in August 1957 when the new minister of citizenship and immigration invited her, along with a handful of men representing other national organizations, to discuss curbing refugee admissions (CWI, Burns, 12 Aug. 1957, 1).

Some coordinating committees developed good working relationships with local immigration authorities while others were sidelined by self-sufficient officers. The Ottawa coordinating committee provided a rare example of a Hungarian Canadian woman attaining a leadership role in the Anglo-Celtic-dominated society of the day by appointing "Mrs. Javorsky, President of the local Hungarian Association," as co-chair with a male counterpart (CWI, Address List 1-2; CWI, Dyson 1-2). The male-dominated Immigration Branch was not always well-disposed to working with the more feminized Citizenship Branch (CWI, Burns, 22 Feb. 1957; Hawkins 96–97). In Montréal, Françoise Marchand either did not face such obstacles or found a way to overcome them. According to Yvan Corbeil, Lisette Laurent-Boyer, and Mireille Richard, Marchand served as "la cheville coordinatrice des efforts que chacun déploya pour venir en aide aux réfugiés [the linchpin in coordinating the efforts of everyone involved in aiding the refugees]" (52, 54–55).

The archives consulted do not show women's associations making the kind and quantity of political intercessions that they had made during the migration of some 190,000 displaced persons to Canada between 1945 and 1952 (Trimble 83–100). Comparing the two movements is complicated, however, by the fact that the migration of displaced persons occurred over a longer period and involved a greater number and diversity of immigrants. Since the Hungarians benefited from considerable political support within government and civil society, women's associations may have concluded that their backing was superfluous. This hypothesis is supported to some extent by a resolution, passed by the National Council of Women in June 1957, that made a link between the generous response to the Hungarian crisis and the desirability of applying that approach to refugees who had been languishing in European camps for years. They, like the Hungarians, were depicted as being fervently anti-communist and thus worthy of asylum despite their age or infirmity (McLean 5).

Women on the front lines in Canada and Europe

Some organizations, other than the local coordinating committees, were formed for the sole purpose of helping Hungarian refugees. Such was the case of Montréal's *Œuvre des réfugiés hongrois* (ORH), created in December 1956 to consolidate Catholic aid among the French-speaking majority (Conseil 21). Gertrude Notebaert, a social worker and director of the Service d'accueil aux voyageurs, also took on the directorship of the ORH. She had an astute awareness of the challenges of providing immigrant services in a province where government and citizens alike were at best ambivalent and at worst hostile to postwar immigration, seen as rarely reinforcing the francophone, Catholic majority. She described her work as being subject to an "[a]lternance de popularité, d'impopularité, d'indifférence" [alternating popularity, unpopularity, indifference], but the Hungarian refugee movement, thought to be composed principally of Catholics, created "[u]n ouragan de miséricorde pour des persécutés du communisme [a hurricane of mercy for the persecuted by communism]" (1–6). Notebaert's work facilitated the admission of Hungarian refugees to Quebec and their settlement in the French-speaking milieu.

On November 5, 1956, Peggy (Mrs. Douglas) Jennings assumed the direction of the newly created Canadian Hungarian Relief Committee, organized to help the Canadian Hungarian Federation with fundraising that had begun during the Hungarian uprising (DMCI, Grant 1). The creation of the relief committee dovetailed with a shift in responsibility for fundraising from the federation to the Canadian Red Cross Society, which worked with associations such as Jennings's committee to raise and distribute funds. Dreisziger described how men and women of Hungarian origin were supplanted "by prominent Canadians, many of them women, who in turn could call upon influential Canadian individuals or institutions to help" ("Toward a Golden Age" 205). Jennings's involvement in Hungarian refugee initiatives reached a point where the Department of Citizenship and Immigration arranged for her to spend a month in Austria in December 1956. A Toronto member of Parliament (DMCI, Hellyer) outlined the expectation that upon her return she would use her "new knowledge and up-to-date information" to help with fundraising and to work with voluntary agencies to aid refugees. It is difficult to fathom how Jennings obtained such support for this undertaking. There is no indication that she had any special training, but she apparently satisfied other criteria. As a member of the conservative Imperial Order Daughters of the Empire, she and Mrs. B. B. Osler had created Canadian Scene in 1951 to provide the ethnic press with an alternative perspective to possible communist propaganda (Imperial Order Daughters 4; Niinistö n.d.). In other words, her cold warrior credentials were well established.

In December 1956 the Canadian Red Cross sent a team of seven people to Austria to run a refugee camp in Wiener Neustadt. The positions of director and doctor were reserved for men, but all other positions—nurse, social worker, nutritionist, administrator, and clothing specialist—were filled by women (DMCI, Stanbury 1956 and 1957). In May 1957, Olive Zeron, the camp's social worker and former director of the Windsor YWCA, shared her perceptions of Hungarian refugees in a YWCA publication. According to Zeron, young Hungarians were forced to work in factories far from their families and were thus deprived of a "home life" and "moral or mental education." Unused to so-called "normal life," the refugees would need time and the aid of Canadians to adjust. Thanks to their "Christian heritage" and democratic values, Canadians were well equipped to help with this process and teach attitudes such as gratitude, since the Hungarians had "never been taught to be thankful" (7–8). A June 1957 YWCA workshop report echoed the sentiment that Hungarian refugees lacked gratitude, but the author had sufficient insight to question what YWCA women expected from doing charitable work (Frontiers of Faith 2). The accounts of women refugees often speak of gratitude, thus suggesting a disconnect between the expectations of some Canadians and the modes of expression of some refugees (Romvary 93; Mihály 145). Zeron concluded her article by predicting that the intelligence and adaptability of the refugees, combined with Canada's proven capacity to receive the world's poor and persecuted and turn them into contributing Canadians, would finally win out. Instead of drawing upon her professional training to develop a deeper understanding of the Hungarian experience, Zeron reinforced stereotypes of the moral superiority of countries like Canada based on Christian and democratic tropes. Historian Franca Iacovetta has indicated that this interpretive frame was not foreign to other Canadians working in the field of social welfare during the Cold War (487–88).

In February 1957, Jean Huggard, another Canadian social worker, was sent by the Department of Citizenship and Immigration to teach English in a camp in the Netherlands. Huggard offered less moralistic predictions of refugee adaptation than Zeron. She believed that although "some [would] certainly adapt readily and do well, others [would] just as certainly have many rough times (107)." In her assessment, housewives "seemed to be less worried about the future. Perhaps because they had never assumed any active part before, they felt a good measure of security as long as their own family unit was maintained" (274–75). This interpretation of the lived experience of Hungarian housewives seems colored more by the perspective of a woman used to working outside the home than informed by a professional lens. As demonstrated by Iacovetta, the social work lens of the time was as much influenced by cold war ideologies as by a "family ideology" of breadwinning fathers and dependent wives focused on home and children (484, 489–91).

Change of government, change in Canadian attitudes

In the summer of 1957, the Hungarian refugee movement fell victim to the newly elected Progressive Conservative government's fears of an economic downturn. On July 11, 1957 the Cabinet accepted the recommendation of the acting minister of citizenship and immigration, E. D. Fulton, to discontinue the admission of refugees without "pre-arranged" employment. Friends, voluntary agencies, and church groups were removed from the list of authorized sponsors (DMCI, Press Release, 26 July 1957; DCI, Fortier, 10 June 1957, 1-4; Hawkins 116). Curtailing the movement had been in the works since at least mid-April, with the Liberal government still in power (Hidas 126–27). A memorandum had been sent to all immigration offices in Europe on May 1, 1957 explaining that "selection [was] to be restricted" to refugees who had been visaed prior to the date of the memorandum; to those who had wintered in specially arranged camps in the United Kingdom, the Netherlands, and France; and to refugees being selected by "special teams" in Austria, Italy, and Yugoslavia. Thereafter, visas would only be issued to refugees sponsored by close relatives and/or with prearranged employment (DMCI, Acting Chief). Ultimate decisions regarding further admissions or restrictions were to wait until after the upcoming general election on June 10, 1957 (DCI,[3] Ignatieff; DMCI, Fortier 16 May 1957).

On August 7, 1957 Phyllis Burns attended a meeting between Minister Fulton and representatives of major national voluntary organizations. The minister justified curbing the admission of Hungarian refugees by indicating that public opinion

---

3 Department of Citizenship and Immigration fonds.

seemed to be turning against them, a trend likely to worsen if the winter brought "serious unemployment." Burns regretted the negative impact this curtailment would have on Canada's international reputation, as Austria would be left with the burden of caring for some 30,000 remaining refugees while a "have" country like Canada closed its doors. Burns and Joseph Kage, of the Jewish Immigrant Aid Society, also challenged the department's plan to fund return trips to Hungary for "ringleaders" of refugee discontent. They suggested that these situations warranted further investigation to determine whether the refugees had "legitimate grievances or specific personal problems," in which case offers of help would be more appropriate (CWI, Burns, 12 Aug. 1957, 3, 6–7).

Women's views on the continued admission of Hungarian refugees were decidedly divergent as the movement approached the one-year mark. The Lethbridge, Alberta chapter of the Imperial Order Daughters of the Empire was concerned about the burden cities would bear for unemployed refugees once the Department of Citizenship and Immigration's one year of support came to an end (2 Oct. 1957; compare DMCI, Press Release 1956). In December 1957 Etta Burko of the Montréal Council of Social Agencies confirmed a decline in public sympathy for the Hungarians. That same month Margaret Peck, a social worker in Montréal, tried to enlist the support of the Committee on the Welfare of Immigrants to speak out against the government's decision to "shut off" the immigration of refugees. The committee decided that getting involved in admission issues was beyond its remit, thus reflecting a refusal to link admission and settlement policies (CWI, 4 Dec. 1957, 5; CWI, 11 Dec. 1957, 4).

On May 10, 1958 Minister Fulton sent a proposal to the Cabinet to pay travel costs for a maximum of 3,500 refugees provided they had applied for visas before the end of April 1958 and would arrive before the end of the year. Ellen Fairclough inherited these dormant recommendations when she became minister of citizenship and immigration on May 12, 1958. She immediately came under pressure from the United Nations High Commissioner for Refugees and the Intergovernmental Committee for European Migration to participate more wholeheartedly in clearing Hungarian refugee camps. In a June recommendation to the Cabinet, she maintained the limit of 3,500 but extended the deadline for visa applications to 31 August 1958 (DMCI, Fairclough 1–3). Being a woman did not make Fairclough more inclined to compassion or less concerned about Canada's economic situation. In her memorandum to the Cabinet, she made it clear that once the deadline or maximum number had been reached, Hungarians would have to apply for admission as ordinary immigrants and pay their own passage to Canada (3). The limits of Fairclough's compassion were patently obvious when she discussed Canada's potential contribution to "the final settlement of the Hungarian refugee problem" with the other members of the Cabinet in July 1958. She frankly declared that "it might be considered that Canada had done enough, if not too much, in this matter" and it would be sufficient to offer to facilitate the admission of one-third the number that the United States had agreed to take, thus around 1,100 refugees (PCO, Cabinet Conclusions, 14 July 1958, 3-4).

Shortly after Fairclough's appointment, the YWCA's Public Affairs and World Service Education Committee passed a resolution commending the federal government for its "generous treatment of Hungarian refugees" while asking that 3,000 more be admitted (YWCA, Board of Directors 6–7). The board of directors declined to send the resolution to the government without first consulting member associations. In the version sent to local associations, 3,000 was replaced with "a number." Although the majority of respondents decided to support this lukewarm resolution, in some cases it provoked "lively" discussion. In St. Thomas (Ontario) those opposed to the resolution pointed to "rising unemployment figures and the failure on the part of many Hungarian immigrants to make any attempt to integrate" (YWCA, Replies from Associations 1-4). The middle-class women involved in women's associations were not only sensitive to the vagaries of the economy, but they also had very specific ideas of how the refugees should behave after their arrival in Canada. The Hungarian refugees experienced upheavals that ranged from the hope in October 1956 of establishing more democratic institutions, through brutal repression that cost the lives of relatives and friends, to exile a few weeks later (Dreisziger, "Refugee Experience" 73). Yet only a few months after their arrival, some Canadian women reproached them for their difficulty in settling into an entirely new situation. These women, by expressing their disappointment at this lack of enthusiasm for what they saw as the great gift of living in the "free world," contributed to a climate that closed the doors to all but a few more refugees.

Voices of Hungarian refugee women

The voices of women refugees were certainly not the most resounding in the Canadian public sphere. The Department of Immigration and Citizenship archives consulted revealed only one letter from a woman refugee and one from a Canadian woman of Hungarian origin. In the latter case, Mrs. R. Virag received a letter from relatives, dated 26 January 1957, describing their desperate situation in a French camp managed by private companies that made them work for miserable wages and housed them in rudimentary conditions. Mrs. Virag forwarded a translation of the letter to the Canadian Red Cross, which in turn sent it to the deputy minister of citizenship and immigration (DMCI, Wilson 1957). In December 1956 Minister Pickersgill had arranged to have France accommodate 3,000 refugees during the winter of 1956–1957. Camp conditions and the forced wait fostered mistrust and discontent among refugees quartered in France and in similar camps in the Netherlands and the United Kingdom (Butler; M. T. qtd. in Kocsis 37).

In her letter, refugee Maria Egger sought to know why she could not find a position teaching English to Hungarians despite her Ph.D. in English from the University of London and her years of experience in Hungary (DMCI, Egger). Apprehensions about the ability to continue one's career in Canada were widespread among the refugees and women shared this concern. Egger's letter raised the question of the discriminatory barriers refugees faced in finding work even when language and skill transfer were not issues. Márta Mihály, a forestry student from Sopron University, was appalled by the expectation that she and her classmates take menial jobs during the vacation period, a real waste of skills in her opinion (146–47). Eve Gabori (1978), a librarian in Hungary, and her husband adopted a perspective more in keeping with the Department of Citizenship and Immigration's expectations: believing that their exile had reduced them to nothing, they would take any job. Fortuitous circumstances and a spirit of initiative enabled Mrs. Gabori to resume her career as a librarian in a relatively short time.

One refugee, Mrs. Gabor Gido, became the subject of a long memorandum from Deputy Minister Fortier to Minister Fulton due to letters she had sent—two to the prime minister, four to Queen Elizabeth, and one to President Eisenhower—asking for help in returning to Europe. In January 1957, the Gidos had been placed with a family in Edmonton. Mrs. Gido soon began to complain about this arrangement, the lack of opportunities for her husband to practice his trade, and the perception that her family was receiving less assistance than other Hungarian refugees. She threatened to go to Ottawa to protest, gathering other refugees to her cause along the way. Fortier advised Fulton not to respond to Mrs. Gido, whom he described as "a chronic complainer" (DMCI, 5 Sept. 1957). She may very well have been the type of person Burns and Kage saw as needing support to overcome a difficult transition rather than dismissal as a troublemaker.

Refugees protested the policy of dispersing them across the country in areas they considered too provincial. One woman and her family, sent to Vancouver, saw the dispersal policy as a circumventable inconvenience because "they turned around and headed back to Toronto straight away" (J. G. qtd. in Kocsis 74). Susan (Zsuzsa) Romvary managed to convince immigration officials in Montréal to allow her family to remain there instead of continuing to Edmonton (91). In March 1957 Pickersgill declared that refugees were not "sent anywhere without their own consent" (CWI, Pickersgill 4-5). Yet, Judy Bing Stoffman's parents, accustomed to life in a "police state" (Stoffman), assumed that their only option was to remain in Vancouver even though they had friends and relatives and the prospect of work in Montréal. When Marta Hidy and her husband, both classical musicians, learned that their destination was Winnipeg, they asked an immigration officer if they could go to Montréal or Toronto instead. He explained that the government was sending refugees to different cities and provinces to tap into the resources necessary to help them. Canada being a free country, they could choose later to go wherever they wanted. They remained in Winnipeg for years, giving life to the music scene there before their careers took them to Toronto (Hidy).

The relationship between Hungarian refugees and Canadians played a role in admission by opening the door to other refugees. In her autobiography, Eva Kende provided a vivid description of the encounter between Hungarian refugees and charity women in Winnipeg in February 1957. Kende descended from the train as one of a "ragtag group" of refugees welcomed by well-dressed women ready to set them on the path to "becoming Canadian." Kende found the women sincere, "even if their understanding of [the refugees'] plight was somewhat deficient." Positive relationships developed in the context of the government's plan to house refugees in private homes could be used to persuade other families to accommodate refugees. They also made for good press. In May 1957, the women's magazine *Chatelaine* published an article about the Mayers, a couple hosted by an affluent surgeon's family (Locke, "Can the Hungarians Fit In?" qtd. in Korinek). Historian Valerie Korniek described the article as "romanticizing" the refugees and praising the generosity of Canadians and the "democratic consumer paradise" that was Canada (285). Mrs. M. Filwood, a reader responding to the article, was impressed that Katarin (Katey) Mayer "ironed clothes for the doctor's wife and . . . did other helpful duties for her, just out of sheer enjoyment of helping" (Filwood). Neither the author of the article nor its readers looked beyond the surface to consider the challenges of feeling indebted to one's hosts, obligated to work as a cleaner in a hospital, and compelled to change one's name in order to "Canadianize."

Although their voices were seldom heard in public debates about admitting the Hungarians, women refugees played a symbolic role in those debates. Stories of escape from the clutches of communism fascinated most Canadians, who not only consumed them for their compelling nature, but also because such stories confirmed their worldview (F. L. qtd. in Kocsis 86). Agota Gabor, who arrived with her mother on one of the first refugee flights, said her youth attracted the attention of the assembled journalists. Before she could greet her father and brother, who had been in Canada since 1948, the journalists impelled her to "touch the ground of freedom" (Gabor), thus spoiling the family reunion but providing images and storylines that fit Canadian constructions of the refugee movement. On January 25, 1957, a member of Parliament extolled Canadian generosity toward the Hungarian refugees, while foregrounding women and children: "We are dealing with babies, little children, mothers and others who . . . have done more than all others to unmask communism and indicate to the world the true nature of this vicious force." (Canada, Parliament, 25 Jan. 1957, 675). The "and others" were the men who made up the majority of refugees and certainly the majority of those admitted to Canada. By April 30, 1958 22,764 male refugees of all ages had been admitted as compared with 13,150 female refugees (DCI, "Hungarian Refugees"). The speaker clearly saw women and children as poignant victims who inspired sympathy. Saving babies and mothers also painted Canada in a more heroic role than receiving relatively healthy young men would. Yet, part of the Department of Citizenship and Immigration's early reluctance to respond to the crisis by admitting large numbers of refugees was due to mistaken information suggesting that most of the refugees were women, children, and old men. During a Cabinet meeting on 14 November 1956, Minister Pickersgill expressed the opinion that such refugees would be better assisted by sending relief to Europe and that Canada should only admit refugees "who could find employment" or offers of sponsorship (PCO, Cabinet Conclusions, 14 Nov. 1956, 7–8).

The case of Ibolya Grossman, a widowed mother of an adolescent son, seems to suggest that the disinclination to admit women without men abated relatively quickly, since she did not report any difficulty in obtaining her visa in December 1956. The assistance that she and her son received from Jewish organizations and employers in Austria and in Canada may well have facilitated her entry into the country (Grossman 79-80, 83, 85, 97). It is also possible that the Department of Citizenship and Immigration became more open to the admission of unmarried women when it became apparent that they represented a very small portion of the refugee population. Eighty-two percent of adult women who arrived in Canada were married, as compared with fifty-two percent of adult men (Hidas 134). Admitting women as part of a couple presented less of a risk than admitting single women since the wife could always be supported by the "male breadwinner," in keeping with the 1950s view of the division of labor between husband and wife (Prentice et al. 337). Eve Gabori and her husband were flabbergasted at the ease with which the decision to accept them was made. When Mrs. Gabori met Canadian officials in Austria, she found them so nice that their attitude seemed suspicious. She was also surprised by their lack of interest in her religion and her excuses for joining the communist party (Gabori). Both Minister Pickersgill and Deputy Minister Fortier had made it clear to their Royal Canadian Mounted Police colleagues, responsible for security screening, that the refugees should not be considered as security risks unless there was strong evidence to support such a charge (Whitaker 85; DCI, Fortier, 6 Nov. 1956, 26 Nov. 1956). Their desire to flee Hungary was generally seen as sufficient proof of their rejection of communism.

Women among the Hungarian refugees were, according to Susan M. Papp, "better educated . . . , younger and more adaptable to life in Canada" than pre-World War II immigrants (42). They joined the women's committees of cultural centers and churches linked to Hungarian Canadian communities and breathed new life into associated activities. Despite their political choice in seeking refuge in Canada, becoming involved in political issues in their host country, including immigration policy, was not a priority for the majority of Hungarian women who arrived between 1956 and 1958 (Kocsis 103).

Conclusion

The Hungarian refugees' sacrifices in rejecting Soviet-style communism won the admiration of many Canadians, including women and women's groups, who expressed support for their admission to Canada in letters to government and through their various actions to help the Hungarians resettle. Long concerned with the "Canadianization" of immigrants (Prentice et al. 54–74), many of these women thought that the refugees' anti-communist rebellion made them ideal candidates for rapid and successful integration and deserving beneficiaries of the assistance of well-meaning Canadians like themselves. Their good intentions began to subside in the face of an economic downturn and their judgment that the Hungarians were not sufficiently grateful for the generosity of Canadians and the opportunity of living in Canada. The election of a Progressive Conservative government in June 1957 and its uneasiness about the economic situation emboldened those calling for an abatement of the Hungarian refugee movement. As minister of citizenship and immigration, Ellen Fairclough viewed adjusting to a less favorable economic situation as more important than humanitarian concerns for refugees that had already benefited significantly from Canadian largesse. Some women's associations also saw the Hungarians as overshadowing their ongoing crusade to convince Canada to accept the "hard core" of displaced persons still languishing in European camps, a deserving anti-communist population that had suffered longer than the Hungarians (Vancouver Young Women's 2).

The Hungarian refugee movement also brought to the fore the growing influence of professional women working for social agencies that were increasingly turning their attention to immigrant welfare. The expertise of these women, mostly social workers, and the increasing importance of the organizations they worked for facilitated their access to immigration policymakers. The Canadian Welfare Council's Committee on the Welfare of Immigrants and its secretary, Phyllis Burns, were prime examples of the trend towards feminized professionalization of immigrant services. Although women welfare professionals promoted approaches to Hungarian refugee settlement that were more adapted to the refugees' needs than the government's budget, their interpretations of refugee backgrounds and aspirations were still colored by Canada's Cold War and family ideologies. The government's need to draw on civil society to access sufficient resources to resettle the large mass of refugees created an opportunity for both volunteer and professional women to try to influence the policy contours of Hungarian migration to Canada. Yet, neither of these groups of women escaped the gendered expectations of the types of contributions they could make or that they play subordinate roles to male immigration officers.

Despite their advocacy on behalf of the Hungarian refugees, mainstream women's associations and immigrant serving agencies remained dominated by the Anglo-Celtic majority. They welcomed immigrant and ethnicized women as lambda members or volunteers, but seldom promoted them to leadership roles (Iacovetta 488–89). Women organizers from the dominant society had few qualms about supplanting women of Hungarian origin in the fundraising campaign on behalf of refugees, since they saw themselves as possessing the skills necessary for a better-organized and more professional approach (Wipper 86–89).

Women were solidly outnumbered in the Hungarian refugee movement, but well over 8,000 adult women arrived and expressed, sometimes through action rather than words, their opinions of the arrangements they encountered in Canada. Refugee women were also present in political debates on the admission of Hungarian refugees when their stories were used to influence public opinion. Language and cultural barriers and their subaltern positioning made it difficult for them to make demands related to their admission or that of other refugees, but their stories reveal their efforts to shape their own Canadian destinies.

Works Cited

Archival records and government publications

Individual records and publications
Atkinson, Mrs. H. 9 Nov. 1956. Letter to J. W. Pickersgill. Jack Pickersgill fonds. MG32 B34. Vol. 57. File I-2-5545-J. Library and Archives Canada. Ottawa. Qtd. in Hidas 71.
Canada. Parliament. 28 Nov. 1956. House of Commons Debates. 22nd Parliament. 4th Session. Vol. 1.
Canada. Parliament. 25 Jan. 1957. House of Commons Debates. 22nd Parliament. 5th Session. Vol. 1.
Conseil des œuvres de Montréal. 22 May 1957. Rapport général des activités, 1956–1957. Montréal: Centre populaire de documentation.
Department of External Affairs fonds. 16 Nov. 1956. Memorandum to Canadian Embassy, Vienna. RG25. Vol. 160. File 5475-EA-4-40. Library and Archives Canada. Qtd. in Hidas 64.
Dominion Bureau of Statistics. Table 32. Population by Origin and Sex, for Provinces and Territories, 1951. Ninth Census of Canada, 1951. Vol. 1. Population, General Characteristics. Ottawa: Queen's Printer and Controller of Stationery, 1953.
Imperial Order Daughters of the Empire, Alberta Chapter fonds. 1951-1952. Summary of Reports. PR067 1983.456. Vol. 3. File 42. Provincial Archives of Alberta, Edmonton.
---. Lethbridge Municipal Chapter. 2 Oct. 1957. Minutes, regular meeting. Alberta Chapter fonds. PR067. Municipal Chapter series. PR0267.003, ACC PR 1985.198/0006. Provincial Archives of Alberta.
Local Council of Women of Toronto fonds. 12 Feb. 1957. Minutes, sub-executive meeting. F805. Vol. MU6363. File F805-1-0-13. Toronto: Archives of Ontario.
McLean. Mrs. Graeme. June 1957b. Paper Prepared in Support of Halifax Resolution and Read at Annual Meeting of N. C. W. in Montréal. National Council of Women of Canada fonds. MG28 I25. Vol. 125. File 4. Library and Archives Canada.
Notebaert, Gertrude. 17 June 1965. Rapport de la directrice. Assemblée annuelle. Service d'accueil aux voyageurs et immigrants. Vol. 48. File 575. Fédération des Œuvres de Charité Canadiennes Françaises fonds. F03 302. Archives de Centraide du Grande Montréal.
Panaro, Mrs. M. A. Oct. 1957. Immigration Report. 37th Annual Convention, 19–23 Oct. 1957. Catholic Women's League of Canada fonds. MG28 I345. Vol. 3. File 11. Library and Archives Canada.
Vancouver Young Women's Christian Association fonds. 18 Feb. 1958. Minutes, board of directors' meeting. RBSC-ARC-1588. 3-13-1. Rare Books and Special Collections. University of British Columbia.

Multiple records from specific archival fonds
Committee on the Welfare of Immigrants (CWI). Canadian Council on Social Development fonds. MG28 I10. Ottawa: Library and Archives Canada.
Meeting Minutes
14 Jan. 1957. Special meeting. Vol. 332. File 5.
25 Feb. 1957. Special meeting. Vol. 332. File 4.

8 April 1957. Vol. 332. File 7.
29. Oct. 1957. Vol. 332. File 7.
4 Dec. 1957. Meeting Concerning the Payment of Cash Assistance to Immigrants. Vol. 332. File 8.
11 Dec. 1957. Meeting Agenda Committee. Vol. 332. File 8.
14 Oct. 1958. Vol. 332. File 10.

Correspondence and other Documents
Address List for Hungarian Committee Meeting Invitations. n.d. [1957]. Vol. 332. File 4.
Burns, Phyllis. 10 Jan. 1957. Memorandum to CWI. Vol. 332. File 5.
---. 22 Feb. 1957. Memorandum to Special Meeting re Hungary Refugees. Vol. 332. File 4.
---. 12 Aug. 1957. Memorandum re Conference on Immigration. Vol. 332. File 7.
"Committee on the Welfare of Immigrants." 17 March 1957. Background information. Vol. 332. File 3.
Dyson, William A. 7 Feb. 1957. Memorandum to Phyllis Burns. Vol. 332. File 4.
"Expected Attendance 29 Oct. 1957" Meeting. n.d. [1957]. Vol. 332. File 5.
Henshaw, Jean. 4 Nov. 1957. Letter to George Nowlan, Minister of National Revenue. Vol. 332. File 9.
McCutcheon, M. Wallace. 12 March 1957. Letter as President, Canadian Welfare Council to J. W.
    Pickersgill, Minister of Citizenship and Immigration. Vol. 332. File 8.
Pickersgill, J. W. 25 March 1957. Letter to M. Wallace McCutcheon. Vol. 332. File 7.

Department of Citizenship and Immigration fonds (DCI). RG76. Library and Archives Canada.
Fortier, Laval. 6 Nov. 1956. Memorandum as Deputy Minister of Citizenship and Immigration to L. H.
    Nicholson, RCMP Commissioner. Vol. 167. File 3-25-11-40. Qtd. in Whitaker 85.
---. 26 Nov. 1956. Memorandum to J. W. Pickersgill. Vol. 167. File 3-25-11-40. Qtd. in Whitaker 85.
"Hungarian Refugees Granted Landing Status, Age Group, Sex, and Marital Status, Eighteen Months
    ended 30 Apr. 1958." Vol. 863. File 555-54-565. Qtd. in Hidas 134.
Ignatieff, George. 14 May 1957. Memorandum as Ambassador to Yugoslavia to External Affairs. Vol.
    864. File 555-54-565-9. Qtd. in Hidas 129.

Deputy Minister of Citizenship and Immigration fonds (DMCI). RG26. Library and Archives Canada.
Acting Chief, Operations Division. 1 May 1957. Memorandum. Vol. 111. File 3-24-12-1.
Butler, R. A. 25 Feb. 1957. Letter to J. W. Pickersgill, Vol. 112. File 3-24-12-6.
Cabinet, 23 Nov. 1956. Record of Decision. Vol. 111. File 3-24-12-1.
Egger, Maria. 15 Jan. 1957. Letter to Immigration Minister. Vol. 111. File 3-24-12-1.
Fairclough, Ellen. 24 June 1958. Memorandum to Cabinet. Vol. 111. File 3-24-12-1.
Fortier, Laval. 16 May 1957. Letter to Jules Léger, Under-Secretary of State for External Affairs. Vol.
    112. File 3-24-12. Qtd. in Hidas 129.
---. 10 June 1957. Memorandum as Deputy Minister to Acting Minister (E. D. Fulton). Vol. 111. File 3-24-
    12-1.
---. 5 September 1957. Memorandum to Acting Minister. Vol. 111. File 3-24-12-1.
Grant, Charity. 7 Nov. 1956. Memorandum to Françoise Marchand. Vol. 117. File 3-24-34-1.
Hellyer, Paul T. 6 Dec. 1956. Letter to Mrs. Douglas (Peggy) Jennings. Vol. 117. File 3-24-34-1.
"Hungarian Refugee Movement." N.d. [1959]. Report. Vol. 111. File 3-24-12-1.
Manion, J. L. 7 Jan. 1957. Memorandum to Constance Hayward. Vol. 117. File 3-24-34-2.
McCarthy, E. E. 6 Dec. 1956. Memorandum as A/Chief, Operations Division to All District
    Superintendents. Vol. 117. File 3-24-34-1.
Meeting Respecting Hungarian Refugees, 27 Nov. 1956. Minutes. Vol. 111. File 3-24-12-1.
Press Release, 20 Dec. 1956. Vol. 111. File 3-24-12-1.
Press Release, 26 July 1957. Vol. 111. File 3-24-12-1.
Stanbury, W. S. 11 Dec. 1956. Letter as President of Canadian Red Cross Society to Laval Fortier. Vol.
    117. File 3-24-34-2.

---. 2 Jan. 1957. Letter to Laval Fortier, with attached document: Summary of Personnel Representing the Canadian Red Cross Society in Austria. Vol. 112. File 3-24-12-5.

Wilson, Margaret E. 18 March 1957. Letter on behalf of Canadian Red Cross Society to Laval Fortier with letter attached: "Dear relatives." 26 Jan. 1957. Vol. 111. File 3-24-12-4.

Privy Council Office fonds (PCO). RG2. Library and Archives Canada.

Catholic Women's League. 6 Nov. 1956. Letter to Prime Minister. B-2, 1990-91/154, 108/H-17-1(a). Qtd. in Hidas 46.

Cabinet Conclusions. 14 Nov. 1956. Series A-5-a. Vol. 5775.

Cabinet Conclusions. 14 July 1958. Series A-5-a, Vol. 1898.

Young Women's Christian Association of Canada fonds (YWCA). MG28 I198. Library and Archives Canada.

Frontiers of Faith (III). June 1957. Draft Reports of Workshops. Vol. 3. File 13.

Board of Directors. 22 May 1958. Meeting Minutes. Vol. 12. File 2.

Replies from Associations re Refugee Resolution. 23 July 1958. Report. Vol. 18. File 6.

Secondary sources

Armstrong-Reid, Susan, and David R. Murray. *Armies of Peace: Canada and the UNRRA Years*. Toronto: University of Toronto Press, 2008.

Bourbeau, Amélie. "Une expertise de terrain: L'expérience en travail social des prêtes et religieuse montréalais (1930–1970)." *Chrétiens et Sociétés XVIe- XXIe siècles* 21 (2014): 97–111.

Corbeil, Yvan, Lisette Laurent-Boyer, and Mireille Richard. *L'Œuvre des réfugiés hongrois et l'adaptation à Montréal d'un groupe de réfugiés hongrois* [The Work of Hungarian Refugees and a Hungarian Refugee Group's Adaptation to Life in Montréal] Thesis. Montréal: University of Montréal, 1960.

Dirks, Gerald E. *Canada's Refugee Policy: Indifference or Opportunism*. Montréal, Kingston: McGill-Queen's University Press, 1977.

Donaghy, Greg. "An Unselfish Interest? Canada and the Hungarian Revolution, 1954–1957." *The 1956 Hungarian Revolution: Hungarian and Canadian Perspectives*. Ed. Christopher Adam, Tibor Egervari, Leslie Laczko, and Judy Young. Ottawa: University of Ottawa Press, 2010. 256-74.

Dreisziger, Nandor F. "The Biggest Welcome Ever: The Toronto Tories, the Ottawa Liberals, and the Admission of Hungarian Refugees to Canada in 1956." *Hungarian Studies Review* 35.1–2 (2008): 41–83.

---. "The Refugee Experience in Canada and the Evolution of the Hungarian-Canadian Community." *Breaking Ground: The 1956 Hungarian Refugee Movement to Canada*. Ed. Robert H. Keyserlingk. Toronto: York Lanes Press, 1993. 65–85.

---. "Toward a Golden Age: The 1950s." *Struggle and Hope: The Hungarian-Canadian Experience*. Ed. Nandor F. Dreisziger, Martin Kovacs, Paul Bődy, and Bennett Kovrig. Toronto: McClelland and Stewart, 1982. 195–219.

Harris, Bessie, and Harold Beals. "The Nova Scotia Association of Social Workers, Part 1: A History 1963–2010." Halifax: Nova Scotia College of Social Workers. 2011. Web. 10 July 2023.

Hawkins, Freda. *Canada and Immigration: Public Policy and Public Concern*. Montréal/Kingston: McGill-Queen's University Press, 1988. Print.

Hidas, Peter I. "Canada and 1956." Unpublished manuscript. N.d. https://independent.academia. edu/PETERIHIDAS/Drafts. Web. 10 July 2023.

Iacovetta, Franca. "Making 'New Canadians': Social Workers, Women, and the Reshaping of Immigrant Families." *A Nation of Immigrants: Women, Workers, and Communities in Canadian*

History, 1840s–1960s. Ed. Franca Iacovetta, Paula Draper, and Robert Ventresca. Toronto: University of Toronto Press, 1998. 482–513.

Kalbach, Warren E. *The Impact of Immigration on Canada's Population*. Ottawa: Dominion Bureau of Statistics, 1970.

Knowles, Valerie. *First Person: A Biography of Cairine Wilson, Canada's First Woman Senator*. Toronto: Dundurn Press, 1988.

Kocsis, Anthony L. *Cultural Integration and Retention: The Dichotomy of the Hungarian '56ers*. Thesis. Guelph: University of Guelph, 1970.

Korinek, Valerie J. *Roughing It in the Suburbs: Reading* Chatelaine Magazine *in the Fifties and Sixties*. Toronto: University of Toronto Press, 2000.

Nakano Glenn, Evelyn. "Racial Ethnic Women's Labor: The Intersection of Race, Gender and Class Oppression." *Review of Radical Political Economics* 17.3 (1985): 86-108.

Niinistö, Juhani. "That Able Organizer from Finland." *Vapaa Sana* (2010). Web. 10 July 2023.

Papp, Susan M. "Hungarian Immigrant Women." *Polyphony* 8.1–2 (1986): 42–44.

Patrias, Carmela. *The Hungarians in Canada*. Ottawa: Canadian Historical Association, 1999.

Prentice, Alison, Paula Bourne, Gail Cuthbert Brandt, Beth Light, Wendy Mitchinson, and Naomi Black. *Canadian Women: A History*. Scarborough, ON: Nelson Thomson Learning, 2004.

Strong-Boag, Veronica. "Home Dreams: Women and the Suburban Experiment in Canada, 1945–1960." *Rethinking Canada: The Promise of Women's History*. Ed. Veronica Strong-Boag, Mona Gleason, and Adele Perry. 4th ed. Don Mills, ON: Oxford University Press, 2002. 313-34.

Trimble, Sheena. *Femmes et politiques d'immigration au Canada (1945–1967): Au-delà des assignations de genre?* [Women and Canadian Immigration Policy: Beyond Assigned Gender Roles?]. Diss. Angers: University of Angers, 2015.

Whitaker, Reg. *Double Standard: The Secret History of Canadian Immigration*. Toronto: Lester and Orpen Dennys, 1987.

Wipper, Audrey. "Response to Revolution Among Hungarian Canadians: A Study of Organizational Conflict." *Berkeley Journal of Sociology* 6.1 (1961): 73–96.

Autobiographies, oral histories, personal accounts

Filwood. Mrs. M. July. Letter to editors. *Chatelaine* (1957). Qtd. in Korinek 284–86.

Gabor, Agota. Interview. 3 March. 1956 Hungarian Memorial Oral History Project. Multicultural History Society of Ontario. SFU Digitized Collections. Web. 10 July 2023.

Gabori, Eve. Interview. 7 March 1978. 1956 Hungarian Memorial Oral History Project. Multicultural History Society of Ontario. SFU Digitized Collections. Web. 10 July 2023.

Grossman, Ibolya Szalai. *An Ordinary Woman in Extraordinary Times*. Toronto: Multicultural History Society of Ontario, 1990.

Hidy, Marta. Interview. 8 Feb. 1976. 1956 Hungarian Memorial Oral History Project. Multicultural History Society of Ontario. SFU Digitized Collections. Web. 10 July 2023.

Huggard, Jean. 10 March 1957. Letter. Repr. in Joseph Kage. "The Settlement of Hungarian Refugees in Canada." *Breaking Ground: The 1956 Hungarian Refugee Movement to Canada*. Ed. Robert H. Keyserlingk. Toronto: York Lanes Press, 1993. 105–07.

---. 1 February 1958. From Emigrants to Immigrants. *Canadian Welfare* 33.6 (1958): 271–76.

Kende, Eva. The Tale of One Refugee. 2002. *Looking in . . . : Portraits of the Canadian Soul*. Ed. M. D. Benoit. Ottawa: Electric eBook Publishing. Web. 10 July 2023.

Mihály, Márta. "Remembering 1956: Invited Immigrants—the Sopron Saga." *Hungarian Studies Review* 35.1–2 (2008): 143–50.

Romvary, Susan. *Zsuzsa Not Zsazsa: Balance with a Smile*. Ste-Anne-de-Bellevue, QC: Shoreline Press, 1992.

Stoffman, Judith, née Bing. The Immigration Story of Judith Stoffman (Hungarian Refugee). Canadian Museum of Immigration at Pier 21. Jan. 2011. Acc. n. S2012.2339.1. Web. 10 July 2023.

Verrall, Olga. *Missing Pieces: My Life as a Child Survivor of the Holocaust.* Calgary: University of Calgary Press, 2007.

Zeron, Olive. "In a Refugee Camp." *The YWCA Journal* (May 1957): 6–8, 18.

Mária Palla

Food Memories Across Borders: Narratives of Emigration from Hungary to Canada

Béla Szabados (1942-) and Erika Gottlieb (1938-2007) fled Hungary escaping to Canada in 1957 and 1958, respectively. This chapter examines the stages of their journey from the war zones of Hungary to the contact zones of various refugee camps in Austria and the space of a new life in Canada in the late 1950s through their life writing. The border crossings of their protagonists closely resemble their own life stories and the journeys recalled involve multiple ways in which the two books' main characters are impacted by various cultural influences ultimately leading to the characters' re-evaluation and reconstruction of their personal and ethnic identities. These identities shift in various directions, often invoked as a source of pain, but more often as an opportunity for adventure and personal growth for Szabados or as a prospect for new beginnings offering liberation and agency for Gottlieb. Striking in both life narratives is the presence of embodied memories related to food, signifying climactic emotional moments and turning points in the protagonists' awareness of themselves and the meanings of their relationships. Szabados's life writing offers itself for an analysis of how the psychological responses given to the somatic experience of eating express the protagonist's position in his sociopolitical environment, while in Gottlieb's narrative the complexity of the relational identity is explored through food memories.

The memories in Szabados's first published book, *In Light of Chaos* (1990), an "ethno-autobiography" (Molnár 90), reveal his attachment to the Hungarian native country, his fascination with the new land after his arrival in Montréal, and the desire to understand the complexities of what is in between. All three locations provide Béla, the protagonist, bearing the name of the author, with experiences that significantly influence his development from a little boy into a young adult. This process is foregrounded by the three-part spatiotemporal structure of Szabados's volume, each part including food memories indicative of his subjectivity in the given phase of his life. The first part depicts his childhood in Hungary (1943-56), the second part is a narrative of his life in a refugee camp in Austria (1956-58), and the third is the story of his "emigration to, and then citizenship in, Canada (1958-66)," where "each ends with a momentous border crossing–geographical, historical and dated, autobiographical and ambiguous, and generic" (Kadar, "Reading Ethnicity" 74).

The only book-length semi-fictional work by Erika Gottlieb (née Simon), *Becoming My Mother's Daughter: A Story of Survival and Renewal* (2008), is an account of the protagonist Eva Steinbach's life, starting in her native Hungary and continuing in Canada, into which the intersubjective narrative of four generations of her family is incorporated. The narrative also follows the stages of Eva's escape from ravaged Budapest after the Revolution of 1956 against the Soviet domination of Hungary is brutally crushed by the invading Soviet forces. The threatening atmosphere created by the fierce street battles make Eva fear for her life; her terror is exacerbated by the haunting memories of the trauma caused by the persecution she and her family were subjected to during the Holocaust hardly more than a decade earlier. After a brief stay as refugees in Austria, Eva and her elder sister eventually find peace and safety in Montréal in 1957. The recollections of the family's past in Hungary, as well as the chronicle of subsequent events in Eva's life on the North American continent, closely follow, if not directly mirror, the real-life experiences of the author herself, who, like Szabados, was among the more than thirty-seven thousand Hungarian refugees to whom Canada granted asylum in the wake of the tragic events of 1956. Gottlieb and Szabados also represent the fifty per cent of the roughly 200,000 Hungarian emigrants fleeing their home country after the Revolution was put down who were under twenty-five (Nóvé 24).

After completing high school in Montréal, Szabados first attended Sir George Williams University (now Concordia), then he did doctoral work at the University of Toronto and at the University of Calgary, where he received his Ph.D. in Philosophy. Currently he is Professor Emeritus of Philosophy and Classics at the University of Regina. He is also former president of the Canadian Society for Aesthetics. His most recent work from 2022, *Far in/Far out: Memoirs of a Philosophy Grad Student 1966-1972*, signals a return to the themes and genre of his first book *In Light of Chaos*.

Before fleeing Hungary, Gottlieb graduated from the High School for Visual Arts in Budapest and started university in 1956, majoring in architecture, before the Revolution interrupted her education. She, like her pseudonymous protagonist, arrived in Montréal a few months later in the winter of 1957. The escape was directly motivated by the violence experienced in the preceding turbulent months, indirectly reminding her of the atrocities her family as members of the Jewish community had been exposed to during the Holocaust, especially when they were forced into the ghetto of Budapest in the winter of 1944–45. In Canada, Gottlieb continued her studies first enrolling in the same Sir George Williams University as Szabados, eventually earning a Ph.D. in English Literature from McGill University. She was an academic with artistic ambitions: a painter, fiction writer, poet, and literary critic in addition to being the author of numerous scholarly articles and books as well as a dedicated teacher. Today Gottlieb's paintings can be seen at permanent exhibitions at Seneca College, Mount Sinai Hospital, and Baycrest—all locations in Toronto—as well as in several private collections.

Due to the work of numerous literary figures including Szabados and Gottlieb, the Hungarian-Canadian literature of the period after 1956 is "characterized by the diversification of themes, styles, and aspirations, and a greater range of quality," claims George Bisztray, critic and late chair of Hungarian Studies at the University of Toronto, also remarking that this was the beginning of first-rate Hungarian literature in Canada (24). Writing in 1987, Bisztray also notes, however, that "it is unfortunate that so few Hungarian-Canadian writers have cultivated [the sub-genre of the memoir] with any artistic success," as he believes that it "can be a particularly useful tool from Canada's point of view in the understanding of the roots and background of New Canadians" (62). As it happens, the 1990s saw a "memoir boom" in North America (Rak 240). What is also of relevance here is that the representation of minority positions in Canadian life writing was on the rise, too, in the last quarter of the twentieth century (Egan and Helms 216), to which Hungarian-Canadian authors added their share. The annotated list of Hungarian-Canadian life narratives, ranging from short stories to book-length publications either in English or in Hungarian, compiled by John Miska in 2012, includes more than thirty such works (147), the majority of which were published in the period after 1990, coinciding with the overall boom of the memoir. It was in 1990 that Szabados's *In Light of Chaos* came out, while Gottlieb also completed the manuscript of *Becoming My Mother's Daughter* around this time, which was only published posthumously in 2008.

Egan and Helms point out an important factor which in fact necessitated the kind of life writing that Gottlieb's belongs to, which is related to her Jewish descent. Among the unique reasons why she embarked on her life writing project in the 1980s was the passing of her mother, a Holocaust survivor, in 1982. It was a time when Holocaust survivors, people able to tell their own stories, started to reach old age in increasing numbers, which meant that the preservation of personal witness accounts of the Holocaust became more urgent (Egan and Helms 227). According to Marlene Kadar, the publication of such testimonies in autobiographies or the related genres of life writing and family memoir is a generational phenomenon in this case. Writing in the early 2000s, she notes that "the autobiographers who were born before 1945 are dying" and "[s]urvivors in the diaspora . . . have realized late in life that the time has come to tell or recall their experiences" ("Wounding Events" 84). Whether or not Kadar's observations were inspired by Jan Assmann's highly influential book *Das kulturelle Gedächtnis* of 1992, published in English translation as *Cultural Memory* in 2011, Assmann's more general theoretical observations concerning the urgency, prompted by the fear of memories fading, is worth quoting at some length:

> Over the past ten (now twenty-five) years, the generation that experienced the traumatic horrors of Hitler's persecution and annihilation of the Jews has been confronted with this situation. That which continues to be living memory today, may be only transmitted via media tomorrow. This transition was also evident during the 1980s when there was a spate of written testimonies by survivors and an intensified accumulation of archive material. (36)

That Erika Gottlieb's book was only published posthumously in the 2000s in spite of having been completed more than two decades earlier—precisely at the time identified by Assmann as the period seeing the "spate of written testimonies by survivors"— is due to the peculiar workings of the publishing industry (Gottlieb, Personal Correspondence). The fact that she did not give up on publishing her book can be explained partly by her being a child survivor of the Holocaust wanting to present her own testimony: she had suffered the trauma of living, at a young age, under the threat of being deported to a death camp or executed on the bank of the river Danube at any moment in the darkest days of World War II, when Hungary became a puppet state of Nazi Germany controlled by the anti-Semitic Arrow Cross Party and its leader Ferenc Szálasi, from October 1944 to the end of the war. Apart from this political aspect of her life writing, Gottlieb, a mother of two, must have had a personal reason for persisting, too, feeling "the urgent need to educate future generations [including her own children] in the history of this period and in the dangers of hatred and discrimination" (Egan and Helms 227). One cannot help assuming that in her final years, when struggling with her fatal illness, Gottlieb must have wanted to ensure that her eyewitness account of persecution together with various memories passed on to her by generations of her family did not disappear with her.

Although Szabados belongs to the same generation of Hungarian-Canadians as Gottlieb, his experience of the brutality of World War II while living in the war zone of Hungary differs from Gottlieb's: he is not Jewish; therefore, he and his family were not threatened by the same kind of persecution as the Gottliebs. His family's decision to leave Hungary was also motivated by slightly different reasons: they found themselves living in a war zone again when the Soviet aggressors returned to the country to ruthlessly crush the Revolution. Having lost all hope for a democratic society in Hungary that would have ensured equal opportunities for all in a free world, in their disappointment the Szabadoses made their way to the West. However, the general claim made by literary scholar Geoffrey Hartman along the lines of Assmann and Kadar is true for Szabados as well. Hartman argues that as a crucial turning point had been reached with respect to World War II since the witnesses were gradually dying, it became urgent in the 1980s and 1990s to educate the young about it all and sustain the collective memory. Hartman also emphasizes the role of personal and active recall to prevent the alienation of that memory from the public at large (qtd. in Carr 57). For Szabados, the events to be recounted in a personal voice did not only include those he had witnessed during World War II, but also the events of Hungarian history in 1956 together with the story of his and his family's subsequent immigration to Canada. That his intentions when writing his narrative involved passing down the familial and national memories to the young, just like for Erika Gottlieb in her memoir, is obvious from the dedication of his book, according to which he wrote it for his only son. Further details are provided in a volume edited by Heather Hodgson: *In Light of Chaos* "was intended as a way of introducing to his son, Imre, his father as a boy and young adult, as well as capturing a beehive of memories that cried out for telling waking him up at nights. He wanted to recreate a Hungarian childhood for his son, whom he tragically lost to a car accident in 1990, the same year that the book *In Light of Chaos* was published" (Szabados 222).

Béla Szabados's narrative covers twenty-three years in the life of the narrator-protagonist between 1943 and 1966. Its three main parts are subdivided into diary-like numbered entries, though they are less transparent and less factual than a diary. Béla is only a one-year-old toddler when first introduced, which might explain why this part is the most fragmented section and why it contains the largest number of comments by the older narrating self. That the little boy passes out on so many occasions signals his lack of full understanding of what is happening to and around him, the "Nothing" in the title of this part.

In spite of his age, young Béla does not miss noticing the aggression, terror, and deprivation he sees around him. He lives a precarious life in a single-parent family looked after by his mother only, which is explained subsequently by the fact that his father was captured and taken to a forced labor camp in Siberia. Béla also has first-hand experience of the murderous and looting Nazi soldiers passing by his home during their retreat to Germany, who are soon supplanted by a drunken Russian officer quartered in his family home only to be replaced, in his turn, by the all-powerful terrifying members of *ÁVO*, the Hungarian State Security Police in young Szabados's hometown. Later, under the sinister communist dictatorship of the 1950s, his sisters are prevented by the party authorities from entering grammar school because of their "systemic, inverse discrimination against the children of the bourgeois, against those whom they perceive to be 'the professional class'" (38). Szabados's father, who miraculously returns from Siberia, works in the capacity of city engineer, so he is a professional and as such is stigmatized by the party apparatus claiming to represent the real working people. After the father's death caused by an incurable illness, the Szabados house is also "expropriated" and the family is moved to a dark, cold, and wet one-room apartment because they are deemed to be reactionaries and, as such, connected with the regime before the war (25).

The contrapuntal arrangement of themes and experiences, characteristic of the whole book, is also introduced in this part. In the atmosphere of dread and confinement, Béla's life is not, however, without joy. What provides him with pleasure and a sense of exhilaration over the following years is enjoying sports, music, reading, and learning languages. He is enthralled when noticing "[that] words of different languages can have the same meaning [which] gives [him] a sense of discovery, something that [he] can not [sic] articulate. [A foreign language] is possessed of an aura of mystery and significance" (30). When English is forbidden and Russian is made compulsory for political reasons, his love of foreign tongues overcomes even "the intense hatred of the occupiers' language" (35).

This is a time when Béla's world expands to include a broader range of sensory and sensual experiences, too. The recalled sense-related memories are almost exclusively gustatory, which is not accidental. Neurologist Gordon M. Shepherd's "research reveals that senses and emotions share the same brain nerve pathways that store experiences as memories. Another neurologist, John S. Allen . . . [,] elaborates this connection by explaining how the hippocampus is the brain structure responsible for both 'the formation of declarative or explicit memories' as well as the regulation of drives and emotions" (152). This research provides the physiological basis for understanding how *food* informs people's memories and narratives" (Abarca and Colby 5, emphasis added).

Szabados's embodied memories of food and the concomitant emotional responses to ingesting food and the situations in which such stimuli occur are as wide-ranging as Szabados's social encounters and intellectual endeavors. The scarcity of food in Hungary during and after the war is a recurring memory in both Szabados's and Gottlieb's work. Besides its nutritional value, food is important in the narratives as an indicator of the protagonists' psychosomatic condition. Where Béla feels unwanted and is treated in an unfriendly manner, as in his aunt's home, he barely eats anything and develops "an acute stomach ache" (13). After seeing the slaughterhouse and smelling the "stench of death and excrement: the stench of fear" (16) there, he refuses to eat meat. When he does, because he is forced to, he runs a fever. But when Béla is successful at obtaining bread from the local bakery after queuing there for hours, his much-enjoyed reward for himself is a salted crescent, or *sós kifli*, whose origin the narrator explains by noting how "Hungarian bakers celebrated the ousting of the Turks from Budapest by creating this marvel" (30). Food serves as a connection between *petit histoire* and national history in both sets of examples: in the former case, the psychosomatic negative reactions of the boy are expressive of the general mood of the oppressed in the period of austerity in Hungary, while in the latter food is a marker of the joyous feeling of victory in both personal and national history.

Pleasure and guilt, contradictory as they are, can be attached to the same food memory. Little Béla discovers that "goodies like tortes" are available if one has enough coins. He also discovers that his mother puts coins in a jar at home. Taking some, he buys the intensely coveted sweets and starts eating them "with a sudden unusual appetite. I am dimly conscious of this not being altogether right. I look out through the window [of the confectionary] and am looking straight at my sisters and my mother, aghast at the spectacle I present. I am reprimanded" (15). As Smith and Watson explain, "the remembered pleasure of eating a food [may be intertwined] with the politics of hunger and scarcity as a sign of class or economic positioning" (149), which, in this case, invokes the impossibility of a content and happy life in post-war Hungary.

Unsurprisingly, the fourteen-year-old Béla is jubilant when news of demonstrations in Budapest reach him in 1956. He joins the revolutionaries demanding freedom for Hungary and celebrates the formation of a new government, the withdrawal of the Soviet troops as well as the democratization of the country. After the return of the Russian tanks to Hungary to crush the uprising, he finds himself in a war zone once again. Hopeless, disappointed, and fearing for their lives, the family make their first border crossing from occupied Hungary into the West. Although this march across the border is terrifying and hazardous, at its end the protagonist experiences "a feeling of glorious, absolute freedom" (55) coupled with his first taste of an orange, an exotic fruit only heard of before, which signifies the beginning of a new phase of life full of fresh opportunities for him. The meaning of freedom is a key idea he problematizes further on. In this particular instance, it mingles with Béla's sense of grief and frustration over abandoning his home and people dear to him. His final comment closing this part of the narrative is: "I keep on crossing this border for ten years. At night. In my nightmares" (56). It is at the end of these ten years that the narrative of the book will finish.

The second part presents a transitory period, the life of the refugee spent mainly in a camp in Austria, the grey zone, which is "Neither Nothing, Nor Something" as the title of this section indicates. Béla feels displaced, bored; there is a sense of stagnation, aimlessness, and uncertainty. In the alien environment he is made to face the dilemma of his identity for the first time as he ponders the question, "How can one be a Hungarian boy somewhere where people have never heard of Petőfi [a prominent Hungarian poet and revolutionary in the 19th century]?" (68) Yet, his fascination with languages continues: he starts learning German and continues improving his English.

This is his first contact zone, to employ the term originally coined by Mary Louise Pratt in the early 1990s. In her use, it is a social space "where disparate cultures meet, clash, and grapple with each other, often in highly asymmetrical relations of domination and subordination—such as colonialism and slavery, or their aftermaths as they are lived out across the globe today" (7). As Pratt emphasizes interaction between cultures in the contact zone, the term is deemed to be appropriate for the examination of diasporic writing such as Szabados's and Gottlieb's here.

When Szabados's protagonist first meets boys and girls his age outside the refugee camp, food indicates who the haves and who the have nots are. Although Béla is offered a few sandwiches from the picnic baskets of the local youth, communication between them falters, his attempts at flirting are rebuffed, and when he applies for the secondary school these young people attend, he is flatly rejected and lines are drawn between those of different national, economic, and cultural backgrounds. Eventually, it is a school for Hungarians in the Austrian Alps where Béla finds both intellectual and bodily nourishment enjoying to the full his literature and language classes, encounters with representatives of the opposite sex, as well as the delicious crepes Suzette served in the mornings.

In the end, the family makes the decision to emigrate to Canada to reunite with one of Béla's elder sisters already there. However, when crossing the border again, this time the border between Europe and America embodied by the ocean, its vastness makes him conclude that "it is inviting and full of mystery and possibilities" (82). But if the possibilities are expressed in terms of food, more specifically the jello offered on board the ship, it raises questions about a smooth transition or integration into the new country. As his mother comments, *"Anyone who can eat this stuff is either North American-born or is a North American no matter where he was born!"* (82).

Literary critic Judit Molnár observes that the first two parts of Szabados's book "are set in highly politicized spaces," which, it may be added, make the narrative a memoir. Molnár then continues, "in the third [section] there is a shift towards social and behavioural spaces" (91), where, it can be argued, the representation of the self is foregrounded bringing about generic changes, among others, suggested by the title of the part "Something Else": the narrative approximates an autobiography proper.

Upon entering the new geographical territory of Montréal, Béla "escape[s] into the fresh air and freedom" (85) of the city, which resembles his earlier experience of border crossing into a free world in Austria. His joy is increased by his being reunited with his family. However, the difficulties of integration in the new contact zone are foreshadowed by embodied experiences again when Béla remarks, "I am beginning to think I am unsuitable for North America—one needs nourishment to live and none of it, the indigenous stuff, do I find edible" (86). After starting work and familiarizing himself with more areas of the city, he discovers ice-cream and French fries, which become "a central feature of [his] staple on Saturdays" (93), signaling a new phase of his gradual and willing acculturation.

In spite of his willingness to adapt to his host country, he has to learn how to deal with discriminatory remarks and racist incidents in social spaces such as the football pitch or the pubs. Béla has to face the limitations of multiculturalism and, consequently, of his freedom when realizing that his choices are not unbounded. He has to make a compromise as to which school he can attend, what kind of accommodation he and his family can afford, and what sort of job he can have. He also has to break up with his girlfriend as he cannot marry her: she is Jewish and he is not, which turns out to be a barrier that prevents them from having a future together.

Understandably, he is troubled by questions of authenticity and distinctiveness in his lifestyle and identity; nevertheless, he receives support on various levels: he is backed by his family, his friends in the Italian immigrant community, and the Hungarian diaspora in Montréal represented by the helpful librarian Erika Gottlieb at the university or her father, Dr. Simon, the chief chemist at the paint factory where he gets a temporary job. On the political level, the Canadian state also officially recognizes him as one of its own. His recurring nightmares of crossing the Hungarian-Austrian border and abandoning his home are recounted four times in this part of the book. The last time he even dreams about his own death, but this trauma is counterbalanced by a rebirth in the form of his taking Canadian citizenship. This does not mean, however, that he gives up his Hungarian heritage since he never discards his Hungarian name. Although people often mispronounce his first name as Bella, because Béla is indicative of his alien culture in the new environment, he consoles himself with finding namesakes, other Hungarian "Bellas" who made it big in North America such as the actor "Bella" Lugossy or the composer "Bella" Bartók (105). At the same time, there are others who do make an attempt at pronouncing his name correctly such as his colleagues or his future professor, who tries to accommodate him as a graduate student in Calgary by insisting on getting his name right.

On the whole, his painful experiences are outweighed by the more pleasant ones. Education is the main source of satisfaction for him, but his education is manifold: it is not only intellectual but also sexual. Therefore, the reference to another Hungarian-Canadian author, Stephen Vizinczey's, novel *In Praise of Older Women* (1965) is not accidental. As Kadar sums up, Béla's border crossings "are substitutes for rites in a more stable community" ("Reading Ethnicity" 74) leading to the creation of a mature self whose education, like the book, is yet incomplete but points to a hopeful and promising future.

Playing a walk-on part in Szabados's life writing, Erika Gottlieb is the pseudonymous protagonist of her fictionalized recollections. As her daughter Julie Gottlieb, Professor of Modern History at the University of Sheffield, points out in an article on her mother's work, "Erika never denied her Jewishness, nor did she hide her past [in Hungary], but she did not want to dwell on either of these identities" ("Memory, Mourning" 23). This does not mean, however, that the question of personal identity and belonging was of no concern to Erika Gottlieb, as it is amply demonstrated by her book *Becoming My Mother's Daughter*. The fictional protagonist, Eva Steinbach, now living in Canada, struggles to recollect and preserve familial memories against the backdrop of her native country's traumatic history, a history spanning roughly four decades from the 1910s to the 1950s. The task is made imperative by the distance separating her and her children from their ancestral past in Europe, initially the result of the immigrants' geographical dislocation. Yet, spatial distance becomes temporal, too, as the full timespan of the volume covers the years between the 1910s and the 1980s. Worries concerning the loss of connection with the ancestral past and the likely concomitant shifts in identity over the generations are exacerbated by the passing away of family members, most importantly that of the protagonist's aging mother, Eliza. The resulting narrative becomes a transgenerational family memoir on one level, chronicling the transmission of memories, mostly traumatic but some also heart-warming, through four generations of the protagonist's family, a search for identity on another, while on a third plane, it is also the testimony of Eva, a child survivor of the Holocaust, which provides a larger historical perspective for the personal narrative.

A satisfactory completion of the tasks involved in these three strands of Gottlieb's life writing depends on how successfully memories can be preserved by recalling them in a controlled manner without allowing them to paralyze or repeatedly traumatize the remembering subject. Gottlieb's narrative is also intricately linked to her artwork, which, together with the verbal images, further enhances the protagonist's attempts to understand herself. While the multi-layered text is consciously constructed in a non-linear structure, the sketches and paintings added to it are employed to fulfill various functions, thus they appear as illustrations of characters and locations at times, while on other occasions they are made to serve as structural devices. When it describes or presents existing artwork, the text also turns into ekphrastic writing at certain points, multiplying the interpretative possibilities through aesthetic impressions (for more on this, see Palla 2022). In this, Gottlieb's book is based on the Western episteme with its perceived preference for the visual and the textual (Howes 3), which is fully understandable given the author's personal and professional background. However, as this chapter demonstrates, Gottlieb transcends these preferences when she includes the impact of gustatory experiences on the mind and emotions of her autobiographical self in at least two key episodes of her narrative.

Unsurprisingly though, being the inventions of a visual artist and a one-time student of architecture, the titles of the chapters already reveal a peculiar emphasis on visuality in the book. All the titles, except for the last one, denote structures of architecture: a bridge, a maze, and various tunnels. Characteristically, they also acquire symbolic or allegorical meanings. The first chapter is called "The Bridge," and the first sketch in the volume is also entitled *The Bridge* (Figure 1).

Figure 1: *The Bridge*[1]

The artwork in question depicts the Chain Bridge in Budapest, anchoring the story in a specific place. Although the opening of the narrative is set in Toronto in the early 1980s, the most powerful memory evoked by the protagonist's mother Eliza is of her own mother, Ethel, while they were living in the war zone of Hungary in the late 1910s and is related to this bridge. This episode is also an instance of embodied memory connected to food. Eliza recalls how it all happened when she "was still a boarder in

---

1 All the sketches and paintings by Erika Gottlieb are reprinted here with the kind permission of Wilfried Laurier University Press.

the convent, when [she] was six. This was right after the Great War, in 1919, during the occupation of the city by the Romanians" (6). Her mother, Ethel, has to cross the Chain Bridge "[c]rawling on her stomach, crawling along that long bridge under fire" to reach her hungry daughter and offer her some rare nourishment in the form of buttered crisp rolls with a slice of ham on top of each—"worth their weight in gold" (6).

The episode does not only introduce the theme of survival included in the subtitle of Gottlieb's volume, which is inextricably linked to food in wartime, but the incident also draws attention to the problematic relationship between mothers and daughters when Eliza comments, "I . . . remember feeling overwhelmingly grateful to that grim young woman who risked her life to bring me [food]. I was overwhelmed by gratitude, but I also felt guilty. Guilty for still not being able to love her" (7). The inability to fully embrace the love of her mother originated in the fact that Eliza was born out of wedlock. Although her parents, Ethel and Stephen, loved each other dearly, Stephen's family opposed their marriage due to class differences. As a result, Eliza was sent away to the countryside to be looked after there in her early years, while her mother tried to earn a living in Budapest. Her parents eventually got married and offered the teenage Eliza great care and comfort, yet she found it difficult to relate to Ethel throughout her whole life. Although the repetition of the initial letter in each of the three names of the mothers may be a coincidence, as the fictional names are based on real ones, it also functions as a highly meaningful literary device: the names of Ethel, Eliza, and Eva stress their relational identity, which emphasizes the unbreakable bond between these women and the generations they belong to. This bond, however, is both a source of supporting strength and a distressing opportunity to transmit trauma from one person to the other, from one generation to the next, creating a conflict for Eva to resolve.

In this light it is not so surprising that the tone established on the first few pages of the book is rather gloomy: it is that of mourning since two mothers' deaths are the focal points here. When Eva is first introduced, she is on a visit to her ailing mother Eliza, treated in a Toronto hospital. By the end of the opening chapter, Eliza herself is gone, leaving Eva wondering whether

> the mother's life . . . has become part of the daughter's, to be handed down, in due course, to the daughter's daughter. Floating bridges between generation and generation. Bridges over endless dark seas. Where are you leading? Bridges between mothers and daughters? Through mothers and daughters? (11)

The notion of familial relations spanning great expanses of time to connect successive generations so prominent in the chapter makes its title "The Bridge" poignantly meaningful. Beyond metaphorically expressing the ties between the women in the family as well as the ties between the past and the present, the image and the chapter title also point out the mother-daughter plot as central to the whole narrative.

This metaphorical meaning of the physical structure verbally formulated in the first part of the book is visually reinforced when, not quite unexpectedly, it appears again in the very last sketch also bearing the title *The Bridge* (Figure 2) on the penultimate page (165).

Figure 2: *The Bridge*

Both the opening and the closing scenes of the book are set in the Toronto of the early 1980s, framing the family memoir of the past. The bridge, however, is more than just a framing device with its new pictorial image at the end of the book made up of family members, echoing Eva's verbal image: "My arms cradling the baby are joining the arms of others; my arms, my body, my baby all become part of the bridge" (164). Graphic image and verbal image, the latter being one of the numerous ekphrastic passages of the book, reinforce and expand each other's meaning.

Another key episode of Gottlieb's book involving an embodied memory is also set in war-torn Budapest, but this time it is World War II and involves the six-year-old Eva, her elder sister, and their mother Eliza locked up starving and freezing in the crowded Jewish ghetto during the siege of Budapest in 1945. Eliza's yellow leather handbag, acquiring greater and greater significance as the narrative progresses, appears to be a source of life support in the physical sense and, later, in a metaphorical one. Here

Eliza manages to secretly store some life-saving bits of sugar and chocolate, means of their survival, to be shared among the three of them when they are absolutely desperate. It is the same handbag in which Eliza takes with her some family photos to Canada when crossing the Atlantic, turning the handbag into a container of family history needed to maintain the identity of the family members and to provide them with a sense of belonging. At the same time, "that heavy handbag . . . is like a burden, yet also full of gifts, of treasures" (27).

In the ghetto Eva is also entrusted with a chunk of chocolate. "Hard, unsweetened baking chocolate. I'm to guard it in case someone from the family needs it. Probably [Mother is] also thinking that if we get separated, I should have something edible with me" (104). When both Eva's mother and sister fall ill and would desperately need a piece of that chocolate to gain some strength, Eva is shocked to discover that she must have eaten it all: "Not that I ever wanted to eat it. At least, not the whole thing. Having little, a very little bite every once in a while, yes maybe. But all the time I was telling myself that I was saving the big slab of chocolate for all of us nevertheless" (105). Food, a symbol of survival, is expected to be shared, a rule Eva unwittingly violates in a manner similar to young Béla, who steals coins from the jar in the family home to buy cakes for himself. As a result, the episode foreshadows Eva's later guilt as a survivor, which she is only able to assuage forty years later. It is only after piecing together the inherited photographs, postcards, letters, and diaries in the family album, creating her testimony, and giving visual expression to her painful emotions of suffering that Eva is psychologically able to deal with her survivor's guilt, to forgive herself, to transcend the paralyzing effect of the past while accepting its everlasting influence on her. She gains agency and at this point she is finally able to cross the Atlantic and reintegrate into the smaller world of her family and the larger world of Canada.

Coincidentally, Gottlieb must have been working on her Orwell monograph at about the same time when writing the manuscript of *Becoming My Mother's Daughter*. The coping mechanism she presents in her life writing, and relied on to deal with her own emotional turmoil caused by her memories, is much the same as the psychological process in which the guilt-ridden protagonist Winston Smith in Orwell's *Nineteen Eighty-Four* finally succeeds "in bringing [a] suppressed memory to the surface" and is finally released from "his neurotic bondage to the past" (Gottlieb, *The Orwell Conundrum* 72). The memory in question involves the young Winston selfishly taking the family's chocolate ration with him knowing that his mother and sister were dying and were in great need of any nourishment available. That is why he accuses himself of murdering them with his thoughtless act, the suppressed memory of which causes him recurring nightmares. Even a whiff of the scent of chocolate "stirred up some memory which he could not pin down, but which was powerful and troubling" (Orwell 128). Gottlieb explains that Winston eventually recognizes that "there is a way to redeem himself for that childish betrayal" (*The Orwell Conundrum* 72), which is equally true for her in her life writing and, possibly, for Szabados grappling with his similarly guilt-ridden recollections.

There is not much said about the events of 1956 in Gottlieb's book, that year being only significant as another time of aggression when, however, the borders were left temporarily unguarded, and Eva and her sister had the chance to flee Hungary. The march to the Austrian border is described as painful and terrifying as in Szabados's work and the relief upon arrival in the safety of the West is expressed in terms of food as well: "Twenty minutes later they were in the refugee camp, revived by mugs of hot cocoa and a strange, orange-colored Canadian cheese that was spread thickly on slices of white bread" (135). Food is an expression of welcome but at the same time its alien quality is pointed out, which reflects the mixed emotional response of the refugees–as it does in Szabados' other autobiographical piece already discussed.

Figure 3: *Escape from Hungary*, 1956

Eva is amply compensated for her suffering by a grant enabling her to attend the Academy of Fine Arts in Vienna. Paradoxically, though, the two sisters have to travel farther to ensure a quicker reunion with their parents through immigration. But, understandably, the farther away they are from Hungary, the safer they feel. Although Montréal is bitterly cold, the food they can afford is scarce, they have to work at two jobs each to raise enough money in order to bring their parents and younger sister to Canada, their life is not in danger anymore. In fact, in Canada there is an abundance of food; it is their economic position deriving from their refugee status that makes certain types of food inaccessible to them. When there is some choice food to be had, it marks a special occasion such as Eva's nineteenth birthday, for which she gets half a pound of glazed peanuts she shares with her friends.

When the family is reunited in Canada, "they want to break with everything they have ever been used to, as if to demonstrate their willingness to reshape themselves . . ." (143). They all take the opportunities they find to educate themselves and to work. Even the father is ready to start anew at the age of fifty-six. It is the second generation that later gives voice to concerns about social interactions outside the family where they experience life in a contact zone. Eva's children try to avoid being considered outsiders in Canadian society by not dwelling on their ethnic differences, while her sister's elder daughter chooses an alternative solution to eliminate culture clashes by preventing the meeting of cultures represented by her and her fiancé's respective families.

To conclude, the fictionalized selves of Béla Szabados and Erika Gottlieb both make the journey from Hungary to Canada via Austria as refugees in the wake of the Revolution of 1956 and reunite with their families never expressing a wish to return to their places of birth. In the process of recalling their experiences of the warzone of Hungary and the contact zones they enter after their escape, embodied memories often play a key role. For Gottlieb, food memories from Hungary are always symbolic of survival, while in the New World, they express pleasure, joy and are coupled with a tremendous degree of safety in spite of the recognition of a sense of unfamiliarity involved. In Szabados's life writing, the psychological reactions given to the somatic experience of eating express the protagonist's relation to his sociopolitical environment. In Gottlieb's narrative, food consumption and individual identity are understood as relational and, in the end, the remembering self comes to terms with the realization that her relationship to her mother, her family, and the traumatic past of two world wars and the Holocaust will always remain part of her personal identity. On the other hand, Szabados's writing is more closely based on the once "common critical trope, that of the primacy of autonomous individualism" in autobiographical works in which "white male writers were essentially concerned with the reassembling of individualistic, autonomous selves who rose above their cultural and social environs" (Ingram 30). Although his protagonist, who has gained a mature identity in the course of the narrative, harbors doubts about his decision to leave his family behind for his graduate studies in Calgary, he is seen boarding his flight on the last page of the book. At the same time, neither narrative expresses paralyzing cross-cultural frustrations or unresolvable conflicts in the new country because the adjustments to be made are accepted as the facts of life there.

Works Cited

Abarca, Meredith E., and Joshua R. Colby. "Food Memories Seasoning the Narratives of Our Lives." *Food and Foodways* 24.1-2 (2016): 1-8. DOI: 10.1080/07409710.2016.1150101. *Taylor, Francis Online.* Web. 25 July 2023.

Assmann, Jan. *Cultural Memory and Early Civilization: Writing, Remembrance, and Political Imagination*. Trans. David Henry Wilson. Cambridge: Cambridge University Press, 2011.

Bisztray, George. *Hungarian-Canadian Literature*. Toronto: University of Toronto Press, 1987.

Carr, Graham. "War, History, and the Education of (Canadian) Memory." *Contested Pasts: The Politics of Memory*. Ed. Katharine Hodgkin and Susannah Radstone. London and New York: Routledge, 2003. 57-79.

Egan, Susanna, and Gabriella Helms. "Life Writing." *The Cambridge Companion to Canadian Literature*. Ed. Eva-Marie Kröller. Cambridge: Cambridge University Press, 2004. 216-41.

Gottlieb, Erika. *Becoming My Mother's Daughter: A Story of Survival and Renewal*. Waterloo: Wilfried Laurier University Press, 2008.

---. *The Orwell Conundrum: A Cry of Despair or Faith in the Spirit of Man?* Ottawa: Carleton University Press, 1992.

Gottlieb, Julie V. "Memory, Mourning and Maternal Inheritances: A Daughter's Reading of her Mother's Holocaust Memoir." *In the Shadows of Memory: The Holocaust and the Third Generation*. Ed. Esther Jilovsky, et al. London: Vallentine Mitchell, 2016.

---. Personal Correspondence. 23 Oct. 2019. E-mail.

Howes, David. Introduction: "To Summon All the Senses." *The Varieties of Sensory Experience: A Sourcebook in the Anthropology of the Senses*. Ed. David Howes. Toronto: U of Toronto P, 1991.

Ingram, Shelley. "Food and the Autobiographical Self in Harry Crew's *A Childhood: The Biography of a Place*." *Food and Foodways* 24.1-2 (2016): 30-47. DOI: 10.1080/07409710.2016.1142778. *Taylor, Francis Online*. Web. 25 July 2023.

Kadar, Marlene. "Reading Ethnicity into Life Writing: Out from 'Under the Ribs of Death' and into the 'Light of Chaos'—Béla Szabados's Narrator Rewrites Sándor Hunyadi." *Writing Ethnicity: Cross-Cultural Consciousness in Canadian–Québécois Literature*. Ed. Winfried Siemerling. Toronto: ECW Press, 1996. 70-83.

---. "Wounding Events and the Limits of Autobiography." *Diaspora, Memory, and Identity: A Search for Home*. Ed. Vijay Agnew. Toronto: University of Toronto Press, 2005. 81-111.

Miska, János. *Magyar irodalom Kanadában* [Hungarian Literature in Canada]. Pomáz: Kráter, 2012.

Molnár, Judit. "Spatial Layouts in a Hungarian Immigrant's Journey to Canada: A Case Study of *In Light of Chaos* by Béla Szabados." *Other Language: Otherness in Canadian Culture / L'autre langue: L'altérité dans la culture canadienne*. Ed. Vladislava Felbakov and Jelena Novaković. Beograd: Tibet, 2005. 89-95.

Nóvé, Béla. *Magyar emigrációtörténeti kézikönyv* [A Handbook of Hungarian Emigration History]. Budapest: Országos Széchényi Könyvtár, 2023.

Orwell, George. *Nineteen Eighty-Four*. 1949. London: Penguin, 1990.

Palla Mária. "Immigrant Memories of Healing: Textual and Pictorial Images in Erika Gottlieb's *Becoming My Mother's Daughter*." *Hungarian Journal of English and American Studies* 28.2 (2022): 453-73.

Rak, Julie. "Life Writing." *The Cambridge Companion to Canadian Literature*. Ed. Eva-Marie Kröller. 2nd ed. Cambridge: Cambridge University Press, 2017. 239-60.

Smith, Sidonie, and Julia Watson. *Reading Autobiography: A Guide for Interpreting Life Narratives*. 2nd ed. Minneapolis and London: University of Minnesota Press, 2015. DOI: 10.5749/minnesota/9780816669851.001.0001. *Minnesota Scholarship Online*. Web. 25 July 2023.

Szabados, Béla. *In Light of Chaos*. Saskatoon: Thistledown P, 1990.

---. "Béla Szabados." *Saskatchewan Writers: Lives Past and Present*. Ed. Heather Hodgson. Regina: University of Regina Press, 2004. 221-22.

Victor Kennedy, Kristian Kolar, and Neža Bojnec Naterer

"Outsider": The Influence of Migration Experience on the Life and Work of Hungarian-Canadian Songwriter B.B. Gábor

"After all the horrors spawned by ideological rigidity in our century, the notion of a variety of histories, as opposed to a single history, is to be celebrated."

Modris Eksteins

Figure 1: B. B. Gábor performing at the Canadian Juno Awards, 1982. Photo courtesy of John Rowlands.

Gábor Hegedűs (1948–1990) was a musician whose life history defined his art. He and his family emigrated to Great Britain, and then to Canada, to escape the Soviet invasion of Hungary in 1956. Settling in Toronto in 1972, he launched his music career playing at Queen Street music clubs becoming known by the stage name B. B. Gábor. In 1980 and 1981 he released two albums that received popular and critical acclaim;

a third, recorded in 1985, remains unreleased to date. Many of his song lyrics include social and political satire based on his early experiences, and two in particular, "Nyet Nyet Soviet (Soviet Jewellery)" (Gabor and Armstrong, 1980) and "Moscow Drug Club" (Gabor, Stevenson, and Keldie, 1980), were released in Canada, the UK, Europe, and Australia (although not in the US) and received widespread airplay in Canada and on Radio Free Europe (Linden "B.B. Gabor").

Hegedűs himself was ambivalent about the popular and critical acclaim accorded to his satires on the Soviet Union, often stating to interviewers that he did not want to be stereotyped for what he considered to be merely jokes. In an interview with Evelyn Erskine of the *Ottawa Journal*, he said that "he does not intend to make a career on an anti-Soviet platform: 'I'm not a gimmick merchant'" (Erskine 35); Erskine points out that several of his other songs, such as "Consumer" (1980) and "Metropolitan Life" (1980), satirize Western society as well. In interviews, he claimed to be apolitical but accepted that his life history and migration experience had an inescapable influence on his music. He often said that he felt like an "outsider," and he transformed this feeling of displacement into a perspective from which he was able to criticize both East and West. He enjoyed a brief period of fame in the early 1980s, when his witty and intelligent style was fashionable on the Canadian New Wave scene, and although his uncompromising attitude toward his art soon alienated his commercially oriented recording company, Anthem Records, who dropped him from their roster after his second album, he had a lasting influence on, and maintains continued respect among, the Canadian artistic community. Sadly, he succumbed to what his friends and colleagues described as life-long depression and took his own life on January 17, 1990.

B. B. Gábor's European roots and migrant trajectory were vital to his musical vision; his personal experience as a refugee from a war zone gave him a deep understanding of the fragility of modern society and civilization, and an insight into the illusory nature of the "peace, order, and good government" that his adopted nation, Canada, claims in its constitution (Constitution Act, 1867); he communicated these insights clearly in his songs. In this chapter we examine the historical, political, and geographical contexts that shaped his life and art before analyzing his national and global reception by music reviewers and audiences, with reference to the concept of "heterotopia," a term used to describe the sense of loss and isolation often felt by immigrants and refugees (Mead; Drewniak; Szamosi). We also draw upon Will Straw's concepts of cultural fluidity, the blending of domestic and foreign influences in the construction of Canadian culture, the inherent time lag in such a construction, and the effect of commodity consumerism on Gábor's work and career (Straw, "Pathways," "Music from the Wrong Place"). We explore themes in Gábor's songs and lyrics and show how he develops them using verbal and musical imagery, symbols, and metaphors. His choice of words and images, drawing upon his life, heritage, and cultural experiences, was unique for a popular songwriter in Canada in the 1980s, and it was this distinctive voice that contributed to his Canadian and international recognition.

Like many immigrants to Canada, Gábor struggled to find his identity. In an article entitled "Soviet Misfit: The Life and Music of BB Gabor,"[1] Imran Khan provides a detailed chronology of his life, along with useful biographical information gleaned from an interview with his brother, Istvan:

> Clearly, there was much weighing on the young Gabor's life. His debut reads like a wide-eyed immigrant surveying his new surroundings with wonder, fright, and the emerging desire to connect with everything around him. It also reads like the collective musings of a typical Torontonian, resigned to the routines of his home city. It's this contradiction of emotional proclivities which seems to have defined much of Toronto living among migrants during the early 80s. (2016)

This duality of vision is an integral part of Canadian identity, and it forms one of the major themes of Canadian literature and the culture it describes. From its beginnings as a nation, Canada has been a country of immigrants, with large communities hailing from Britain, Europe, and Asia. Historically, Canada has prided itself on being a multicultural society and Toronto is a cosmopolitan city with many immigrant communities. Canada today officially welcomes immigration, but inevitably there are difficulties adjusting to new surroundings and a new culture (Papp; Venkovits). Khan addresses this process of adjustment, which forms a major current in Canadian literature and culture, in his discussion of Gábor's songs: "The lyrics are especially telling; Gabor demonstrates the absurdity of irrational fear in a satirical comment on xenophobia; implicitly, migrants contending with displaced identities and projected fears" ("Soviet Misfit").

The feeling of displacement, often described by critics and theorists as "heterotopia," is a major theme in Canadian literature and academic writing. Walter Russell Mead defines "heterotopia" the following way: "Utopia is a place where everything is good; dystopia is a place where everything is bad; heterotopia is where things are different—that is, a collection whose members have few or no intelligible connections with one another" (13). Heterotopia "describe[s] places and spaces of otherness that are neither here nor there and that are simultaneously physical and mental" (Szamosi 89), illustrating the experience of immigrants who feel caught between past and present, the old country and the new. This feeling is experienced by refugees in search of safety and security and find it in a safe place like Canada, but

---

1 Throughout this chapter we use the Hungarian spelling of Gábor's name, except for passages and titles quoted from Canadian newspapers, magazines, and recordings, where we quote the spelling as printed. There are also inconsistencies in the way Canadian journalists and his record company spelled his stage name "BB Gabor," "B. B. Gabor").

who then feel loss, alienation, and isolation, all of which can define one's identity (Drewniak 24–26).

These concepts are often used as aids to understanding novels and stories written by immigrants to Canada, but may also be applied to poetry and songs, including those by B. B. Gábor, whose lyrics contain themes of loneliness, alienation, and discomfort illustrated with the experience of marginalized people in both the Soviet Union and Canada. We argue that the concept of heterotopia helps provide an understanding of his recurring theme of being an "outsider."

In interviews, Gábor acknowledged the influence of his early life on the themes of his songs: "In a 1980 interview with Paul McGrath of the *Globe and Mail*, B.B. Gabor recalled that his family escaped Hungary just 'one step ahead of the Russian tanks'" (McGinnis). In a *Music Express* interview, he explained how he came to Canada:

> The revolution started on October 23, 1956 and there were two weeks of really amazing freedom. Everyone in Budapest thought that finally, the whole yoke had been shaken off, that we had liberated ourselves from the Soviet line of communism—that we had done what Tito had successfully done in 1948. It seemed like that to the Russians too, which is why they sat back for two weeks and allowed the state of freedom. Public opinion was also in favour of the revolt.
>
> Then at the end of those two weeks, the Russians realized the West wasn't going to step in and risk a war over Hungary. So in they came, and it was two weeks after they came that we decided to leave. (Linden "Gabor Says Nyet")

Gábor and his family were among the more than 37,000 Hungarians who found asylum in Canada after the 1956 Russian invasion, the largest intake of refugees in Canadian history. As Tamsyn Burgmann reported in *The Toronto Star*,

> More than 200,000 Hungarians fled their homes in the Iron Curtain country in 1956 and 1957, after a two-week uprising that began in Budapest on Oct. 23 with university students rallying for basic human rights—and, mainly, to get the Soviets out. Hundreds of Hungarians were executed, 2,500 died fighting, and 20,000 were injured. ("Hungary's Loss")

A 2007 Hungarian-language magazine article provides more information about Gábor's early life, his route to Canada, and his aspirations, and provides another insight into why he moved to Canada:

> Gábor Hegedűs was an unhappy guy. In 1956, at the age of eight, he emigrated with his parents to London, where he later became a taxi driver. He didn't dream of a music career, though music was really important to him, especially the black dance music that he learned from Motown Records in Detroit. When he left London, he thought he was going there, but the cheapest charter flight was to Toronto, so there was no argument against that. Canada was a boring place, as always, but the wind of the new wave blew over it, so Gábor became established there. From a combination

of B. B. King and Zsa Zsa Gabor, he created a new name for himself, added a guitar, and it only took a few backing musicians to be an international star for fifteen minutes. (Marton)[2]

These early experiences provided the inspiration for his two biggest hits, "Moscow Drug Club" and "Nyet Nyet Soviet (Soviet Jewellery)," which found an audience in his native Hungary as well as in Canada.[3] In 2014, Péter Kocsis wrote, "Played here more than once, B. B. Gábor's hit, 'Nyet Nyet Soviet (Soviet Jewellery),' is a song which still holds its place today. The musician himself would have deserved a mention . . . even in the years immediately before the change of regime." Musicologist Tamás Szőnyei mentions B. B. Gábor in his 1992 book *Az Új Hullám Évtizede 2* [The Decade of New Wave Music 2] (341), and Gábor also has an entry in the *Az égben lebegők csarnoka: A magyar zenei élet elhunyt csillagainak emlékoldala* [Memorial Page of the Deceased Stars of Hungarian Music Life] Facebook site.[4] During the 1980s, Canadian fans were aware of this international airplay, and it formed part of the appeal of his music there:

> Istvan Hegedus says of his brother, Gabor, "his music was broadcast to Hungary via Radio Free Europe, as some of his songs, like 'Soviet Jewellery' and 'Moscow Drug Club' had definite Cold War dimensions. Apparently he had a following in Hungary, as well as here in Canada. (McGinnis)

Much of the appeal of Gábor's songs lay in their satire. Many Canadian listeners had similar life stories to Gábor's and could identify with the themes in his lyrics, while others who grew up in Canada during the Cold War could remember bomb shelters in the basement, nuclear attack drills in school, and the Cuban Missile Crisis (1962), so his critique of Russia struck a resonant chord in a wide audience.

For European listeners, there was the added appeal of forbidden fruit. The situation of international music performance, broadcasting, and marketing, and the influence of Western music and musicians on Eastern European and Russian musicians and audiences during the Cold War (1947–1991) has been well documented. Radio Free Europe began broadcasting into Eastern Europe in 1950 (Puddington 1). For most of the second half of the twentieth century officials across Eastern Europe and the Soviet Union regarded Western music as ideologically suspect. Martin Lücke points out that from its introduction in the Soviet Union in the 1920s, through the Stalinist era, the government alternated between encouraging and banning jazz (1). Radio playlists and concert performances were carefully monitored; music considered subversive could be banned, and performers could be imprisoned (Von Faust).

---

2 All translations from original Hungarian sources in this paper are by Neža Bojnec Naterer.
3 A 1986 recording of a Radio Free Europe (Hungary) broadcast of his music is available on YouTube. https://www.youtube.com/watch?v=X3RRhhs-OT4.
4 Available at https://www.facebook.com/profile.php?id=100063705091629.

In Hungary, the authorities blocked and censored Western music, but musicians and audiences found ways to listen to it, which was sometimes a risky endeavor: "In Hungary of the 1950s, jazz music was a dangerous pastime—but music lovers got some clandestine help from the United States government" (Gorondi). Jazz was broadcast on The Voice of America, Radio Free Europe, Radio Liberty, the BBC World Service, Radio Luxembourg, and other stations available in Eastern Europe and the USSR.

Genres such as blues, rock, and punk received similar treatment in the following decades. Musicians who fell afoul of the authorities could find themselves in trouble, far more so than their Western counterparts (Kürti). For example, in 1973, the band Illés (Hungarian name: *Illés Együttes*, that is, *Elijah Ensemble*) broke up after having been barred for one year (plus a fine) from the capital because of an interview they released while staying in Britain in which they criticized the Hungarian government. In the early 1970s, Illés had also been banned from recording. In an even more extreme case, all four members of the band CPg were sentenced to two years' imprisonment for political incitement in 1983 (Hegedűs).

Gábor's satire, however, targeted not just Russia and Eastern Europe, but Western culture as well. *BB Gabor* (1980) and *Girls of the Future* (1981) contain songs including "Metropolitan Life," "Consumer," "Hunger, Poverty and Misery," and "Girls of the Future" that take a satirical, anti-consumerist stance criticizing Western capitalism. His witty, edgy lyrics fit in well with the burgeoning Toronto New Wave music scene of the late 1970s and early 1980s, which featured many songwriters and bands, such as Rough Trade and Pukka Orchestra, who had a similar satirical style and message (Kennedy).

New Wave was a popular genre in Canada and around the world in the early 1980s; although it is often described as having a humorous or quirky pop approach, many performers added a serious, satirical element: R.E.M., from Athens, Georgia, formed in 1980, and their first single, "Radio Free Europe" (Berry, Buck, Stills, and Stipe), dealt with the same themes as "Nyet Nyet Soviet (Soviet Jewellery)" and "Moscow Drug Club." Similarly, Nena's 1983 hit "99 Luftballons" (Fahrenkrog-Petersen and Karges) is a well-known satire on East German politics. All of these works reflect a widespread popular movement of criticism and rebellion that culminated in the fall of the Berlin Wall in 1989 and the collapse of the Soviet Union in 1991.

Gábor often acknowledged that his experiences as a refugee shaped his life and art, and provided themes, images, and symbols for his song lyrics, musical arrangements, and stage persona. In the interview with Erskine, he said, "The form that it is presented in is a little humorous, but you look at the lyrics and you look at what I'm trying to say in those songs and you'll know that this message hits hard at the Soviets" (35). His satire on the KGB, the Soviet secret police, in "Nyet Nyet Soviet (Soviet Jewellery)," and his critique of Soviet repression in "Moscow Drug Club" attracted the most critical and popular attention of all his songs.

"Nyet Nyet Soviet (Soviet Jewellery)" is a straightforward lyric built around a forthright metaphor, SOVIET JEWELLERY = HANDCUFFS, and repetition of the word "nyet" ("no" in Russian): "Nyet nyet Soviet, Soviet jewellery / I say no no no no no no no no no—they shouted 'Yes!' / And snapped the Soviet jewellery around my wrists." For listeners used to simple, polarized "us vs. them" Cold War rhetoric, this lyric confirms Western stereotypes, but on closer examination, the song contains some interesting layers of irony. The lines "I'm just a little dec-a-dec-a-dec-a-dent / I smoke my tea in the bed" equate being suspected of being decadent with proof of being a dissident in KGB logic. The ambiguous nature of the word "tea" reflects the arbitrary nature of state oppression. If "tea" is taken literally, then the speaker is being persecuted just for being different; if it is interpreted as slang for cannabis, then possessing it is a crime under the 1934 Criminal Code of the Soviet Union (Conroy; Kramer). There is little information available about drug use in the Soviet Union from the 1920s until 1990 because information about drug use other than alcohol was officially suppressed (Conroy). Possession of cannabis was a crime in Canada in the 1980s, but the usual punishment was a fine and/or short term of imprisonment; Gábor's lyric implies a more serious outcome in the USSR. The clear message of the song is that being a dissident in any way, such as performing decadent acts like smoking marijuana, would be punished harshly by arrest and worse at the hands of the KGB. The lines "They call me a dissident / When you're better dead than red?" contain the slogan "better dead than red," which was current during the 1950s, along with its inverse, "better red than dead" (Doyle et al.). As used in "Nyet Nyet Soviet (Soviet Jewellery)," it implies that in a police state, where something that would be judged a minor infraction elsewhere is interpreted as proof of committing a crime against the state, life is hardly worth living.

There is a similar use of idioms with more nuanced imagery and symbolism to satirize state repression in "Moscow Drug Club": "Underneath the grey streets, where the grey people walk / There's a small secret nightclub, where subversives sit and talk." The musical accompaniment parodies Russian folk music, with instrumentation comprised of accordion, balalaika, string bass, piano, acoustic guitar, vocal harmonies, and verbal interjections ("Nyet!"; "da svidanje"), creating the impression of being in a noisy club; the overall effect has been described as "Brechtian" (Harrison, "Real B.B. Gabor"). The lyrics use multiple plays on words to satirize Soviet society and government: in the opening line, Russians are described as "grey people," symbolizing both their nondescript dress and the tedium of everyday life. Inside the club, however, where the patrons add color to their lives by taking drugs, the "Reds" (a metonym for "Communists") "play the blues": "Smoking Georgian Gold, they refuse to do what they are told—'Nyet!' / Moscow Drug Club, secret rendezvous / Moscow Drug Club, where the Reds play the blues." The "blues," like jazz, a musical genre imported from the West, was associated in the minds of Soviet officials with decadence and dissidence; the other meaning of "blues" is, of course, sadness. "Georgian Gold" is a play on "Acapulco Gold," a potent strain of marijuana popular in the United States in the 1960s, often mentioned in popular films and songs, such as Led Zeppelin's 1973 song "Over the Hills and Far Away" (McClure). Gábor's pun here replaces Acapulco, a city in Mexico and source of much of the marijuana consumed in North America, with Georgia, one of the republics of the USSR, and, according to the CIA, one of the country's major sources of drugs (CIA.gov).

There is a double play on words in the lines "They take little "red" pills to stay awake / Under the Kremlin's gaze / Being a beatnik Russkie's risky now-a-days." The little "red" pills are a metaphor and a pun, combining the tenor of communism with the vehicle of drugs, putting a new interpretation on the Marxist axiom "opiate for the masses": in these times, drugs, not religion, are the escape of choice for common people. The original quote from Marx was interpreted as "religion is an opiate for the masses" (Meyer), but Gábor's pun, in an ironic reversal, replaces "religion" with "drugs."

Another example of transborder intertextuality appears in an allusion to a well-known popular song in the line "you don't hear balalaikas because they're playing saxophones / They ignore the party line, and disconnect the telephone"; this is a pun on the old-fashioned use of shared telephone lines, or "party lines," and prevailing political dogma, and an echo of The Beatles' "Back in the U.S.S.R.," in which Paul McCartney sings, "Honey, disconnect the phone," and "let me hear your balalaikas ringing out" (McCartney, 1968). Gábor's allusion draws on a vein of parody with a long history in rock music: "Back in the U.S.S.R." is a satire on Chuck Berry's "Back in the USA" (Berry, 1959) and the Beach Boys' "California Girls" (Wilson, 1965); The Beatles' lyrics subvert Berry's patriotic sentiments about the United States, and their list of Ukrainian, Moscow, and Georgian girls is a send up of The Beach Boys' ode to American girls. The "party line" is another multifaceted jab at Soviet officials' hypocrisy: undoubtedly, Soviet telephony was developed primarily to create total domination in the Soviet regions. Though telephony in the USSR became much more casual in the 1970s, it still retained its surveillance character:

> Direct telephone lines between the capital of the USSR and major Ukrainian cities offered a means of control that bypassed the republic level authorities. This control imperative, coupled with the goal of political education in the annexed territories, ensured that the western regions received "privileged treatment" in the provision of technology and equipment. . . . Telecommunications technologies were expected to establish Soviet political authority in these areas, while preserving their image as "prosperous regions" in the eyes of their residents. (Roth-Ey and Zakharova)

Gábor's lyrics counter the premise of the official plan—how could anyone achieve surveillance/prosperity if the "party line" is constantly ignored? "Moscow Drug Club" is thus a multi-layered parody. The penultimate line of the song, "Moscow Drug Club, the 5-Year Plan is just a joke," points to the fact that, in the Soviet Union, Five-Year Plans, first implemented in 1928 by Stalin, were notorious for leading to disaster (Goldberg).[5]

---

5 They are also mentioned in the Creedence Clearwater Revival song "Who'll Stop the Rain" in the lines "Five-year plans and New Deals / Wrapped in golden chains" (Fogerty). Cyril Montrose's "The

The line "Listening to illegal jazz, ten years behind the Western fads" introduces two themes; first, although Western music, including jazz, was at times outlawed behind the Iron Curtain, this, according to contemporary accounts, did not prevent audiences from listening to it, but turned it into a "forbidden fruit," with jazz recordings smuggled into the country and broadcast from Western radio stations (Troitsky). Jazz was not the only genre made attractive by the ban. Rock music by artists including Little Richard, Chuck Berry, Hank Marvin and the Shadows, and many others was broadcast via western stations throughout Europe, even though authorities went to great lengths to intercept such illicit cargo by jamming broadcasts, intercepting mail, and circulating lists of banned musicians and songs (Von Faust). In discussing the line, "ten years behind the Western fads," Will Straw proposes a theory about time delay:

> In popular and critical understandings of music, distance from a center is presumed to institute a delay of influence, a "lateness," as when Soviet jazz or Bollywood thriller movie funk are mocked (or, these days, relished) for their tardy absorption of innovations from elsewhere. ("Ten years behind the Western styles," Hungarian Canadian new-waver B.B. Gabor sang, mockingly, of Soviet jazz, in his 1980 song "Moscow Drug Club.") . . . The implicit model here is of a broken communications system through which news of stylistic change arrives at the margins too late and too faintly to be understood and credibly acted upon. (Straw 121–22)

The time delay is reinforced by the line "They do the shimmy and the shake," specific references to outmoded Western styles: the shimmy and the shake are dances dating from 1919 and 1965 respectively (Piron). The assumption of a time delay resulting from censorship and repression is the subject of debate; however, Lücke puts the delay at five years, starting in the early 1920s (1); Radio Free Europe began broadcasting into the Eastern Bloc in 1950 (Puddington), and jazz musicians there were well aware of the latest recordings:

> [Hungarian] Drummer Ferenc Ruttka, later a famous painter and art director in Xlms, recalled that jazz was a "forbidden fruit" in the 1950s but said many musicians managed to stay abreast of the rapidly changing scene by getting their hands on smuggled recordings. (Gorondi)

Radio Free Europe playlists from 1980–1982, the same time that Gábor's "Nyet Nyet Soviet (Soviet Jewellery)" and "Moscow Drug Club" were released, show that audiences in Hungary, the USSR, and other Eastern Bloc countries were fully up to date with Western music releases. The idea that listeners behind the "Iron Curtain" were behind the times is one of the Western stereotypes about the East that Gábor

---

Five-Year Plan" (1939), a Trinidadian calypso, was a protest against colonial government, and, more recently, "Five-Year Plan" by Chance the Rapper (2019) uses the phrase as a simple metaphor for a bad idea.

satirizes in his songs; the stereotype lingered because it allowed a sort of constructed cultural nostalgia, and because memories of the old country tend to be fixed in the minds of émigrés at the time they left.

Overall, the ekphrastic color and sound symbolism in the lyrics creates a vivid mental picture that, with the juxtaposition of the satiric text and anachronistic accompaniment, develops the main ironic theme of the song: unlike Ian Dury's "sex and drugs and rock and roll / are very good indeed" (1977), mixing politics, drugs, and music in the Soviet Union was not very good at all.

In contrast to his Russian records, several of Gábor's songs, such as "Metropolitan Life" (Gabor and Stevenson, 1980), satirize Western society: "Give me half a minute and I'll tell you what I'm thinking / I get so excited when you're waving that knife / It's driving me crazy but I know I can't blame you / For the deserving man this metropolitan life." The song's title and refrain are a play on the name of the Metropolitan Life Insurance Company (one of the world's largest corporations) and The Municipality of Metropolitan Toronto (where Gábor settled in Canada). Life in Canada, in Gábor's telling, is no bed of roses either. Urban decay is portrayed in verbal images such as "you're waving that knife," "getting high," and "sweeping up the sidewalk after every fight," which result in feelings of fear, hopelessness, and cognitive dissonance that drive the speaker "crazy," since the gap between expectations and reality "don't make no sense." The fear was not imaginary; a Statistics Canada report on homicides in Canada between 1980 and 1989 showed a 23 percent rise in knife crime ("Number of Homicide Victims"). The lines "Left wing politicians, loose women, and musicians / Try to make a living off a regular guy" provide an ironic juxtaposition, as Gábor includes himself in the group about which the speaker, "a regular guy," is complaining.

The second verse ironically compares the life of the "regular guy" in the urban first world to that of people living in third world deserts; the "concrete" desert of the city gets people "down on their knees": "Third world people well they got their situation / Living in the desert where there ain't no trees / Well look around downtown, everywhere there's concrete / And people getting down on their knees." The line "You can survive, but it all depends" is open ended; it depends on what? The answer is that despite the trappings of civilization, "[t]elevision, saturation, sanitation for the nation," life in a modern capitalist city can be dangerous, brutal, and for some, nearly hopeless. Gábor's ironic commentary on Canadian society exposes the central division at the heart of western capitalist culture: while wealthy, privileged members of society live comfortable lives, those at the lower end of the social hierarchy might as well be living in third-world countries.[6]

---

6 A similar observation was made by Gábor's Canadian contemporaries, the Pukka Orchestra, whose song "Cherry Beach Express" (1981) exposed police brutality against marginalized members of Toronto society.

Two of Gábor's songs that appear diametrically opposed, based on their titles, but which actually share a core theme, are "Consumer" (Gabor and Stevenson, 1980) and "Hunger, Poverty and Misery" (Gabor, 1980). "Consumer" criticizes capitalism and the way advertising uses sex to compel people to keep spending at ever-increasing rates: "Discount prices people scrambling shoppers mall is mesmerized / Pretty salesgirls very charming their eyes are there to hypnotize . . . TV ads and high-priced fads the merchandise is so seductive." "Mesmerize," "hypnotize," and "seductive" recall the use of psychological manipulation in techniques described at length in Vance Packard's 1957 exposé of the advertising industry, *The Hidden Persuaders*. The repetition in the lines "It's ten to nine you'd better get in line consumer / It's ten to nine you'd better be on time consumer" emphasizes the pressure felt by inhabitants of this world to work hard in order to be able to afford to buy the unneeded products that keep the wheels of industry greased and the economy growing. The terms "media," "masses," and "productive," in the line "The media controls the masses making sure that you're productive," and buzzwords like "daily intake" and "price wars" all sound as if they were taken from a sociology or economics textbook, indicating a self-reflexive Marxist criticism from the point of view of someone who can see behind the veil hiding the manipulation of consumer capitalism.

The lyrics to "Hunger, Poverty and Misery" are straightforward, full of literal description and few symbols or metaphors, other than the dead metaphor "razor's edge," but the message is the same: "There are things in life other than money / Hunger poverty misery." The song contains many concrete images that evoke the disparity between rich and poor in Canadian society: while the audience is addressed as "comfortable people" who "have all you want to eat," implying that they are middle class, if not wealthy, the fact that "I know that some of you would like to / Live a little closer to the street" suggests a desire among many to live a more bohemian, adventurous lifestyle; however, Gábor observes that "I guess that you've decided / That the razor's edge is not for you." In this consumer-based capitalist society, to try to live the life of an artist is living on "the razor's edge": "I don't think I have to be reminded / What life without money can do." The theme of this song is similar to that of "Metropolitan Life": while life in Canada is safe and easy for the haves, it is dangerous and difficult for the have-nots. The chorus contains a surprising twist, as the line "There are things in life other than money," which sounds like a standard maxim, setting up the expectation of a conventional list of items such as "love" or "happiness," is followed by the ironic asyndeton "Hunger poverty misery." Gábor here undercuts the uncritical assumption of Western citizens that they are safe in a prosperous society with the voice of experience from one who experienced the destruction of a democratic society in the 1956 Russian invasion of Hungary.[7]

---

7 Prior to the Soviet invasion on November 4, 1956, Hungarian protesters had demanded free, multiparty elections and the withdrawal of Soviet troops from Hungarian territory ("The Days of Freedom," http://www.rev.hu/history_of_56/ora3/ora3_e.htm).

Taken together, these three songs paint a bleak picture of modern urban life in Canada, where citizens are pressured to consume more than they need, but are still always aware that hunger, poverty, and misery await those who fail to conform and perform according to society's demands. Gábor's gritty, realistic criticisms of the West contrast with his stylized, stereotypical pictures of life behind the Iron Curtain, although there is, we argue, a great deal of truth to the latter. There is an immediacy to his descriptions of life in Canada that contrasts with the more ambiguous imagery of his Russian songs.

Several of Gábor's songs provide a more personal insight into his life and his psyche. On a psychological level, the song "Outsider," from his second and last album, *Girls of the Future* (1981), is a nightmarish vision of paranoia that could apply anywhere, East or West, and at any time, in the Cold War of the past or a dystopian future: on a "dark night" with "nowhere to hide," "He's walking behind you / But you don't see him / He has no motive / You have no chance." The narrator is addressing the target of a psychopathic killer who has "no motive"; the setting is night, beside a river, and the victim has "no chance," because the stalker has killed before: "They know his work / But they never see his face"; "they," it is implied, are the police. The imagery supports the theme, with the repetition of "dark," "night," "the moon," and light reflected in a "gleam" off the water. Repetition of the word "odd" in the chorus, in the phrases "odd man out," "odd man outside," "odd man inside," and finally, "outsider," emphasize the various connotations of "oddness": different, strange, alienated, rejected, and psychologically broken. The "outsider" can be interpreted as a foreigner, someone feeling the effect of the "heterotopia" described earlier, or someone who is psychologically estranged from society, a "loner" who feels no connection to others. The song is neither satire nor political or social commentary, but a glimpse into a tortured, paranoid worldview, conveying a feeling of overwhelming anxiety. A comment by Gábor in an interview in *The Province* provides insight into the song's origin:

> There's a part of me that's from Budapest, a part from London and a part from Toronto. I don't know if that's good. Sometimes I wish I was more a part of one community. I'm the kind of person who is a permanent outsider. (Harrison, "Silence Ends")

The song's narrator is distanced from the drama unfolding between the addressee and his killer, but interviews reveal that Gábor identifies with both; he himself acknowledged that he had emotional and psychological problems: "I would like to think that I'm the nicest and most easy-going guy in the world, but I know I really can't look into a mirror and say that" (Hayes). These problems affected his professional activities, as a member of his band recalls:

> B. B. was emotionally unpredictable. He behaved like a bipolar person but I don't know if he was ever diagnosed as such. He would go from overconfident and gregarious to completely withdrawn and unable to perform. Sometimes in the same show. Genius often comes at a high

price. One instance stands out. During a set B. B. was quickly becoming less confident and began withdrawing. Halfway through the last set he stopped playing and crawled under the keyboards and went into fetal position. The keyboard player at the time was Dave Stone, now in Vancouver. Dave crawled under the keyboards with him and held him for at least 20 minutes while the crowd just watched. I don't think we finished the night. (Griffiths, Tom. Personal Communication, 26 Apr. 2021)

Another of Gábor's bandmates tells a similar story of the effect of his troubled personal life on his art and life philosophy:

Gabor [was] a very intelligent and interesting man. Very present and intuitive, a good communicator and often edgy. Something was troubling him deep down inside, yet his song messages were insightful and wanted the world to wake up from our painful dream and habitual frenzy. He pointed to the manipulation of the masses and wanted us to resist. There was an underlying compassion for our plight as programmed consumers, caught in a trap of projected expectations that were never to be fulfilled in the ways made available by the mainstream bourgeois lifestyle we are cultured into. (Justice)

"Outsider," his own words in interviews, and the accounts of his bandmates, offer glimpses into Gábor's mind that add to our understanding of the themes of his other songs. Some writers create personas through which they can explore issues and themes without acting out those ideas; David Byrne and Mick Jagger were not psycho killers, even though they sang about them (Byrne, Frantz, and Weymouth, "Psycho Killer," 1977; Jagger and Richards, "Midnight Rambler," 1969).[8] Writers also create art from personal experience, however, and "Outsider," along with Gábor's statements regarding his feelings of alienation as an immigrant in Canada, professional rejection by his record company, being misunderstood by audiences, and the subject of negative criticism in the Canadian music press, indicates a tangible autobiographical element in his lyrics, in conjunction with his critique of society, and foreshadow his descent into depression and eventual death by suicide.

From the same album, *Girls of the Future*, the title song is another social satire, with another personal statement at the end: "Girls of the future will be from the east / They'll be imported, trained to be obedient / Girls of the future will be wrapped in cellophane / Sealed at the factory far in the Orient." Like David Bowie's "China Girl" (1977; 1983) and Pukka Orchestra's "Rubber Girl" (Williamson, 1981), "Girls of the Future" satirizes the commodification of women. Unlike Bowie's real girl, and Williamson's plastic inflatable sex doll, however, Gábor's is a *Stepford Wives*-style robot (Levin): "Girls of the future will be programmed to serve / Girls of the future printed circuit well." In this science fiction-inspired lyric, Gábor envisioned with

---

8 Jagger and Richards have never explicitly said that that the song was about serial killer Albert DeSalvo, but the line "You heard about the Boston . . . [Strangler]" refers to the nickname given to him in newspaper headlines. David Byrne has said that "Psycho Killer" was based on The Joker and Hannibal Lecter, not on the real-life David Berkowitz.

trepidation the inevitable future of a capitalist society that values profits over people and commodifies basic human needs and human bodies with a description of life-sized, mass-produced plastic sex dolls that was quite prophetic: "I'm a little bit scared by the girls of the future."

In an article about the social and political effect of current popular music, Alexander Herbert notes that "Pussy Riot has mobilized some Russians to inject their music with a dose of political consciousness that turns the abstract neo-Nazi and bureaucratic state into concrete realities, not distant boogiemen" (227). B. B. Gábor did the same for Canadian music in the 1980s with song lyrics written with a political consciousness that shone a light on global culture from the perspective of an artist with personal experience of life in both the communist and capitalist systems, with insights that appear to have come, at least in part, from a difficulty coping with life in either context. Some of his more commercially oriented songs, such as "Laser Love" (1979) and "Jealous Girl" (1981), were produced to satisfy the demands of his record company; in interviews, he often railed against commercial pressure to conform, and his resistance to do so led to his being dropped by Anthem, which may have contributed to his eventual descent into obscurity, depression, and finally, suicide (Marton). However, he was able to transform his experiences into an insightful view of the world that spoke to many people. Gábor's dislocated identity, briefly supported by the multiculturalism of Canada, underlay a critique bound to neither west nor east, but heterotopic. His lyrics paint a picture of an artist who felt stranded between two worlds, at home in neither of them. Despite these existential difficulties, he was able to transform his experiences and feelings into an art form that resonated with many listeners; in the words of a musician who performed and recorded with him, "He was a genius and I was honored to have played with him . . ." (Griffiths). Thirty years after his death, his music is still played on Canadian radio stations, discussed by music critics around the world, shared on social media, and kept alive by a British band who named themselves Moscow Drug Club after the title of one of his songs.[9]

Acknowledgements

Thanks to John Rowlands for granting permission to reproduce his photograph of B.B. Gábor taken at the 1982 Juno Awards, to Corinne Lynn Osko, administrator of the Facebook group *BB Gabor—Moscow Drug Club*, for sharing her archive of newspaper and magazine articles and record and CD covers, and to Martins Zvaners, Acting Director, Communications and Public Affairs—RFE/RL, Inc., for his assistance in researching the Radio Free Europe archives. We would also like to thank Dr. Julie Adam for performing a survey of awareness of B.B. Gábor and his music among Hungarian-

---

9 Available at: https://www.youtube.com/watch?v=b6VzmE3NW_M.

Canadians and for providing historical information about Hungarian emigration to Canada. Thanks also to Tom Griffiths for sharing his musical experiences with B. B. Gábor, to Tony Duggan-Smith of Pukka Orchestra for information about the Canadian music scene in the 1980s, and to Professor Michelle Gadpaille for editorial advice.

Discography

Berry, Bill, Peter Buck, Mike Stills, and Michael Stipe. "Radio Free Europe." Single. Winston-Salem, North Carolina: Hib-Tone, 1980.

Bowie, David, and Iggy Pop. "China Girl." *The Idiot*. By David Bowie. Hérouville, Munich: RCA, 1977. Re-released, 1983.

Byrne, David, Chris Frantz, and Tina Weymouth. "Psycho Killer." *Talking Heads: 77*. By Talking Heads. New York: Sire Records, 1977.

Dury, Ian, and Chaz Jankel. "Sex & Drugs & Rock & Roll." Single. By Ian Dury. London: Stiff Records. 1977.

Fahrenkrog-Petersen, Jörn-Uwe, and Carlo Karges. "99 Luftballons." *Nena*. By Nena. West Berlin: Epic, 1983.

Fogerty, John. "Who'll Stop the Rain." *Cosmo's Factory*. By Creedence Clearwater Revival. Los Angeles: Fantasy, 1970.

Gábor, BB. *BB Gabor*. Toronto: Anthem Records, 1980.

---. "Girls of the Future." Gabor, *Girls of the Future*.

---. *Girls of the Future*. Toronto: Anthem Records, 1981.

---. "Hunger, Poverty and Misery." Gabor, *BB Gabor*.

---. "Jealous Girl." Single. Toronto: Anthem Records, 1981.

---. "Laser Love." Single. Toronto: Pye Records, 1979.

---. "Metropolitan Life." Gabor, *BB Gabor*.

---. "Outsider." Gabor, *Girls of the Future*.

---, and Leon Stevenson. "Consumer." Gabor, *BB Gabor*.

---, Leon Stevenson, and Dennis Keldie. "Moscow Drug Club." Gabor, *BB Gabor*.

---, and Paul Armstrong. "Nyet Nyet Soviet (Soviet Jewellery)." Gabor, *BB Gabor*.

Jagger, Mick, and Keith Richards. "Midnight Rambler." *Let It Bleed*. By The Rolling Stones. London: Decca/ABKCO, 1969.

McCartney, Paul. "Back in the U.S.S.R." *The Beatles*. By The Beatles. London: EMI, 1968.

Page, Jimmy, and Robert Plant. "Over the Hills and Far Away." *Houses of the Holy*. By Led Zeppelin. New York: Atlantic, 1973.

Piron, Armand J. "I Wish I Could Shimmy Like My Sister Kate." New York: Clarence Williams Music Publishing Co. Inc., 1922.

Williamson, Graeme, and Tony Duggan-Smith. "Cherry Beach Express." *The Pukka Orchestra*. By The Pukka Orchestra. Toronto: Solid Gold Records, 1984.

Williamson, Graeme. "Rubber Girl." Single. By The Pukka Orchestra. Toronto: Solid Gold Records, 1981.

Works Cited

Burgmann, Tamsyn. "Hungary's Loss, Canada's Gain." *Toronto Star*. 24 Jun. 2007. Web. 27 Apr. 2021.

Conroy, Mary Schaffer. "Abuse of Drugs Other Than Alcohol and Tobacco in the Soviet Union." *Soviet Studies* 42.3 (1990): 447–80. Web. 22 May 2021.

Doyle, Charles Clay, Wolfgang Mieder, and Fred R. Shapiro, eds. "Better Red Than Dead." *The Dictionary of Modern Proverbs*. New Haven: Yale University Press, 2012. Web. 22 Jan. 2022.

Drewniak, Dagmara. *Forgetful Recollections: Images of Central and Eastern Europe in Canadian Literature*. Adam Miczkiewicz University, 2014. Web. 25 Apr. 2021.

Eksteins, Modris. *Walking since Daybreak: A Story of Eastern Europe*. Boston: Houghton Mifflin Harcourt, 1999. Print.

Elder, Miriam. "Pussy Riot Sentenced to Two Years in Prison Colony over Anti-Putin Protest." *The Guardian* 17 Aug. 2012. Web. 14 Apr. 2021.

Erskine, Evelyn. "B.B. Gabor Is Always Welcome at the Nifty Moscow Drug Club." *Ottawa Journal* 12 Mar. 1980: 35. Web. 28 Jan. 2021.

"Georgia." *The World Factbook*. Central Intelligence Agency. N.d. Web. 3 Mar. 2022.

Goldberg, Maren. "Five-Year Plans." *Encyclopedia Britannica*. Ed. Adam Augustyn. 2009. Web. 22 Feb. 2022.

Gorondi, Pablo. "Hungarian Musicians Recall Secret Jazz Recordings from 1956." *Business Insider* 26 Oct. 2016. Web. 14 Apr. 2021.

Harrison, Tom. "Real B.B. Gabor Starting to Emerge." *The Province* 1981. Web. 10 May 2021.

---. "Silence Ends." *The Province* 13 Jan. 1985: 51. Web. 10 May 2021.

Hayes, David. "Rock and Roll Catalyst." *Canadian Composer* Dec. 1980: 4-9. Web. 28 Jan. 2021.

Hegedűs, Barbara. "Punks under Socialism." *Courage: Connecting Collections*. 2019. Web. 10 May 2021.

Herbert, Alexander. *What About Tomorrow? An Oral History of Russian Punk from the Soviet Era to Pussy Riot*. Portland, OR: Microcosm Publishing, 2019.

Justice, Gary. "B.B. Gabor and New Wave." *revsound.ca*. N.d. Web. 10 May 2021.

Kennedy, Victor. "Breaking Taboos in 1980s Toronto New Wave Music." *Words, Music and Gender*. Ed. Michelle Gadpaille and Victor Kennedy. Newcastle Upon Tyne: Cambridge Scholars Publishing, 2020. 67–91.

Khan, Imran. "Soviet Misfit: The Life and Music of BB Gabor." *Pop Matters* 13 Mar. 2016. Web. 5 Jan. 2021.

Kocsis, Péter. "Itt a Szabad Európa Rádió . . ." [This is Radio Free Europe . . .]. *nyugat.hu*. 2014. Web. 25 May 2021.

Kramer, John M. "Drug Abuse in the USSR." *Social Change and Social Issues in the Former USSR*. Ed. Walter Joyce. London: Palgrave Macmillan, 1990. 53–79. Web. 22 May 2021.

Kürti, László. "Rocking the State: Youth and Rock Music Culture in Hungary, 1976–1990." *East European Politics and Sciences*. Ed. Ivo Banac. Thousand Oaks: SAGE Publishing, 1991. 483–513.

Levin, Ira. *The Stepford Wives*. New York: Random House, 1972.

Linden, J. J. "B.B. Gabor—An Unusual Artist, an Unusual Career." *Records, Promotion* 22 Mar. 1980: 26–27. Web. 28 Jan 2021.

---. "Gabor Says Nyet to Soviets." *Music Express* Mar. 1980: 23. Web. 10 May 2021.

Lücke, Martin. "Vilified, Venerated, Forbidden: Jazz in the Stalinist Era." *Music and Politics* 1.2 (2007). Trans. Anita Ip. Web. 25 Apr. 2021.

Lynskey, Dorian. "Nelson Mandela: The Triumph of the Protest Song." *The Guardian* 6 Dec. 2013. Web. 15 May 2021.

Marlyn, John. *Under the Ribs of Death*. Toronto: McClelland and Stewart, 1964.

Marton, László Távolodó. "Narancs-Ásatás: Menekülthullám (Spions, BB Gabor, Geza X, Monty Cantsin)" [Orange-Digging: A Wave of Immigrants]. 2007. Web. 22 Apr. 2021.

McClure, James. "Led Zeppelin's Top Marijuana Moments." *Civilized* 2021. Web. 10 Feb. 2022.

McGinnis, Ray. "#738: Nyet Nyet Soviet (Soviet Jewellery) by B.B. Gabor." *Vancouver Pop Music Signature Sounds* 2018. Web. 1 Apr. 2021.

Mead, Walter Russell. "Trains, Planes, and Automobiles: The End of the Postmodern Moment." *World Policy Journal* 12.4 (1995/1996): 13–31. Web. 25 Apr. 2021.

Meyer, Alfred G. *Karl Marx. Critique of Hegel's "Philosophy of Right."* Trans. Annette Jolin, and Joseph O'Malley. Ed. Joseph O'Malley. New York: Cambridge UP, 1970.

"Multiculturalism." *Government of Canada*. N.d. Web. 1 Mar. 2022.

News, BBC. "Joan Baez Arrested in Vietnam Protest." *BBC News* 16. Oct. 1967. Web. 24 Apr. 2021.

"Number of Homicide Victims, by Method Used to Commit the Homicide." *Statistics Canada*. N.d. Web. 22 Feb. 2022.

Packard, Vance. *The Hidden Persuaders*. New York: D. McKay Co., 1957.

Papp, Susan M. "Hungarians in Ontario." *Polyphony: The Bulletin of the Multicultural History Society of Ontario, Double Issue* 2.2–3 (1979–80): 3–16. Web. 27 Apr. 2021.

Puddington, Arch. *Broadcasting Freedom: The Cold War Triumph of Radio Free Europe and Radio Liberty*. Lexington: The University Press of Kentucky, 2000.

Roth, Andrew. "Kremlin Bears Down on Moscow Bureau of US-Funded Radio Station." *The Guardian* 5 May 2021. Web. 5 May 2021.

Roth-Ey, Kristin, and Larissa Zakharova. "Communications and Media in the USSR and Eastern Europe." *Communiquer en URSS et en Europe socialiste* 56.2–3 (2015): 273–89. Web. 27 Apr. 2021.

Straw, Will. "Music from the Wrong Place: On the Italianicity of Quebec Disco." *Criticism* 50.1 (2008): 113–32. Web. 29 Jan. 2021.

---. "Pathways of Cultural Movement." *Accounting for Culture: Thinking through Cultural Citizenship*. Ed. Caroline Andrew, Monica Gattinger, M. Sharon Jeannotte, and Will Straw. Ottawa: University of Ottawa Press, 2005. 183–98. Web. 29 Jan. 2021.

Szamosi, Gertrud. "Heterotopic Narratives of Identity in Tamas Dobozy's Short Stories." *The Central European Journal of Canadian Studies* 14.1 (2019): 87–96. Web. 25 Apr. 2021.

Szőnyei, Tamás. *Az Új Hullám Évtizede 2* [The Decade of New Wave Music 2]. Katalizátor Iroda, 1992. Web. 25 May 2021.

Troitsky, Artemy. *Back in the USSR: The True Story of Rock in Russia*. Winchester, MA: Faber and Faber, 1988.

Venkovits, Balázs. "'The New Mecca of Immigrants': Hungarian Emigration to Canada and the Role of Immigration Propaganda." *Minorities in Canada: Intercultural Investigations*. Ed. Miklós Vassányi, Judit Nagy, Mátyás Bánhegyi, Dóra Bernhardt, Enikő Sepsi. Budapest: L'Harmattan-KRE, 2020. 99–122.

Von Faust, Boris. *Banned in the USSR: Counterculture, State Media, and Public Opinion During the Soviet Union's Final Decade*. Rutgers University, 2014. Web. 25 Apr. 2021.

Yahr, Emily. "Vince Gill Is Still Stunned by How Country Music 'Buried' the Dixie Chicks." *The Washington Post* 24 Oct. 2019. Web. 3 May 2021.

Ludmila Čiháková

From Communist Czechoslovakia to Canada and Back: The Story of a Teacher from Czechoslovakia in Alberta

Introduction

Josef Novotný, a teacher at the State Language School in Prague, published his *Konec medvědí sezóny: rok na kanadské vsi* [The End of the Bear Season: A Year in a Canadian Village] in 1973, only five years after the Prague Spring, followed by the second and third editions of the book in 1976 and 1980.[1] The books were inspired by Novotný's personal experience of living in northern Alberta and teaching at a local high school during the 1969/1970 school year, which provides an unusual setting considering the various travel restrictions imposed by the Czechoslovak state at the time and his family's association with emigration. As also reflected by the publication of three different editions, the narrative about one year spent in Canada provided an attractive reading for Czechs at the time. The books, however, are more than just popular accounts and they provide unique insights into the development of the Czech image of Canada during communism, the history of Czech immigration to North America, and issues of censorship, ideology, as well as micro history. This chapter examines Novotný's books in their broader literary, cultural, and political context, and based on archival research carried out for the first time, reconstructs the life of a Czech teacher and writer who influenced the perceptions of Canada in Czechoslovakia after 1968, while his life story (examined thoroughly for the first time here) and books tell us just as much about Canada as the Czechoslovakia of the time.

Josef Novotný published his book about his Canadian experiences in three editions (he based his book on real-life experience but changed some of the details of his life in the country, he added fictional names, and some details were also fictionalized), but it might be more accurate to say that he published three books in the form of three different genres: adventure fiction, travel writing, and autobiographical travel writing. Generally speaking, the main text remains the same in all three editions, it is the presentation of this text and the paratext that differs (including the foreword, book cover, and so forth). For example, the cover illustration of the first edition was created by Zdeněk Burian (1905-1981), a famous Czech painter and book illustrator

---

1 The chapter is based on the presentation at the international conference Transatlantic Dreams organized by The Canadian Museum of Immigration at Pier 21 and Wirth Institute for Austrian and Central European Studies (University of Alberta), October 2019. Unless otherwise noted, the third edition is used as the source of the quotations.

who illustrated adventure fiction primarily. The book cover suggests to the readers very clearly that they are dealing with adventure fiction, possibly written for young adults. The title and cover illustrations were likely chosen due to their attractiveness, indicating readability by the general public.[2]

Meanwhile, the front cover of the second edition shows a photo of a village built in the New England style surrounded by a fall landscape.[3] This is a rather surprising choice, as Novotný's story takes place in Alberta in 1969 and 1970. The back cover suggests to the readers that they will be reading a piece of travel writing. The second edition was renamed "A Year in a Canadian Village", instead of the original title, which change could be interpreted as a shift from adventure fiction to another genre. It should also be noted that the second title can be seen as more appropriate, as bear hunting and the bear season are somewhat marginal topics in the book.

The third print run of the book comprised 61,000 copies, three times more than the second edition. The increased number of copies indicates the sales success of the previous edition. Moreover, the third edition is longer, including more pages and illustrations and an illustrated preface and letters from the author's former Canadian colleague Jerry (Šámal-Jareš).[4] The book cover stresses the concepts of modernity and urban life. Comparing the second and third editions, one can notice that the second edition shows a village from the early twentieth century. In contrast, the third edition shows a modern town full of cars and electricity, in spite of there being a church discretely hidden among the other buildings. The other paratextual elements (illustrations and preface), despite this "modern cover," indicate to the reader that Indigenous people also represent a key topic of the book.

The text on the inner flap describes Canada as the country of contrasts, wild nature conflicting with technical development, marginalized Indigenous people standing against the descendants of arrogant European newcomers. The text stresses the fact that the book describes Canada as seen by a Central European man hailing from a socialist country. On the one hand, these paratextual elements perpetuate the stereotype about Canada built around adventure and wild nature. On the other hand, they emphasize negative aspects of a capitalist society, as all published books were subject to the ideology and political will of the Communist Party of Czechoslovakia at the time.

2 The book covers are available online, in the ObalkyKnih.cz database providing cover images of books for library catalogs: https://www.obalkyknih.cz/view?oclc=(OCoLC)42185514&nbn=cnb000441278; https://www.obalkyknih.cz/view?oclc=(OCoLC)4907287&nbn=cnb000145525; https://www.obalkyknih.cz/view?oclc=(OCoLC)40079580&nbn=cnb000163882;
3 I would like to thank Lachlan MacKinnon (Cape Breton University) for bringing this fact to my attention.
4 I would like to express my gratitude to Přemysl Šámal, the director of the Institute of Czech Literature of the Czech Academy of Science, and his colleagues Michal Jareš and Jiří Trávníček, who were so kind as to provide me with detailed information about the three editions and respective publishing houses.

Travel accounts represented a popular genre among Czechoslovak readers in the 1970s due to the effective travel restrictions and because sources of information about countries like Canada were scarce and limited. While readers interested in Canada could choose from translations of foreign works, usually providing a merger of adventure fiction and travel writing, Novotny's book was more appealing as it came from a fellow Czech and recounted the story of contemporary events. The book, however, poses several questions for scholars that may be answered only using an interdisciplinary approach at the borderline of historical and literary studies, heavily relying on archival research. Josef Novotný, Jr. claimed that his father's book was among the most borrowed items at libraries in Czechoslovakia during the late 1970s (email by Novotný, Jr.). But what made the book so popular at the time? How could Novotný actually travel to and publish about Canada after 1968? How did his image of Canada fit into the general Czech perception of the country at the time and what factors could influence such an image? To gain a better understanding of Novotný's work and answer these questions, we need to examine the topic within the broader context of Czech emigration as it could serve as an influencing factor on both the journey to Canada and the publication. We need to scrutinize how this popular work fit into the perceptions of Canada in the country at the time, and also how the real life-story of Novotný impacted the books themselves.

The examination of questions like ideology and censorship seems to be especially important as the book was published in the era referred to as the age of normalization in the wake of the Warsaw Pact invasion of Czechoslovakia. As Mariannna Bachledová put it: "the era of normalization was characterized by the powerful influence of ideology on literature that also determined the publishing agenda" (22). Before a book was published, employees of publishing houses investigated the works for "progressive elements" to prevent ideologically undesirable books from reaching the public (Bachledová 23). Josef Novotný's story is rather unusual, as the Czechoslovak Socialist Republic tried to restrict traveling (and especially emigration) of their citizens. Although cases of unsuccessful immigrants returning back to Czechoslovakia are known, legal travelling abroad and returning back could indicate some sort of a collaboration with the Czechoslovak Security Service (*Státní bezpečnost, StB*) that will be investigated in detail below with the initial hypothesis considering the possibility of collaboration. Novotný could have been promised access to a visa, a special exit permit (*výjezdní doložka*), and so on, in exchange for collaborating with and spying for the Czechoslovak Security Service.

Methods and materials

This chapter relies on a variety of research methods, including historical and biographical studies as well as devices of literary scholarship. The questions outlined above demanded the extensive study of archival sources (Security Services Archive, the Archives of the Ministry of Foreign Affairs of the Czech Republic, Prague City Archives), while the analysis of the different editions of the book required the use of literary theory, travel writing studies, and especially Gerard Genette's concept of paratext. As part of my work, I also contacted the Czechoslovak community in Alberta (Czech and Slovak Association of Canada)[5] and was able to interview several people, including the author's son and daughter, who provided me with important details.[6]

Despite the three editions of his book, the Czech National Library could not provide any information about Josef Novotný except for his date of birth and death. Nonetheless, this data enabled me to contact the Service Security Archives. In addition, a dictionary *Slovník českých autorů knih pro chlapce* [Dictionary of Czech Authors of Books for Boys] listed Novotný's name and again his life data. Unfortunately, the archival collections of the publishing houses which published Novotný's book are not accessible to researchers, and the location of one archival collection is unknown. Surprisingly, the Museum of Czech Literature, which gathers the archival materials of Czech writers, does not have any collection concerning Josef Novotný. The research conducted in the Archives of the Ministry of Foreign Affairs of the Czech Republic provided me with general information about travelling to Canada in the given period and about Czechoslovak-Canadian relations during the Cold War, even if the archives did not mention Novotný's name specifically. The "school card" (*školská karta*) of Josef Novotný, deposited in the Prague City Archive (Archiv hl.m. Prahy, fond Školská správa hlavního města Prahy [NAD 1940]), however, helped me uncover precise information about Novotný's personal and professional life.[7] Unfortunately, the archival collection of the State Language School in Prague, where Josef Novotný taught for decades, is not accessible at all. Regrettably, contacting the local archives of the school district in Canada where Josef Novotný was teaching in the school year of 1969/1970 did not yield any results either. Once a former employee turns seventy years of age, the School District destroys their employment records. Thus, with Novotný being born in 1919, the records concerning him would have been destroyed many years ago.[8]

---

5 I would like to thank Libor Ptáčník, the president of the Edmonton branch of this association, for connecting me with Michal Princ and Mirjana Vrba. I would also like to express my gratitude towards Mirjana Vrba for providing me with the details of her family story.

6 Because of the geographical distance between the Czech Republic and Canada, I used a combination of questionnaires sent by email and phone calls to interview Ms. Mirjana Vrba, the daughter of Josef Novotný.

7 I would like to express my gratitude towards my colleagues from the Prague City Archive, (especially Mgr. Zora Damová, Mgr. Jan Schwaller, and Mgr. Veronika Knotková) for finding the school card of Josef Novotný for me.

8 I would like to thank Dr. Evelyn Ellerman for contacting the local archives in Alberta.

Reconstructing Novotný's life

Dr. Michal Princ, a member of the Czech community in Edmonton who had known the family of the writer since his childhood, described Josef Novotný as follows:

> He belonged to the generation of my parents. I remember him as a huge person who walked every afternoon returning from work around my native blocks of flats at the corner of Národní obrany Street and Roosevelt Street via Lotyšská Street towards Place Náměstí interbrigády, where they lived. He was very tall, about 2 metres, slightly corpulent, and always with a pink face. One could get the impression that he was smiling all the time. (Princ)

Using Novotný's school card it is possible to reconstruct his life, educational path, and professional career. Josef Novotný was born on September 11, 1919 in Želeč (South Bohemia, Czechoslovakia) and died on November 12, 1989 in Prague. He passed away due to apoplexy, one week before the fall of communism in Czechoslovakia. He was raised by his grandparents as his father died from Spanish influenza (phone interview with Ms. Mirjana Vrba). During World War II, he was a teacher from 1942 to 1943. Later, he was a civilian forced laborer in the Astonia factory in Prague from 1944 to 1945 (Archiv hl. města Prahy, fond Školská správa hlavního města Prahy, Jiří Novotný; hereafter referred to as school card, Prague City Archives). After the war, he began studying at the Faculty of Law and later he became a language teacher at the State Language School at Národní třída in Prague, teaching English, French, Russian, and German (school card, Prague City Archives). This language school was a rather prestigious one, continuing to some extent the pre-war tradition of the previous language institute.

Novotný studied law from 1945 to 1947 but did not complete his studies. According to his daughter, this was due to his involvement in student movements; in other words, due to political reasons. Nevertheless, these seemingly did not affect his later career or studies. He graduated in 1960 from the Faculty of Education (English and Czech) in Olomouc as a part-time student. According to the school card, he also earned a scholarship to London Polytechnic in 1946. Unfortunately, the school card does not include details regarding his stay in London. Apart from being a teacher, he was also a translator, and translated theatre plays by John Patrick (1905-1955). In literary activities, according to the school card, he won a writing scholarship twice, in 1961 and 1967. The first was offered by the Association of Czechoslovak Writers (*Československý svaz spisovatelů*) and the second by the Czech Literary Funds Foundation (*Československý literární fond*) (school card, Prague City Archives). Presumably, he received these scholarships for his translation work, as several plays translated by Josef Novotný and co-translator Jan Procházka were published in the 1960s (databases of the National Library of the Czech Republic).

In 1967 Novotný was accepted as a teacher at a provincial school (Ridgevalley School) in Alberta in the Ridgevalley School District made possible by his language skills. The school was designated for children from surrounding areas who commuted to school by bus. Their parents were local farmers or Indigenous people, as the local Cree population had lived there since the eighteenth century. Novotný lived in DeBolt, like many of his students (Novotný 40). Though the school originally prepared a three-room apartment for him, in his opinion it was too large, so he instead lived in the sole hotel in DeBolt, a hamlet in Northern Alberta, which remains quite a desolate spot to this day.[9] It is located approximately 350 kilometres from Edmonton. The school probably had issues with hiring new teachers due to its geographical location and harsh weather conditions; specifically, the severe winters. As mentioned by the narrator, almost all teachers were newcomers (from the USA, from India, from Japan, and so on [Novotný 34-35]).

Novotný's daughter provided me with details not mentioned in the narrative. Josef Novotný had a total of three children, two sons and a daughter. The daughter emigrated to Canada with her husband, a theoretical physicist, in 1967. They settled in Edmonton, where their first child was born in 1968. As Josef Novotný and his wife wanted to see their grandchild, they had to make a decision about how to make it happen. The narrative describes a job advertisement sent from Australia to Novotný by his aunt, and Ms. Mirjana Vrba confirmed this. However, the narrative does not mention anything about Novotný's family.

Novotný was allowed to go to Canada with his wife. She stayed in Edmonton with her daughter and her family, and Novotný worked in DeBolt and commuted to Edmonton every weekend. Nevertheless, he returned to Czechoslovakia with his wife after the end of the school year. According to Novotný's school card, he remained an employee of the State Language School during the school year of 1969/1970 as he was on unpaid leave. As his daughter confirmed, he resumed to his teaching position after his return to Prague. Josef Novotný, Jr., a physician, stayed in Czechoslovakia during this time and he could be one of the reasons why his father returned to his home country. According to Mirjana Vrba, Josef Novotný, Sr. had a very cordial relationship with his son. Moreover, Novotný's daughter claimed that her father returned home as he had found it difficult to live in another country outside Czechoslovakia due to his patriotic sentiment. Novotný's daughter stressed the optimistic nature of her father and his positive attitude towards people. These characteristics enabled him to cope with new students and the new environment in Canada (phone interview with Mirjana Vrba).

---

9 Nevertheless, the hamlet has its own entry in Wikipedia. See more: https://en.wikipedia.org/wiki/DeBolt.

Czech immigration to Canada from communist Czechoslovakia and the secret service

The story of Novotný's family can be seen as an example of how liberalization in Czechoslovakia influenced travels to the West. In 1965, a new passport law came into force that made travel more accessible, even if it was not possible for everyone. A traveler had to obtain a special exit permit (*výjezdní doložka*) and be the bearer of a passport. In addition, border control became even more relaxed later in 1968 (Rychlík 89). Therefore, more Ph.D. students, assistants, and researchers were able to travel abroad for university exchanges than before. First, they travelled to Western Europe, but some of them had the opportunity to go to the USA or Canada. The number of Czechoslovak scholars in Canada increased rapidly, as can be seen in the table below—from three scholars in Canada in scholars. It appears that this increase was not controlled entirely by the communist government, as suggested by the Czechoslovak Embassy in Ottawa in a letter addressed to the Czechoslovak Ministry of Foreign Affairs. The Czechoslovak government seemingly lost track of the number of Czechoslovak scholars in Canada at a certain point.[10]

1964	1965	1966	1967	1968	March 1969
3	26	43	73	120	168

Table 1: Number of scholars from Czechoslovakia in Canada.
Source: Archiv Ministerstva zahraničních věcí, fond: Teritoriální odbor FMZV, k. 3, March 1969

The Soviet-led military occupation on August 21, 1968 changed everything. The first secretary of the Communist Party of Czechoslovakia, Alexander Dubček, declared on August 27 that an "agreement has been reached regarding measures aimed at a rapid normalisation of the situation" (Bren 29). This was the start of the new period of hard-line Communism. In April 1969 censorship was re-established. Dubček was replaced by Gustáv Husák on April 17 (Bren 32) marking the beginning of the purge. Well-known reform communists were dismissed, reformist newspapers and journals were permanently abolished, the press, publishing houses, television, and radio underwent drastic personnel changes (Bren 36).

The invasion had severe consequences on emigration, too. Due to the new passport law, many Czechoslovak citizens were outside the country (on holiday, university exchange, and so forth) at the time of the Warsaw Pact-led invasion. They

---

10 Archiv Ministerstva zahraničních věcí/The Archives of the Ministry of Foreign Affairs, fond Teritoriální odbor FMZV, k. 3, March 1969.

faced the difficult decision whether to return home or seek political asylum abroad (for personal stories see Raska 232 and Haváč 80-83). Subsequently, Czechoslovakian cases of emigration after the invasion of their homeland were even more numerous. The communist government estimated that about 150,000 individuals resettled in the West (Raska 234).

Although travelling abroad remained relatively easy until October 1969, government Decree No. 114 practically sealed off the borders to the West for Czechoslovak citizens. Therefore, travel to the West was possible only for two reasons: to visit close relatives who had left Czechoslovakia legally and to take part in expensive group tours. Individual travels depended solely on the discretion of the police (Rychlík 259). Czechoslovak citizens who left Czechoslovakia after August 1968 were seen by the Communist Party as illegal émigrés, who committed "the criminal act of abandoning the Republic" (Raska 307). According to Section 109 of the Communist Criminal Code (adopted in 1961), leaving the Republic was a crime. This law was directed against emigrants; specifically, anyone who had left Czechoslovakia without permission or stayed abroad without permission.

Moreover, the communist regime in Czechoslovakia made an attempt to convince their citizens to return home. As a result, a general amnesty was announced in Czechoslovakia on May 27, 1969 for persons who had fled the state illegally or whose travel permits had expired. Czechoslovak citizens were asked to return home or to legalize their status at a Czechoslovakian consulate or embassy until September 15 (Raska 289). Generally, the communist regime did not give up convincing the emigrants to return to Czechoslovakia until the 1980s (Rychlík 117).

Josef Novotný was therefore extremely fortunate to be able to legally travel to Canada in the summer of 1969 and his case should be seen as unusual. First, together with his wife he travelled legally to Canada, where their daughter had already been living. Secondly, he returned to Czechoslovakia, seemingly without negative consequences to either himself or his career. Thirdly, he was allowed to publish a book about his experiences.

It should be stressed that the communist regime usually did not allow families to be reunited. This statement was confirmed by archival research in the Archive of the Ministry of Foreign Affairs of the Czech Republic. There are numerous documents preserved here (Archive of the Ministry of Foreign Affairs of the Czech Republic/ Archiv Ministerstva zahraničních věcí, Teritoriální odbory-obyčejné 1960-1964, 1965-1969) containing requests written by a husband or wife, or even both parents, who left Czechoslovakia hoping that their family member(s) could be reunited with them in the future. It was very often not possible due to administrative obstacles instilled by the communist regime.

The unusual case of Novotný led me to a hypothesis about possible collaboration with the Czechoslovak State Security (Státní Bezpečnost, StB). State Security could blackmail foreign citizens who were trying to obtain passports and travel permissions to go to Czechoslovakia. Similarly, communist authorities could also blackmail their own citizens who were trying to obtain such documents. To give an example, the famous British actor Herbert Lom, having a Czech background, emigrated to the UK before World War II, while his sister stayed in Czechoslovakia. He had difficulty obtaining a visa to visit her in Czechoslovakia and was blackmailed by State Security. In exchange for collaborating and spying for the Czechoslovak Security Service, he was promised easier access to a visa (Bauer 60-70). Similarly, the Czechoslovak State Security pressured Czech and Slovak refugees in Canada to become spies or information gatherers. Sometimes they even extorted money from the former Czechoslovak citizens who resided in Canada (Raska 335).

To examine this hypothesis, research was conducted in the Security Service Archives (Archiv bezpečnostních složek). This institution administers the records created by the former security services, the Communist Party of Czechoslovakia, and other players. Nevertheless, the research indicated no evidence of Novotný being an informer of the Czechoslovak State Security or a State Security collaborator. Moreover, there is no mention of Novotný in the records kept by the Czechoslovak State Security. Interestingly, the Security Service Archives have records of another Josef Novotný, born exactly one year (11 September 1918) before the writer Josef Novotný (born 11 September 1919). As my research showed, these were two different people. Josef Novotný (born 1918) was a director of a boarding school for foreign students in Houštka, Stará Boleslav and he lived in Stará Boleslav. His professional career and life data are very different from the writer Josef Novotný (born 1919).[11] Therefore, these are two different persons.

A possible explanation could be that Josef Novotný was simply lucky enough to travel and another possibility could be that the records in question were destroyed following the fall of communism in 1989. His daughter, being asked if she knew more about how her father obtained the necessary travel permission, said that she had been surprised at that time that it was possible for him to go to Canada. Nevertheless, she claimed that they had never spoken about this administration process, stating: "We were simply happy to be together." Having pondered my question, she concluded that this was a happy accident (Phone interview).

As previously mentioned, the narrator claimed he had to travel to Edmonton every weekend for "family reasons." The use of the generic term "family reasons" should be seen as a consequence of self-censorship, as the topic of emigration after 1968 was seen as problematic due to political reasons. It should be borne in mind that while many newcomers from Czechoslovakia became permanent residents or Canadian citizens, the communist authorities during the period of normalization refused to recognize their new citizenship and they were treated as persons who had left the state illegally (Raska 322). Moreover, official Czechoslovak media portrayed

---

11 The Security Service Archives, Archiv bezpečnostních složek, Fond I. správa SNB-operativní svazky, sign. MTh 22070 I. S.

emigration to the West as a "driven betrayal of socialism" (Bren 181). Therefore, it was better to avoid the topic in order to ensure that the book would be published. Notably, while Novotný's narrative mentions Czech emigrants, it refers only to the descendants of Czechs who came from the Czech Lands to Canada before World War II, not émigrés who came after 1948 or 1968.

Novotný's books and Czech images of Canada

Novotný's books fit into the traditionally positive Czech attitude towards and interest in North America in general and its Indigenous peoples in particular, and the literary works about Canada which were accessible to readers in communist Czechoslovakia in the twentieth century also provide useful context for Novotný's books. As Canadian scholar Don Sparling, based in the Czech Republic, summarizes: "Of all the countries in Central Europe, the Czech lands have the longest and richest tradition on producing translations of works by Canadian authors and works by non-Canadians that take Canada as their theme or setting" (39). In other words, translations of books about Canada had a strong influence on the image of the country in Czechoslovakia during the twentieth century. Czech translations of Ernest T. Seton and Jack London's books especially shaped the image of Canada in Czechoslovak readers' minds for several generations. Jack London is not a Canadian author, but several of his dog novels (such as *White Fang* and *The Call of the Wild*) are set in Canada. These works definitely helped shape the image of Canada in Czechoslovakia from the pre-war period onwards. The image included the wilderness of Canada (including wild animals), the Prairies, the mountains at their western extremity, unspoiled nature, and home of Indigenous people (Sparling 42, 48).

Canadian authors (or authors considered Canadian) such as Allen Roy Evans (1885-1968), Grey Owl (1888-1938), and Ernest Thompson Seton (1860-1946) were translated in the pre-war period as well as in communist Czechoslovakia. Interestingly enough, Ernest Thompson Seton, an author of adventure fiction, remains the Canadian author most translated into Czech to this day. One of his most popular works in Czechoslovakia was the book *Two Little Savages*, the story of two Canadian boys trying to live as Indigenous people in the province of Ontario. The book could be categorized as young adult fiction and was first translated into Czech in 1925, having been reprinted several times since, most recently in 2005. Moreover, the book served as a practical handbook for life in the woods. Sparling underlines that *Two Little Savages* is "appealing to the general Central European obsession with 'the Red Man'" (42-43). This sort of literature emphasizes Canada's wilderness, natural beauty, virgin forests, and the lives of Indigenous people. In general, these are topics which traditionally fascinated Czech readers (42). As Sparling adds, however, "rather ironically, it was at precisely this period, in the course of the 1920s, that Canada crossed the threshold to becoming an urban nation, with the majority of its population living in the cities" (44).

Considering more contemporary literary sources which had an impact on the perception of Canada in post-war Czechoslovakia, Arkady Fiedler's travel account *Kanada pachnąca żywicą* (in Czech translation, *Kanada vonící pryskyřicí* [Canada Smells of Resin]) translated from Polish should also be considered. Actually, Fiedler (1894-1985) emphasized not only the wilderness, but also the negative aspects of capitalist society such as unemployment, as the original was published in 1955 in communist Poland. The dust jacket of the Czech translation (published in 1958) emphasized "unscrupulous French people, more unscrupulous English people and brave Indigenous people" (Fiedler).

Generally, literature about First Nations had already become very popular in pre-war Czechoslovakia, and this popularity did not change during the communist era (1948-1989) at all. Czechoslovak readers, especially young ones, had a very different image of Indigenous people than their North American peers, which was in part shaped by the German author Karl May (1842-1912), who actually never visited North America. In the 1960s, the popularity of his books increased thanks to movies made in Yugoslavia by Harald Reinl starring Pierre Brice as the main Indigenous hero Winnetou. Actually, several generations of youth in Czechoslovakia were influenced by the books of Karl May and the film adaptations of his stories. As literary scholar Jiří Trávníček noted, all cinema viewers of the era were touched by the last movie of the Winnetou series, in which the main hero is unjustly killed by the enemy (95).

The Communist regime was actually aware of this rather romanticized view of Canada. In the late 1960s, the Czechoslovak Ambassador in Ottawa suggested that "this idealistic image of Canada" should be neutralized in Czechoslovakia.[12] As the image of the country introduced earlier was highly positive, it was not further encouraged by the communist regime for ideological reasons; moreover, the increasing wave of emigration to Canada in the 1960s was especially alarming for them. This drive for neutralization was thus intended to serve as one of the corrective measures of the communist era.

Meanwhile, Canada became more popular in Czechoslovakia thanks to Expo 67 held in Montréal, where Czechoslovakia presented its own exposition. A delegation of Czech actors also travelled to the city and organized several performances. As a result of his personal experience, actor Miroslav Horníček published a book about his participation in the Expo. This definitely helped to spread information about Canada in Czechoslovakia, as the sources of information about Western countries were limited. Compared with Fiedler's travel account, Horníček could avoid stereotypical

---

12 Archive of the Ministry of Foreign Affairs of the Czech Republic/Archiv Ministerstva zahraničních věcí, fond: Teritoriální odbor FMZV, tajný, období 1965-1969, Antikomunismus v Kanadě k. 3, November 1967.

images of a "bad capitalist country" thanks to the liberalization of the 1960s. Therefore, his book was more objective and his narrative provided more information about the history of Montréal and everyday life in Canada. Moreover, Horníček's book describes urban life more extensively than the Canadian wilderness. This general context shaped the expectations of readers in Czechoslovakia, who wanted to read about the wilderness but also about a distant country, to which it was not possible to travel. This was the general cultural and political context in which Novotný's books were written and published.

The End of the Bear Season, or A Year in a Canadian village

Shifting away from the title of the first book, the title of the second and third editions, *A Year in the Canadian Village*, also refers to Czech late-nineteenth-century literary classics written by Mrštík's Alois and his brother Vilém: *Rok na vsi: Kronika moravské dědiny* [A Year in the Village: A Chronicle of a Moravian Village], first published in 1903. The book describes a Moravian village, its life, its inhabitants, and their stories observed over four seasons through a teacher's eyes. Novotný's book seems to follow the same pattern as the story recounts a school year starting in September and ending in June. The other significant common point is the social role of the author, being both a teacher and a newcomer who observes and describes the new place.

The book is made up of different sections: an autobiographical narrative about one year in Canada, excerpts of Novotný's students' essays, and letters written by his former high school colleague Jerry, which were sent to Novotný after his return to Prague. These elements are truly varied and readers could get the impression of a chaotic narrative. However, bearing in mind that the narrator also taught creative writing, the direct quotation of students' essays is not surprising.

Jerry,[13] an important person in the book, became a friend of the narrator. He originally came from North Carolina and started to work as a teacher by accident after a fire ravaged his shop. He taught biology and mathematics and was also known to be a bear hunter. Notably, he had a Czech background himself, having been a descendent of Czech immigrants from the first half of the twentieth century. He later maintained correspondence with the narrator and even visited him in Czechoslovakia.

Key topics addressed include the cultural differences and cultural shock that the narrator experienced during his stay. He was particularly surprised by advertisements, as these were not common in communist Czechoslovakia. He was also amazed by the school equipment (an electronic coffee percolator, a photocopier) in the staff room. He was astonished by clean bathrooms with hand driers, clean towels, and a sufficient amount of soap at local cafeterias. These cultural differences reveal details

---

13 According to Mirjana Vrba, his real name was Joe.

about everyday life in communist Czechoslovakia, which reinforces one of the key tenets of travel writing studies that accounts of foreign lands tell just as much about the author's home as the country they introduce.

The narrator recounts experiences including bear hunting, living in the Canadian winter with minus 40 degrees Celsius, which he enjoyed during the year, often comparing and contrasting the familiar (the self) with the unfamiliar (the other). For example, he took part in moose hunting twice with his colleagues. His friend Jerry in particular turned out to be quite a successful hunter, managing to shoot a grizzly bear (Novotný 58, 95). As the narrator was a teacher, descriptions of his students play an important role in the book. The narrator was not a native speaker, but despite this disadvantage, he was accepted as an English and French teacher, while he also taught creative writing, physical education, and art, in spite of not having any formal qualifications for these subjects (Novotný 43). As a teacher in Canada, he started work at 9 a.m. every morning while he started teaching language courses at 7 a.m. when at home. He was surprised by his students' poor knowledge of French. In the narrator's opinion, the language knowledge of his students in Prague was much better (Novotný 45).

He showed a very positive attitude towards Indigenous students (Novotný 241-42), and indeed the Indigenous children are an important element of the narrative in all three editions; however, it is only the third one where the narrative begins with a powerful story not included in the previous two editions. When the narrator arrives in the village for the first time by car with a local driver, the local Indigenous children begin to throw stones at them. He thinks of himself as an intruder. He is shocked by the fact that they are not allowed to speak their native language, which he compares with the position of the Czech language in the past. The narrator empathizes with the Indigenous students, giving them better marks, and stresses that he has never had any disciplinary issues with them (231). This is in line with other travel accounts available for readers in Czechoslovakia. The narrator's attitude is based on two sources: first, the positive image of Indigenous people in Czechoslovakia, and second, ideology. As literature was meant to educate the public, it was considered desirable to show the citizens of a communist country that human rights were being violated in Western countries, which often criticized the nations of the Eastern Bloc for the same reason.

Besides Indigenous students, the narrator also taught Mennonite pupils and described their beliefs and traditions. He viewed the Mennonite community very critically, which may be explained by the negative image of religion in a communist country, seeing it in opposition with atheism and anticlericalism. He described his personal contacts with the members of the community and also compared the simple Mennonite church with the beautiful baroque Catholic churches he knew from his home country. He found certain Mennonite habits strange and was especially critical of the rigidity of Mennonites' habits, the simplicity of their liturgy, and the unequal position of women in Mennonite society (187).

The author also tried to meet the expectations of Czechoslovak readers who wanted to read about the Canadian wilderness. Even if the biographical aspects of the narrative are omnipresent, the geographical names were changed to meet readers' expectations. For example, the real geographical names of places in Alberta—Valleyview, Grande Prairie, and Crooked Creek—were translated into Czech and replaced by more poetic and appropriate names for wild nature: Moose Valley (*Losí údolí*), Blue Prairie (*Modré údolí*), and Singing Creek (*Zpívající potok*) (Novotný 21, 31).

Censorship, self-censorship, ideology, and ideological elements

Throughout the period of communist rule in Czechoslovakia literary politics were subjected to different interventions with alternating times of repression and liberalization according to political and socioeconomic development.[14] In general, literary politics in the Eastern Bloc were subordinated to the state's mission to reshape society and educate its citizens. Therefore, only books describing Western society in a negative light were seen as acceptable (Wohlgemuth 49). Reading Novotný's narrative, the influence of ideology is clearly discernible, which is not surprising as the book was published after 1968. For the purposes of this chapter, ideology is defined "not in the commonly used sense of a political doctrine but rather as the set of beliefs and values which inform an individual's or institution's view of the world and assist their interpretation of events, facts and other aspects of experience" (Mason 141–56). In André Lefevere's opinion, "ideology is often enforced by the patrons, the people or institutions who commission or publish translations" (Lefevere 19). In this case, the ideology was enforced by state control and the Communist Party of Czechoslovakia.

Marianna Bachledová, analyzing the ideological elements in paratext in Czechoslovakia during the period of normalization (1968-1989), distinguished several thematic groups. As Bachledová argues, these groups were likely required to be mentioned in the paratext. Interestingly enough, these obligatory topics can also be identified in Novotný's narrative in general, not only in its paratexts. These are the following: materialism, the author's political opinions, the exploitation of the working class, freedom, polarization, the opponent's moral shortcomings, images of destruction, the Great October Socialist Revolution, hostility and religion (Bachledová 34-35). Apart from the October Revolution, the author's political opinions, and the exploitation of the working class, all topics are mentioned in Novotný's book as well where the positive self-presentation and negative other-presentation could be observed in the narrative. Czech people are depicted as skillful, tough, and proud of their traditions. Moreover, the stress is put on developed industry, especially textile

---

14 Compare with situation in Eastern Germany (for additional information see Thompson-Wohlgemuth).

and the automobile industry in Czechoslovakia, which should show Czechoslovakia as a modern, developed country (Novotný 111, 114). The narrator's students were especially impressed by the information about long traditions of Czechoslovak car production. On the contrary, local habitants aside from Indigenous people are depicted as spoiled, selfish, and disrespectful of nature. An example could be cited in the narrator's story about hitchhiking during a frosty winter, where he waited for a long time without success due to the selfishness of local drivers (Novotný 83). Contrastingly, his colleagues from the high school are described as pleasant and friendly (33).

Materialism can be identified in the excerpts describing TV advertisements, which did not exist in Czechoslovakia at the time, and the role of the car in Canadian society. He described social pressure to buy a new car every two years (212): "The car is a king of a family budget as—if possible—it is expected to change it every second year. Which is not a bargain. It costs between 2,500 and 6,000 dollars."[15] The narrator also criticized the country for its waste of food and electricity and using paper tissues instead of handkerchiefs (201).

The image of destruction could be identified in fragments describing waste dumps around Canadian cities and used tires lying beside the roads (212). The moral shortcomings of Western society can be identified in the excerpt describing how the narrator read men's magazines (such as *Playboy*) for the first time in his life. This sort of publication would not have been allowed to be sold officially in communist Czechoslovakia. The narrator stressed that he was disgusted by these magazines (206). The potential reader was interested in these details about life in the West, but these topics were usually not approved by literary censorship. As scholar Přemysl Šámal points out, erotic topics in the literature were not allowed during that period, and literary censorship could be classified as prudish (1184).

These mentions probably represented instances of self-censorship, which can be identified in excerpts concerning the narrator's attitude towards Canada, the question of Czech immigration to Canada, and his personal and family life. It is unlikely that a censor had any influence on Novotný's narrative, presumably, the author censored himself, bearing in mind what was deemed acceptable and what was not. Such self-censorship would most probably prevent the author from writing about the more positive aspects of his Canadian stay.

The ideological elements in the book are "obligatory sentences," which include positive images of the author's homeland and negative images of "capitalist" Canada, religion, and other topics such as materialism, the moral shortcomings of Canadian people, and so forth. The presence of these "obligatory sentences" and the author's self-censorship made the book publishable. Interestingly enough, however, excerpts

---

15 Translation mine. "Automobil vládne rodinnému rozpočtu, protože se musí pokud možno každé dva roky vyměňovat, a to není laciný špás – stojí totiž od dvou a půl do šesti tisíc dolarů."

positively describing Canada can also be found in the narrative, and the reader could have the impression that the narrator liked the country and enjoyed his stay even if overall he stressed the negative aspects of life. These positive excerpts often repeat stereotypical images of Canada: the wilderness, the beauty of nature, and the land as a home of the Indigenous people. The latter are described positively in accordance with the Central European literary tradition and probably also because the author was aware of readers' expectations and tried to meet them. In spite of communist censorship laws, several excerpts can be identified in which the narrator expresses his admiration for Canada. His enthusiasm can be seen in this excerpt, for example: "Canada. There are three 'a's in this word. A perfect name to be sung by an Italian tenor. Sweetly, passionately, fervently."[16] He also admits that he would miss Canada; especially its wild nature (and not society): "The landscape reminded me of South Bohemia. But the sky is extremely high and profound. I had been admiring its powerful beauty all the time being here. And I will never forget it."[17]

Conclusion

Defining the genre of Novotný's work poses a challenge. It seems that we are dealing with a literary fictionalization of Novotný's autobiography, the mixture of fiction and reality that is defined as "autofiction." This term was first used by Serge Doubrovsky, who saw his novel as being of a genre between fiction and autobiography, and, as a result, the line between narrator and author became entirely ambiguous (Hutchens 59-60). It is evident that even the publishing houses had difficulties determining the genre of the book. The book was presented first as adventure fiction, secondly as travel writing, and thirdly as autobiographical travel writing. It seems that the paratext of the first edition in particular does not correspond to the character of the narrative. Interestingly, Novotný's name can be found in the *Slovník českých autorů knih pro chlapce* [Dictionary of Czech Authors of Books for Boys], presumably thanks to the first edition of his book. Regardless, Novotný's book should not be classified as a "book for boys," nor as young adult fiction. The book was probably first presented as adventure fiction due to readers' expectations as it was the typical genre for books about Canada and was compatible with the traditional Czech fascination with the American wilderness.

---

16 Translation mine. "Jméno Kanada obsahuje tři a. Jméno jako stvořené pro italského tenora, aby je zazpíval sladce, vášnivě a ohnivě."

17 Translation mine. "Tady už se krajina trochu podobala jižním Čechám, jen nebe je tu nesmírně hluboké a vysoké. Jeho mocné kráse jsem se obdivoval pod celou dobu svého pobytu na severu a nikdy na ně nezapomenu."

After the fall of communism in 1989, the book ceased to be of public interest because of specific ideological elements associated with it. Moreover, after 1989, more books and travel accounts about Canada became available to Czech readers than before. While Novotný's book is firmly placed within the Czech literary tradition going back to the nineteenth century, the narrative should be seen as a typical cultural product of the era, aiming to show Canada in a negative light and trying to negate the romantic image of Canada firmly and deeply rooted in Czechoslovakian readers' minds due to the numerous translations of Canadian adventure literature. The narrative omitted important personal facts due to political reasons and self-censorship, but it should be reiterated that the hypothesis regarding Novotný's possible collaboration with the Czechoslovak State Security has not been proven. There is no evidence of any contact with the Czechoslovak State Security preserved in the State Security Archives. Nonetheless, as mentioned, the communist authorities usually did not grant permission to families to join their other family members residing in Western countries. The book could also be seen as a sort of collaboration with the communist regime, as it can be considered a typical cultural product of normalization. Furthermore, it could be seen as an attempt by the communist authorities to neutralize the aforementioned "romantic image of Canada" to make it less appealing to would-be emigrants.

Works Cited

Primary Sources

Novotný, Josef. *Konec medvědí sezóny: Rok na kanadské vsi*. 1st ed. Prague: Práce, 1973.
Novotný, Josef. *Rok na kanadské vsi*. 2nd ed. Prague: Orbis, 1976.
Novotný, Josef. *Rok na kanadské vsi*. 3rd ed. Prague: Práce, 1980.

Archival Sources

The Archive of the Ministry of Foreign Affairs of the Czech Republic, Prague [Archiv Ministerstva zahraničních věcí České republiky, fond: Teritoriální odbor FMZV, fond Teritoriální odbory-obyčejné 1960-1964, 1965-1969]
Security Services Archive, Prague [Archiv bezpečnostních složek, fond: Hlavní správa rozvědky SNB, Emigrace v Kanadě]
Prague City Archives [Archiv hlavního města Prahy, fond: Školská správa hlavního města Prahy]

Interview

Phone interview with Mirjana Vrba, 2 Oct. 2019.

Electronic sources

Email
Novotný, Josef, Jr. "Re: Rok na kanadské vsi." To Ludmila Lambeinová. 23 Oct. 2019.
Princ, Michal. "Re: Hledání Josefa Novotného." To Ludmila Lambeinová. 6 Sept. 2019.
Sedláčková, Jaroslav. "Nový dotaz Ptejte se knihovny." To Ludmila Lambeinová. 8 Aug. 2021.
Šámal, Petr, and Michal Jareš. "Re: Kniha Josefa Novotného - Rok na kanadské vsi." To Ludmila Lambeinová. 14 Oct. 2021.
Trávníček, Jiří. "Re: Rok na kanadské vsi - kniha Josefa Novotného". To Ludmila Lambeinová. 14 Oct. 2021.

Websites

National Library. *Databases of the National Library CR, Results for: Novotný, Josef, 1919-1989.* 8 Nov. 2021. https://aleph.nkp.cz/F/J4K1MIXMNP8YQ2LB2QSDK9QX4CQ3TB9D6BAYNYELKY3DAGR 44M-18581?func=find-acc&acc_sequence=000658614. Web. 14 July 2022.
Ibadatelna. *Communist State Security. Documentation Portal on the Czechoslovak State Security.* Dictionary entry *Leaving the Republic.* 10 Nov. 2021. https://ibadatelna.cz/en/dictionary/leaving-republic. Web. 14 July 2022.

Secondary Sources

Bauer, Zdeněk. "Zmařené cesty šéfinspektora Dreyfuse: česko-britský herec Herbert Lom v hledáčku 'lovců rudých' i československých zpravodajských služeb." *Paměť a dějiny: Revue pro studium totalitních režimů* 2 (2019): 60-70.
Bachledová, Marianna. "Translators and Publishers in Czechoslovakia (1968-1989): Following and Subverting the Ideology." *Translation, Interpreting and Culture: Old Dogmas, New Approaches.* Ed. Martin Djovčoš and Emília Perez. Berlin: Peter Lang, 2021. 17-41.
Bren, Paulina. *The Greengrocer and His TV: The Culture of Communism after the 1968 Prague Spring.* Ithaca and London: Cornell University Press, 2010.
Fiedler, Arkady. *Kanada vonící pryskyřicí.* Transl. Irena Dvořáková. Prague: Mladá fronta, 1958.
Genette, Gérard. *Seuils.* Paris: Éditions du Seuil, 1987.
Haváč, Ondřej. *Exil a Identita: Komparace českého exilu v Rakousku a Švýcarsku po roce 1968.* Ph.D. thesis. Brno: Masarykova univerzita v Brně, 2018.
Horníček, Miroslav. *Javorové listy.* Prague: Olympia, 1968.
Hutchens, Jack J. B. "Julian Stryjkowski: Polish, Jewish, Queer." *Canadian Slavonic Papers* 1(2019): 57-80.
Kovala, Urpo. "Translation, Paratextual Mediation, and Ideological Closure." *Target* 1 (1996): 119-47.
Lefevere, André. *Translation, Rewriting, and the Manipulation of Literary Fame.* London: Routledge, 1992.
Mason, Ian. "Discourse, Ideology and Translation." *Translation Studies: Critical Concepts in Linguistics.* Ed. Mona Baker. Abingdon, New York: Routledge, 2009. 141-56.
Raska, Jan. *Freedom's Voices: Czech and Slovak Immigration to Canada during the Cold War.* Ph.D. thesis. Waterloo: University of Waterloo, 2013.
Rychlík, Jan. *Cestování do ciziny v habsburské monarchii a v Československu: Pasová, vízová a vystěhovalecká politika 1848-1989.* Prague: Ústav pro soudobé dějiny AV ČR, 2007.
Sparling, Don. "'Canada' in the Czech Lands. *Canada in Eight Tongues.* Ed. Katalin Kürtösi. Brno: Masaryk University, 2012. 39-48.

Studenovský, Tomáš, and Josef Bláha. *Slovník českých autorů knih pro chlapce (a nejen pro ně)*. Prague: Ostrov, 2000.

Thomson-Wohlgemuth, Gaby. *Translation under State Control: Books for Young People in the German Democratic Republic*. New York: Routledge, 2009.

Trávníček, Jiří. *Česká čtenářská republika: Generace, fenomény, životopisy*. Brno: Host, 2017.

Tůma, Oldřich. "Reforms in the Communist Party: The Prague Spring and Apprehension about a Soviet Invasion." *The Prague Spring and the Warsaw Pact Invasion of Czechoslovakia in 1968*. Ed. Günter Bischof et al. Plymouth: Lexington Books, 2009. 64- 76. *ProQuest*. Web. 27 June 2021.

Wögerbauer, Michael, Přemysl Šámal, et al. *V obecném zájmu: Cenzura a sociální regulace literatury v moderní české kultuře 1749-2014*. 2 vols. Prague: Academia, 2015.

Authors of the Volume

Bram Beelaert studied history and journalism in Ghent and Brussels, Belgium. He has published about social, cultural, and migration history and has expertise in the fields of archivism, oral history, heritage studies, museology, journalism, and historical research. He is currently curator and head of research at the Red Star Line Museum in Antwerp.

Peter Bush, Independent Scholar and Teaching Elder, St. Andrew's Presbyterian Church, Fergus, Ontario, Canada, does research on the history of the Canadian Presbyterian Church. He is author of *Western Challenge: The Presbyterian Church in Canada's Mission on the Prairies and North, 1885–1925* and editor of *Presbyterian History: A Newsletter of The Committee on History*. Cross-cultural interactions between Christians of differing ethnicities and languages, and the relationship between The Presbyterian Church and the Indigenous Peoples of Canada, especially with reference to Residential Schools, represent a long-term research interest. He has also written about immigrant Christian communities in late-twentieth- and early-twenty-first-century Canada, and, as a parish pastor, about congregational leadership and congregational worship for the journals *Practical Theology*, *Reformed Worship*, and *Perspectives: A Journal of Reformed Thought*. His book *In Dying We Are Born: The Challenge and Hope of Congregations* was published in 2007.

Ludmila Čiháková (Lambeinová), archivist at the State Regional Archives, Litomerice, the Czech Republic, earned her MA in Polish Philology and History from Palacký University, Olomouc. In 2019, she defended her Ph.D. dissertation in linguistics titled "Characteristics of Polish-Czech Translation of Academic Papers Based on the Texts on the 20th-Century History of Poland" at the University of Warsaw. She was a Research Fellow at the Wirth Institute of Austrian and Central-European Studies at the University of Alberta in 2017-2018. She has been working at the State Regional Archives in Litomerice since 2020. Her research interests include translation, the history of Bohemian nobility, and the 20th-century history of Poland and Czechoslovakia.

Victor Kennedy studied guitar at Berklee School of Music, Boston; astronomy at James Cook University, Townsville, Australia; law at York University, Toronto; and English at the University of Toronto. At various times he has worked as a truck driver, lawyer, musician, scuba diving instructor, lexicographer, and English professor. He taught at the University of Maribor from 1996 until his retirement in 2022. He is the author of *Strange Brew: Metaphors of Magic and Science in Rock Music* (2013) and co-editor of *Words and Music* (2013), *Symphony and Song* (2016), *Ethnic and Cultural Identity in Music and Song Lyrics* (2017), *Engendering Difference: Sexism, Power, and Politics* (2018), and *Words, Music, and Gender* (2020).

Kristian Kolar, holding a BA in English Language, Literature, and History from the University of Maribor, does research on ethnic music in Northern Croatia, the history of Eastern European propaganda, and notions of popular music. He is also a guitarist and songwriter. His publications include "Home as a Motif in Croatian Ethnic and Popular Music" (2021) and "This is (Not) Radio Free Europe: Music that Changed the World" (2022, co-authored with Victor Kennedy). His essay "An Unlikely Revolution: The Impact of Radio Luxembourg on Yugoslav Culture" is scheduled for publication by the University of Graz later this year, in the volume *In Memoriam Hugo Keiper*.

Neža Bojnec Naterer, born in a Hungarian minority community on the Slovenian-Hungarian border, has worked as a translator of German and Slovene and as a language teacher since completing her BA in 2001. At present, she teaches at an adult education center in Maribor. Her professional interests include adult education, translation, and music.

Mária Palla, Assistant Professor, Institute of English and American Studies, Pázmány Péter Catholic University, Budapest, graduated with a dual MA in English and Russian Studies from the University of Debrecen. Having earned her Ph.D. in the Modern English and American Literature and Culture Program at Eötvös Loránd University, Budapest, she did research and taught in Canada, and has taught at various universities in Hungary. Her courses and research focus on postcolonial literatures and theory, with particular emphasis on diasporic writing. She has published several articles on the literary representation of the Hungarian as well as the South Asian diasporas living in Canada and England. She is a member of the Central European Association for Canadian Studies.

Lukáš Perutka is Assistant Professor at Palacký University in Olomouc and at the Charles University in Prague. He has teaching experience at the Institute of Technology in Monterrey, Mexico and the University of California at Berkeley. Among his research interest are the contacts between Central Europe and the Americas in the 19th and 20th centuries. He focuses on diplomatic relations, travelers, and migration. He published several articles and books on these topics including *Checoslovaquia, Guatemala y México en el período de la Revolución Guatemalteca* [Czechoslovakia, Guatemala, and Mexico during the Guatemalan Revolution] and *Za to spasitelské more* [Across the Messianic sea].

Sheena Trimble, Assistant Professor of North American Studies, Université catholique de l'Ouest, Angers [Catholic University of Western France], teaches American history and culture. Her research focuses on women's efforts to influence Canadian immigration policy between 1945 and 1967. The women she studies include immigrants, politicians, professionals, housewives, and members of associations and minority groups. Her 2015 doctoral dissertation, *Women and Canadian Immigration Policy (1945–1967): Beyond Assigned Gender Roles?* examined the subject in depth and she has since published nearly a dozen related articles in academic journals such as *Canadian Studies* and *Canadian Jewish Studies* as well as in publications targeting a non-academic public such as *Bout de papier: Canada's Magazine of Diplomacy and Foreign Service*. She is also co-editor of the most recent edition (no. 48) of the *Cahiers interdisciplinaires de recherche en histoire, lettres, langues et arts*, entitled *Ruptures et* *normes: Déclinaisons et degrés de non-conformité* [Declinations and Degrees of Non-Compliance].

Balázs Venkovits, Associate Professor of American Studies, Institute of English and American Studies, University of Debrecen, teaches courses on American civilization, history, travel writing, and translation. His broader academic interests include migration studies, travel writing studies, nineteenth-century Hungarian travel accounts on Mexico, the United States, and Canada, Hungarian immigration to Canada, and US–Hungarian relations. Among others, he is the recipient of OTKA (2022-26), Jedlik (2013-14), JFK Research Fellowship (2013), and Fulbright (2010-2011) grants. His Hungarian monograph on the perception of Mexico and the United States in Hungarian travel writing was published in 2018 (University of Debrecen Press). His articles and book chapters have been published by Berghahn Books, *AETAS*, *HJEAS*, *Studia Migracyjne—Przeglad Polonijny*, *Journeys: The International Journal of Travel and Travel Writing*, *IdeAs: Idées d'Amériques*, and *Hungarian Cultural Studies*, among others.

Eric Wilkinson is a Ph.D. candidate in philosophy and Vanier Scholar at McGill University, Montréal, Canada. His research interests include meta-ethics, normative ethics, and political philosophy. He also enjoys writing on Canadian history, politics, and literature. His recent work includes an investigation of the relationship between multiculturalism and nationhood, especially as it pertains to Canada, in "The Possibility of Multicultural Nationhood" (2021), published in the *American Review of Canadian Studies*. Another of his research projects involves reconstructing the thought of Indigenous philosophers who lived in what is today Canada during the seventeenth century and earlier.

Acknowledgments

HJEAS Books are co-published by DeGruyter through its subsidiary Sciendo and Debrecen University Press, with substantial financing from the University of Debrecen, the Faculty of Humanities Scholarly Fund and with additional financing by the Institute of English and American Studies.

The project was also supported by the National Research, Development and Innovation Office (NKFIH), grant no. FK 143388.

ʌ **HJEAS** book

HJEAS Books is a new series of peer-reviewed, open-access scholarly books launched by the *Hungarian Journal of English and American Studies*.

Published in 2022:

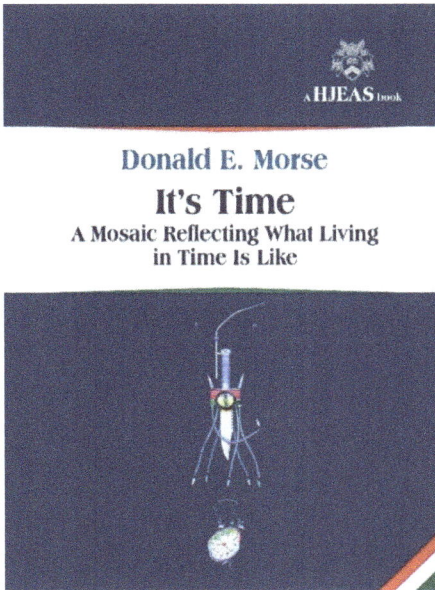

Donald E. Morse
It's Time
A Mosaic Reflecting What Living in Time Is Like

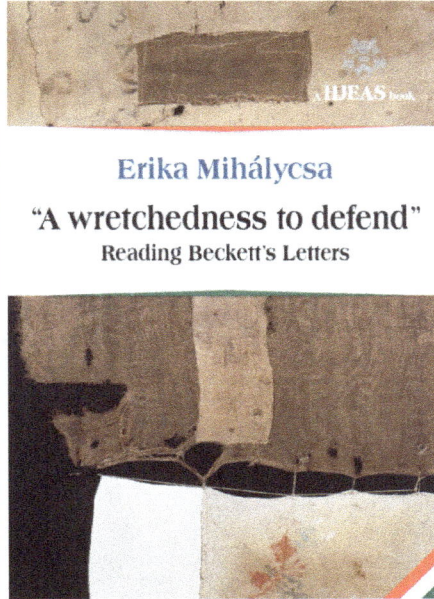

Erika Mihálycsa
"A wretchedness to defend"
Reading Beckett's Letters

In 2023: Mária Kurdi, ed. *Negotiating Age: Aging and Ageism in Contemporary Literature and Theatre*

Forthcoming:
Donald Wesling, *Perceiving-Thinking-Writing: Merleau-Ponty and Literature* (University of California, USA)
COVID19: The Crisis in Care, edited by Eszter Ureczky (University of Debrecen, Hungary)

Other titles in preparation include:
Coetzee and Dostoyevsky, The Female Detective, Ecocritism, American Free Verse, and *Contemporary Irish Literature*.